A HISTORY OF WITHAM

by Janet Gyford

Janet Gyford

For John, Phil and Sue

Published by
JANET GYFORD
Blanfred, Chalks Road,
Witham, Essex, CM8 2BT
www.gyford.com/janet

© Janet Gyford 2005

All rights reserved. No part of this publication may be reproduced, in whole or in part, in any form, without written permission from the publisher

British Library Cataloguing in Publication Data
A catalogue record for this book is available from the British Library

ISBN 0 946434 04 2

Designed by the author, and printed by Owl Printing Company, East Street, Tollesbury, Maldon, Essex CM9 8QD
Tel 01621 869201   Fax: 01621 869811

CONTENTS

Map of Witham	4
Acknowledgements	5
Maps of Witham's surroundings	6
Introduction	7
1. Early days	8
2. Tudor and Stuart Witham	20
3. 1700-1815. 'A good handsome town'	29
4. 1815-1901. 'A radical place' or 'a respectable little town'?	54
5. 1901-1945. Paradise in Cressing Road	93
Walk 1. Round the ancient earthworks	140
Walk 2. The village of Chipping Hill	150
Walk 3. The town centre	160
Other places to see	183
Sources of information	186
Index	190
Colour section	in centre

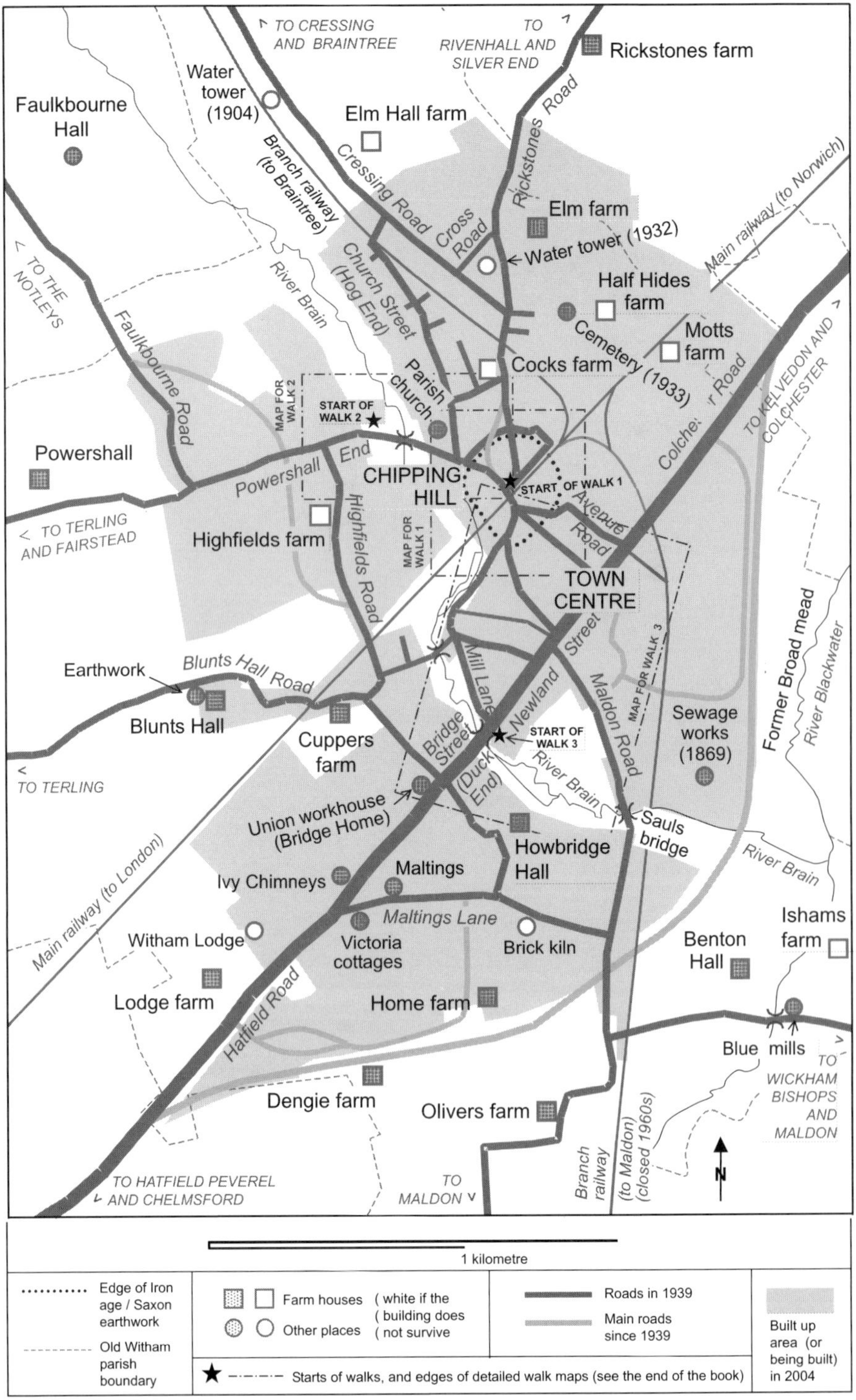
TO CRESSING AND BRAINTREE
TO RIVENHALL AND SILVER END
Rickstones farm
Water tower (1904)
Faulkbourne Hall
Elm Hall farm
Rickstones Road
Branch railway (to Braintree)
Cressing Road
Main railway (to Norwich)
Elm farm
Cross Road
Water tower (1932)
Church Street (Hog End)
River Brain
TO THE NOTLEYS
Faulkbourne Road
Half Hides farm
Motts farm
Cemetery (1933)
Cocks farm
Parish church
MAP FOR WALK 2
START OF WALK 2
Colchester Road
TO KELVEDON AND COLCHESTER
Powershall
Powershall End
CHIPPING HILL
START OF WALK 1
Avenue Road
Highfields farm
TO TERLING AND FAIRSTEAD
MAP FOR WALK 1
Highfields Road
TOWN CENTRE
Newland Street
MAP FOR WALK 3
Former Broad mead
River Blackwater
Earthwork
Blunts Hall Road
Mill Lane
Blunts Hall
Cuppers farm
Bridge Street
START OF WALK 3
Maldon Road
Sewage works (1869)
TO TERLING
(Duck End)
River Brain
Union workhouse (Bridge Home)
Sauls bridge
Howbridge Hall
River Brain
Main railway (to London)
Ivy Chimneys
Maltings
Maltings Lane
Witham Lodge
Victoria cottages
Brick kiln
Benton Hall
Ishams farm
Lodge farm
Home farm
Hatfield Road
Blue mills
TO WICKHAM BISHOPS AND MALDON
Dengie farm
Olivers farm
Branch railway (to Maldon) (closed 1960s)
TO HATFIELD PEVEREL AND CHELMSFORD
TO MALDON
N
1 kilometre
Edge of Iron age / Saxon earthwork
Old Witham parish boundary
Farm houses
Other places
(white if the (building does (not survive
Roads in 1939
Main roads since 1939
Built up area (or being built) in 2004
Starts of walks, and edges of detailed walk maps (see the end of the book)

Acknowledgements

Many people very kindly lent photographs and allowed me to use them. They are listed below, together with just a few of the innumerable people who generously gave all sorts of other help, advice and information: Simon Alderton, David Andrews, Nyria Atkinson, Michael Bardell, Dot Bedenham, Owen Bedwin, Noel Beer, Roy Belsham, David Blake, Jim Boutwood, Braintree District Museum, Elaine Brison, Pat and Arthur Brown, Rosemary and Stewart Brown, Tony Brown, Kevin Bruce, Bessie Bryers, George Capon, Kathy Carpenter, Yvonne Carpenter, Chelmsford and Essex Museum, Dr Bill Cliftlands, Tony Conerny, the Masters and Fellows of Corpus Christi College Cambridge, Fiona Cowell, Ray Cressey, Ariel Crittall, Peter Dean, Tim Dean, Patrick Denney, Angela and Ted Dersley, Ken Doughty, Martyn Drake, Shirley Durgan, Stella Eccleston, Myles Eckersley, Liz Edwards and Trevor Naylor of the Highway Bookshop, Essex County Council, Essex Record Office, Geoff Fairbairn, The Fisher family, Joyce Fitch, Barry Fleet, James Fylan (Dr Bod PC Problem Solving), Roy Gage, Fred Gaymer, John Gyford, Phil Gyford, Sue Gyford, Julia Harrison, Anne Holden, Ian Hook, Kerry Hook, John Horne, Patrick Horner, Keith Howell, Peter Howell, David Humphries, Michael Hurst, Helen Irons, Cecil Joslin, Rosalind Kaye, Rod Lane, Les Larnder, Gina Latner, Nick Lavender, Edward Legg, Daphne Le Sage, Sue Littlewood, Mary Long, Betty Loring, Ted Mawdsley, Peter May, Maria Medlycott, S R Moore, Fred Nash, The National Archives, National Monuments Record, National Trust Photographic Library, Keith Newbitt, John Newman, John V Nicholls, Lionel Oakley, Jim Page, Margaret Paine, David Pattisson, John Pattisson, Walter Peirce, Tony Pennock, Dominic Petre, Lord Petre, Don Pettican, Andrew Phillips, Picturesque, Albert Poulter, Roy Poulter, Lord Rayleigh, the Rector of Kedington, Sue Reichart, Graham Richardson, Lois Richardson, Andrew Robertson, Pam Robinson, Malcolm Root, Royal Greenjackets Museum, Pat Ryan, Betty Scales, Maureen Scollan, Mollie Scott, John Scott-Mason, Lester Shelley, Pat Slugocki, Alan Smith, Alison V Smith, Michael Smith, Peter and Betty Spall, Ben Stevens, Dominic Stinson, Richard Stone, Paul Succony (Wiltshire Clocks), Eve Sweeting, Cyril Taylor, Ruth and Eric Teverson, Mark Thomasin Foster, Ken Thompson, John Thurgood, David Tomlinson, Cyril Wade, Malcolm Wallace, John Walter, Brenda Watkin, David Webb, Peter West, Doreen Williams, Norman Wilson, Witham Library, Witham Town Council, Bob Wood, John Wordley, Jen Young (British Red Cross).

The following people bravely read some of my drafts, or walked the walks, and made many helpful comments: Pat Baker, Chris Goodes, John Gyford, Sue Gyford, Julia Harrison, Dr Jane Pearson, Pat Ryan, Maureen and Michael Scollan, Dr Chris Thornton.

Heartfelt thanks to them all. Also to my family and friends and the members of the Witham History Group and the Essex Local History Workshop for their encouragement. And finally to Martin and John Lord and Lindsay Taylor of Owl Printing for their usual optimism, enthusiasm and efficiency, which made the final production of the book into a pleasure.

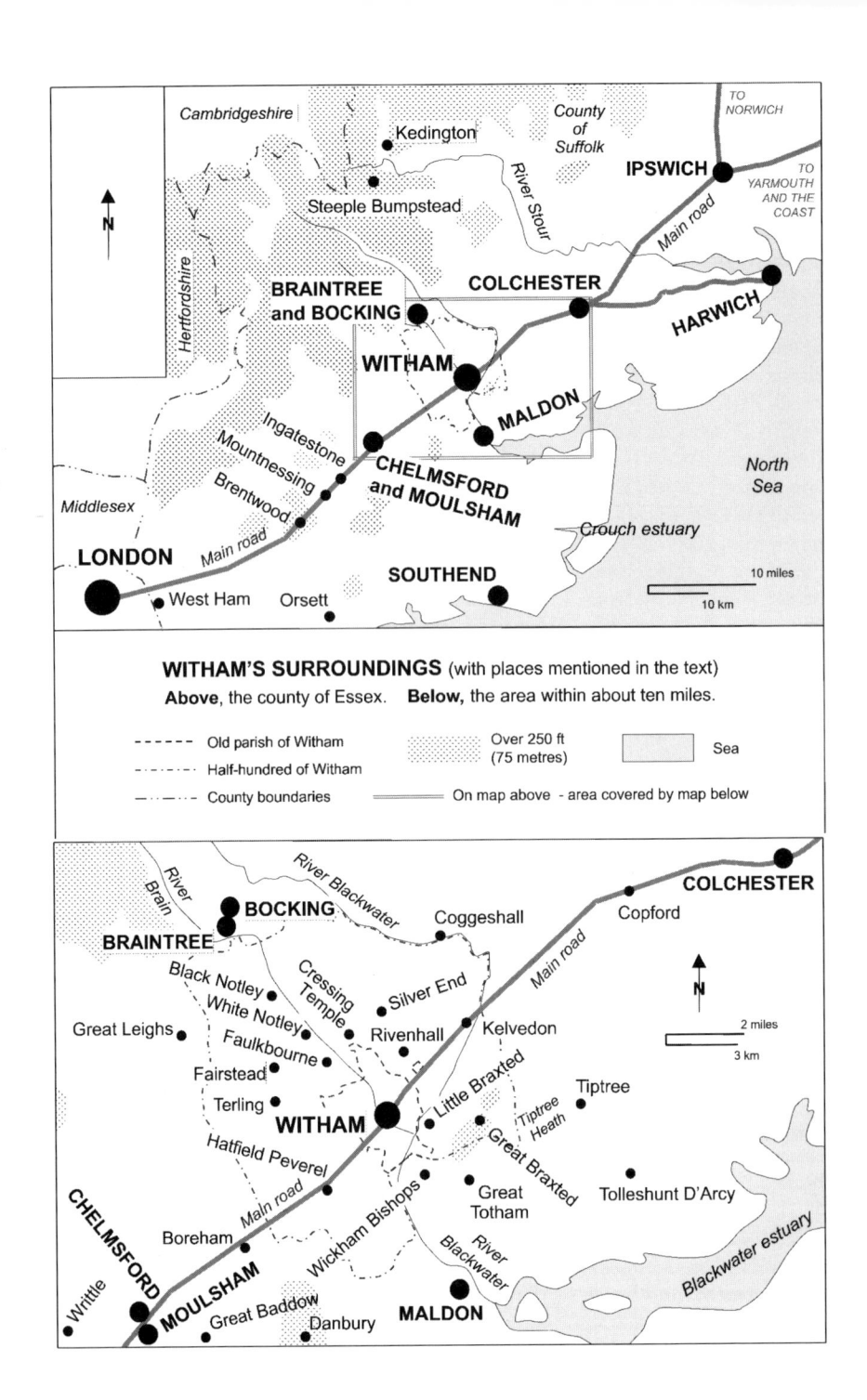

WITHAM'S SURROUNDINGS (with places mentioned in the text)
Above, the county of Essex. **Below**, the area within about ten miles.

- - - - - Old parish of Witham
- · - · - Half-hundred of Witham
——— · · ——— County boundaries

Over 250 ft (75 metres)

Sea

On map above - area covered by map below

Introduction

Not long ago I was talking to some people from another part of Essex. I asked them about their image of Witham. One spoke enthusiastically about how charming it is, and about the lovely little shops. A second reported hearing that many supposedly undesirable people had come to live here during the 1960s. Having arrived in the 1960s myself, I was pleased when a third person leapt to the defence of the incomers, stressing the benefits they had brought with them.

This exchange really summarises the whole history of Witham. Sometimes, the town's chief virtue has been seen as respectability. But from time to time, waves of strangers have arrived, allegedly lowering the tone, but usually bringing new activities and often higher wages, particularly in manufacturing. They have been helped by the town's position, only 38 miles from London, and on the main route to the east coast. This route itself has given employment, with horses and coaches to be looked after, and eventually a busy railway junction and motor cars. The new residents were often suspected by the locals, but stood up for themselves. If they stayed, they became locals themselves in a generation or two.

In a more specific way also, modern Witham is a product if its past. The religious dissenters of early centuries were succeeded by the more settled nonconformists of the 1700s, amongst whom were the Thomasin family, who became prosperous brushmakers. It was in their property that the Co-op set up shop in 1887. The Co-op in turn provided a site for Crittall's metal window factory in 1919-20, which brought in more newcomers and played a large part in making Witham what it is today.

Witham has a long tradition of receiving newcomers. In August 1966, people started moving to Witham as part of a so-called overspill scheme. They and their successors came from London to new houses and jobs. This cartoon shows the first (Templars) estate in Cressing Road. It was drawn by the late Des Choate and published in the *Braintree and Witham Times*.

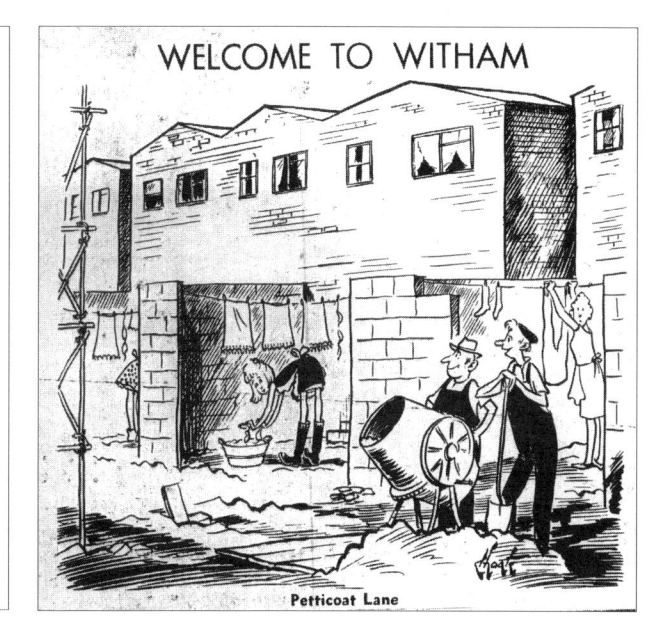

1. EARLY DAYS

Witham is full of surprises. Some of the older ones are now under the ground. This means that within the town, much of the distant past is concealed by newer buildings. Occasionally there are accidental revelations. For instance, men digging the railway in 1843 found three very rare Iron Age pokers. But most of the discoveries of recent years have come from organised excavations in fields around the edges of the town, prior to new building.

Putting all the discoveries together, we find that the river gravels and springs of the Witham area have long been attractive to humans. In some places tools have been found from the Stone Age (before around 2,000 BC), whilst the earliest signs of actual settlement date from the early Iron Age, perhaps about 1,000 BC. It was probably about five hundred years later that Iron Age people built a hill-fort surrounded by two circles of earth banks and ditches on the natural rise next to the river Brain. Covering twenty five acres (ten hectares) it was one of the largest in Essex.

Here by the river Brain, the natural embankment helped the construction of a hill-fort surrounded by earthworks, started in the Iron Age and enlarged in 913 AD. The main railway line was cut through them in 1843. This view is from Armond Road (taken in 1986). See also page 1 of the colour section, and the plan with walk 1 on page 140.

1. EARLY DAYS

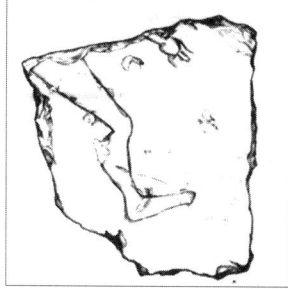

Roman finds from Maltings Lane. The copper-alloy key handle in the shape of a lion is one of the best examples found in Britain. The drawing of the leg and hand is on part of a tile, and was casually scratched by the tilemaker before firing (© Essex County Council).

By the time the Roman emperor Claudius landed in 43 AD to begin his conquest of Britain, much of Essex was settled and cultivated. The Romans continued this activity. The new main road from London to the Romans' 'oldest recorded town' at Colchester cut diagonally across the Iron Age fields. Although Roman items have been found in various locations, the only Witham sites which have been thoroughly investigated are on the southern edge of the town at Ivy Chimneys and Maltings Lane, on either side of the main road (now Hatfield Road).

There were several interesting domestic buildings at these places, but the most spectacular discovery was the sacred site at Ivy Chimneys. It was in use for over two hundred years with a succession of structures (it is shown on page 1 of the colour section). In its first phase, during the second century, the Romans collected early Stone Age hand axes to be used as ritual offerings in a pond within a ditched enclosure. Forty-one axes have been retrieved by archaeologists, a very rare find. Later offerings included carvings, and over a thousand coins. Houses built near Hatfield Road in the 1970s were given Roman street names such as Allectus Way.

The Anglo-Saxons

Saxon people were already arriving in Britain from the continent before the Romans left in 409 AD. Whether they used the old Roman sites is still debated, though there is some evidence for this happening near Maltings Lane. Most of the villages and towns in Essex were once Anglo-Saxon. At first the newcomers lived in small hamlets, some of them probably consisting of scattered houses around greens, detectable today from placenames such as 'Tye' or 'End'. For instance there was Powershall End, which still exists, and 'Rayners att Tye' (later Elm Hall farm).

The hamlet called 'Witham' was just outside the western bank of the old Iron Age earthworks (the area that we now call Chipping Hill). The origin of the name 'Witham' is not known for certain. 'Ham' was an early Saxon word for 'settlement', but 'Wit' could mean several different things, such as a bend (in the river), the general name for a leader, or the name of a particular person. In due course Witham became a very important place. There may have been a Saxon minster church as early as the 600s AD (a minster supervised a wide area). More people probably came here during the 800s when it became usual to gather in larger villages. Then in the following centuries Witham also became the headquarters of one of the new administrative areas called hundreds (in Witham's case known as a half-hundred). The leaders of fifteen parishes, some five or six miles away, came regularly to gather in outdoor 'moots' where they made decisions and dispensed justice. Their meeting place may have been near Moat farm, which stood in Moat Farm Chase until the 1950s and was sometimes called the Moot or Mote in the past.

Witham also had one of Essex's first markets. It probably started in late Saxon times, though the first written reference just says that it existed in the reign of Henry I (1100-1135). It was on Sundays until 1219 and on Tuesdays thereafter. This is the origin of the name Chipping Hill ('ceap' meaning market in Old English). The stalls were probably set up on the green.

The burh

With all these facilities and advantages, it is not surprising that King Edward the Elder should have chosen Witham when he wanted his soldiers to build a fortified site or 'burh' in 913 AD. This was during his successful battles to retrieve eastern England, and particularly Colchester, from the Danes. Most historians and archaeologists think that the burh at Witham was created by strengthening and enlarging the old Iron Age earthworks next to the village at Chipping Hill. As shown on the facing page, the work was considered sufficiently important to be mentioned in the Anglo-Saxon Chronicle. This is one of the most important surviving early medieval documents in the country. It had been started about twenty years previously, and was to be continued and updated by scribes for over two hundred years afterwards.

Anglo-Saxon Chronicle - original text:

[manuscript facsimile]

What the letters mean
Using modern letters except Þ = th; ⁊ = &

1	eadweard cyning mid sumum his ful-
2	tume on east seaxe to maeldune ⁊ wicode Þaer
3	Þa hwile Þe man Þa burg worhte ⁊ getimbrede
4	aet witham ⁊ him beag god dael Þaes folces to Þe aer un-
5	der deniscra manna anwulde waeron

Approximate translation

1	Edward [the] King with some [of] his for-
2	ces, in Es-sex to Maldon, & camped there
3	while the men the burg wrought & stockaded
4	at Witham, & [to] him submitted [a] good deal [of] those people which before un-
5	der Danish men's rule were

Building the 'burh' at Witham, as described in the Anglo Saxon Chronicle. It was a fortified site surrounded by earth banks which had a timber stockade on top. The manuscript itself is reproduced with the permission of the Masters and Fellows of Corpus Christi College, Cambridge.

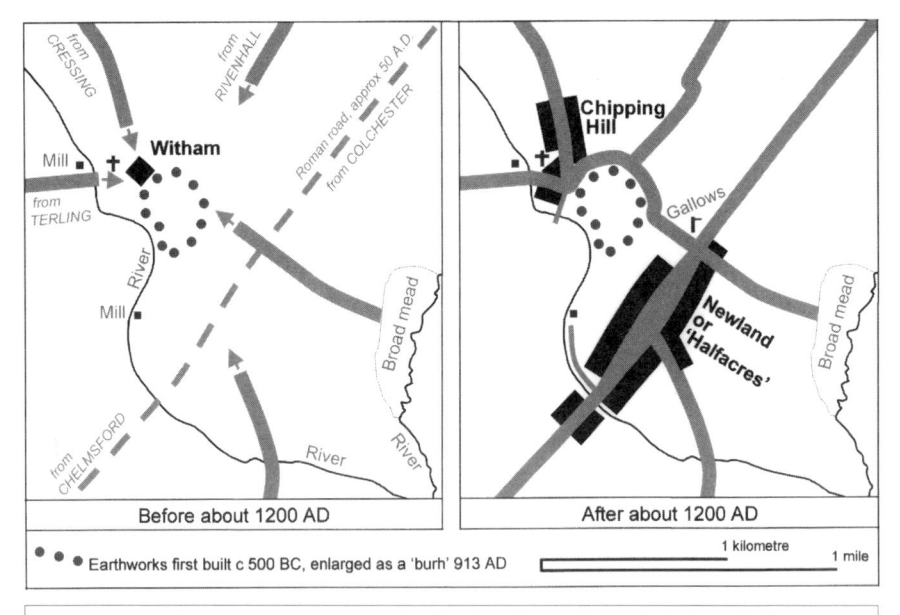

Sketch maps of two phases in the growth of early Witham. Solid black shows built areas, grey lines are roads and tracks. The exact form of the junction at Witham in the first phase is unknown, so I have shown the general direction of the routes with arrows.

The parish

A system of parishes grew up during the 10th and 11th centuries. The parish of Witham covered about 4¾ square miles (twelve square km). It included several estates or 'manors'. The main one, which was itself called Witham, continued to belong to the Crown after King Edward's forces had moved on. Its combination of royal estate, market, moot, minster church, and burh, seems to be unique in Essex. At some time its village at Chipping Hill was extended north in small regular plots, along what was then Hog End and is now Church Street. Three miles up this road was Cressing, which became a separate parish, but to start with probably belonged to Witham manor.

In the same period the Crown granted some of the other manors in the parish of Witham to noblemen or religious bodies. These were Powershall (or 'Little Witham'), Blunts Hall, Howbridge Hall, Benton Hall and Ishams. Later farmhouses survive for all of these today except Ishams (the one at Howbridge is shown on page 4 of the colour section). Blunts Hall has a small early medieval earthwork, possibly the fortification permitted to the

1. EARLY DAYS

baron Geoffrey de Mandeville in 1141 by King Stephen. Other manors with churches of their own, such as Faulkbourne, became separate parishes.

After the Norman conquest in 1066 the Saxon owners of these manors were replaced by new ones with French names. For instance, part of Howbridge manor, belonging to Brictmar, was given to Robert Gernon. The Domesday survey of 1086 recorded that the several manors in the parish of Witham had 140 'tenants' attached to them. Only five other Essex parishes had more. With their families there were perhaps 750 people in all. They may not all have lived in Witham. But those that did had plots of land, and certain rights to use their lords' valuable meadow land along the rivers, as well as the five water mills and the woodland. The biggest wood was in the south-east, where Chantry Wood near Ishams covered a hundred acres (40 hectares). Others were in the north, part of a large area of ancient woodland, some of which still survives in the adjoining parish of Rivenhall as Tarecroft Wood and Rivenhall Thicks.

Much of the Crown's property was taken by the victorious King William,

Chipping Hill, from across the river. This was the centre of Witham until a new town was built at 'Newland' in about 1200 AD. The parish church and some of the houses date from the 1300s and 1400s. Taken in January 2004 after a rare snowfall. Also see page 2 of the colour section.

The medieval barns of the Knights Templar at Cressing Temple, three miles north of Witham. They are some of the oldest timber barns in the world. On the left is the barley barn (built c 1200-1230) and on the right is the wheat barn (c 1257-1280). Witham also belonged to the Templars, but as Cressing was their local headquarters, they only had quite small buildings in Witham, where they did not need a big manor house.

including most of the manor of Witham. At Domesday a noticeable feature of the latter was that 57 of the tenants were called freeholders, the largest single group of these in Essex. They had more independence than other types of tenant, but their significance is not fully understood. In Witham they held small urban plots and also pieces of land of 20-40 acres (8-16 hectares). Soon after Domesday the King gave Witham manor to Count Eustace of Boulogne. For a time Eustace held regular courts of law here for some of his other manors. He had more estates in Essex and Hertfordshire than anyone else.

The Knights Templar

In 1137 Eustace's daughter Queen Matilda and her husband King Stephen gave the Cressing part of Witham manor to the Knights Templar. They were 'warrior monks', who had been formed in about 1118 by Crusaders in Jerusalem. Cressing now became a separate manor and the local headquarters or preceptory of the Templars. In about 1147 they were also given Witham itself. By then the settlement at Chipping Hill was a thriving commercial centre. Its residents included smiths, a mason, a thatcher, and a baker.

1. EARLY DAYS

The Templars' Witham base was in the old earthworks, near where the Albert now stands. They did not need a big manor house because their main centre was at Cressing. But they did have a chapel, a barn, a granary, and a dovecote. There was also a small dwelling probably used by the bailiff. In 1310 its living room was furnished only with a trestle table and two benches. The Templars' local courts of law were held at inns. Thus in 1290 'the whole court' stayed in the house of Richard the Taverner and his wife (probably the predecessor of the George, part of which is now the Town Hall).

The new town

By about the year 1200 England was experiencing a period of greatly increased trade and prosperity, and like many other landowners, the Templars saw a chance to profit from it. As well as having tenants, they kept a large area of land for themselves as their 'demesne'. It stretched for over a mile from near Cocks farm in Braintree Road in the north, to Sauls bridge

Newland Street (High Street) in about 1909. Many of the original plots of the early 1200s have been subdivided into narrower ones over the years. The wide area was once the market place. In the 1400s, some people, like butcher John Herde, turned their market stalls into fixed shops; hence the building projecting to the right of the telegraph pole. Also see page 3 of the colour section.

in the south, and was divided into three or four large fields of about forty acres each (sixteen hectares). A busy road ran through them, approximately following the Roman route from London to the coast. Men were set to work marking out long plots about five rods wide (82½ feet, 25 metres), along both sides of this road. At the lower end, in the west, the road crossed the river Brain, where there had earlier been a small hamlet called Wulversford.

This new settlement was the 'Newland', also known as 'Half Acres', because of the size of the plots (half an acre, one fifth of a hectare). It is now Newland Street, also often called the High Street. In 1212 King John granted the Templars a Thursday market and an annual three-day fair here. There was a market house or cross situated opposite the present Town Hall.

The building of Newland made Witham into a town rather than a village, and it has remained so ever since. The plots extended for over half a mile (800 metres) along the street, and during the rest of the 1200s most of them were built on by tenants who included people like tailors and bakers, drapers and dyers. None of the very first buildings survive today, but we do have a few which contain timber-work from as early as the 1300s.

More changes

About a thousand people may have been living in the parish as a whole during the 1200s, and other parts of it benefited from the flourishing trade of Newland Street. For instance, the lords of Howbridge Hall and Blunts Hall manors set out their own plots in 'Duck End' (now Bridge Street), which was a continuation of Newland Street to the west.

However, the original Saxon centre at Chipping Hill now suffered, because it was nearly a mile away from the commercial centre at Newland and the main road. By 1290 it was known as the 'old market' and in 1379 Richard II formally acknowledged the transfer of its weekly market to Newland Street.

The departure of commercial activity from Chipping Hill has helped to preserve its antiquity – there has been little pressure for change. Some of the fine houses which still stand there today date from before 1400. The parish church of St Nicholas remained at Chipping Hill also (spelt St Nicolas since the 1930s). The Bishop of London appointed the first vicar here in 1223, and much of the flint structure of the church building dates from the early 1300s.

The Knights Hospitaller

The Templars were disbanded by the Pope in 1312 after various disputes, and their property given to another military religious group, the Knights Hospitaller. This brought the Witham area to the fore during the Peasants' Revolt of 1381. The King's Treasurer, Robert Hales, was Master of the Hospitallers and lord of the manors of Cressing and Witham. So Cressing Temple was attacked during the early stages of the disturbance. Some goods were also stolen from Thomas Benington, probably at Benton Hall, and later William Berkeweye was killed by three men who worked for the lord of Blunts Hall. After the rebels had been to London and killed Robert Hales in the Tower of London, Robert Rykedon's house at Powershall was captured by another group. Two weeks later the rebellion was defeated near Billericay.

During the 1300s Britain's previously vibrant economy slowed down. The situation was aggravated by natural disasters such as harvest crises and particularly by the Black Death of 1348, when probably one third to one half of the people in the country died. In Spring 1349 Denise Bacon could not sell her pastures at Blunts Hall in Witham 'on account of the common pestilence in the country', and in 1355 Alice Faucelon was told to rebuild her ruined tenement called Goldings. Population numbers had been declining already, so there may have been only about five hundred people here by the 1400s. The parish church suffered financially from the smaller congregations, so in 1349 its buildings, mud walls, and dovecote were in decay. By 1360 they were worse, and the dovecote had disappeared altogether.

At the same time the Hospitallers began to lease much of their own demesne land to individuals, and in the 1430s some of the manorial buildings on the old earthworks were demolished. Two cartloads of the old timber were given to John Brown to repair his ruined house in Cressing. Another change in late medieval times was that small tenants began to pay their rent in money instead of being obliged to perform services for the lords of the manors.

Everyday life in the 1400s

The town centre at Newland declined less than other parts of the parish. It still benefited from being on the main road. Even the royal household and its officials stayed occasionally. In 1320 three of the king's carters with two carts and eleven horses lodged at an inn in Newland Street and were said to have been robbed by their hosts. The commercial opportunities and the freehold land had allowed individual tenants to have some success here. For instance the family of John Page of Newland Street built up sizeable estates.

Another important resident of Newland Street was John Basset, a woolmonger. He was part of the rural cloth industry of north Essex, which was well established by about 1300, and, after various setbacks, peaked in the late 1400s. Witham also had some dyers, and many weavers and fullers. Fulling is soaking and beating cloth to thicken it; Witham's water mills were used to mechanise the process in the 1400s. A group of fullers' men were in trouble in 1433 for taking rabbits from the manor's rabbit warren.

The river was also used for processing skins and making leather. Two leather workers were given pieces of land by the river Brain in the 1430s. In return, one of them, John Welde, was obliged to make a leather bag in which the steward could keep the manor court rolls. The river and the millponds were also important for fish. In 1435 red eels were kept at Chipping mill in a special floating box fastened with nails and bolts, but nevertheless a fuller and a shoemaker managed to break into it at night carrying swords and cudgels, and steal forty-three of the eels.

Much of our information about later medieval Witham comes from some manor records which survive for the first part of the reign of Henry VI (1423 to 1442). The court had the use of stocks and a pillory to punish the guilty. The stocks at Chipping Hill were broken in 1432; this was said to be 'to the great prejudice of the whole town of Witham'. Offenders included people who did not clear their ditches, causing them to flood and roads to be filled with dirt. There were also butchers and fishmongers who sold meat or fish

Medieval ploughing. In early medieval times, tenants had to do 'services' for the lord of the manor. In Witham these included sheep dipping, ploughing the demesne, and carting corn at harvest. But by 1400, most rents were paid in money instead (occasionally with a fowl or goose as well), and if tenants worked they were given wages.

1. EARLY DAYS

which was bad or too expensive, curriers (leather workers) who did not do their work properly, and bakers whose bread was underweight.

Sometimes there were assaults, with weapons such as sticks, daggers and swords. In 1423 Joan Busshegge was found to be a common scold, to the distress of her neighbours. She and her husband Thomas were also said to be eavesdroppers. In addition Joan had attacked Ellen Trippe with a pair of fire tongs. In 1426 seven Witham men were accused of breaking down the hedges of the lord and his tenants with branches of wood. They were all 'common players at ball', so perhaps the destruction took place during a game, with branches as sticks.

This man may be poaching like John Frer of Witham in 1442. In addition he was also a 'common player' of dice, chess, 'penyprik' and 'tenys' by day and night, which was also disapproved of. Tennis was originally played with the hands; penyprik was another ball game but its exact nature is unknown.

In the same documents we read about people who were tailors, carpenters, millers, bakers, yeomen, skinners, smiths, leather dressers, butchers, fishmongers, wheelwrights, innkeepers, and labourers, as well as a tiler, a fletcher, a chapman, a thatcher, a thresher, a shepherd, and a shoemaker. Sometimes there are lists of possessions taken to meet a debt, or found after a theft. For instance in 1425, John Rydel, the miller at Newland mill, had to forfeit the following: a fur-lined blue gown, a russet gown, a kirtel (tunic), a red cap 'called a langcappe', two linen sheets (one decent and one worn), and a worn blanket. In 1430, goods found 'abandoned' included two pairs of worn bags, a stewpan, a breadknife, ten wooden dishes and cups, three wooden spoons, a worn canvas doublet, a worn linen sheet and a wooden garlic mortar. More luxurious stolen goods in 1436 comprised three silver bowls, a silver lid, a maplewood bowl with silver decoration and gilding, six silver spoons, a pair of silver dishes and two belts with silver decoration.

Most of this diverse picture of Witham's everyday life would also hold good for the century after 1485, when the Tudor dynasty came to the throne. But at about that time we also begin to get information about some of the parishioners' enthusiasm for the more elevated disputes of Church and State, so much of the following chapter will concentrate on that.

2. TUDOR AND STUART WITHAM

Christopher Raven

During the early 1500s it was dangerous to criticise Catholicism, which was then England's state religion. But this did not deter Witham tailor Christopher Raven and his family, who lived in Church Street. He was so critical of the Pope and the Catholic church that he was summoned to London to explain himself to the authorities in both 1511 and 1527. He and his friends said that they repented, so they escaped being burned at the stake. But in fact both Christopher and his wife Joan continued in their beliefs.

They were part of a national movement often known as Lollards. Some of them were constantly on the move. For instance a well-known London preacher called John Hacker sometimes visited Witham, where he taught 'that in the sacrament of the altar was not the very body of god', that 'worshipping images, and offering and going on pilgrimages, was nought'. Another traveller was Thomas Hills, one of Christopher Raven's own assistants. In 1526 he visited London and bought Tyndale's forbidden version of the New Testament from a famous friar who was later executed. It cost three shillings (worth about £70 today). He used to read it aloud to his friends at Witham and elsewhere in Essex, and eventually sold it to the curate of Steeple Bumpstead, twenty-five miles north along winding roads.

The Ravens were very friendly with gentleman Christopher Royden, who lived across the road. The Roydens shared the Ravens' religious beliefs but probably escaped trouble. Very rich people do often seem to have been able to worship as they wished. And even the ones who were criticised by officials might be treated well in their home parish. So the Ravens and the Roydens all played a full part in Witham life. Christopher Raven even left twenty pence in his will to repair the parish church (perhaps £20 today).

The Dissolution of religious houses

By the time Christopher died in 1542, some of the Catholic traditions that he had criticised had been abandoned. This was part of the complicated series

2. TUDOR AND STUART WITHAM

of changes called the Reformation, which in due course officially turned England from a Catholic country into a Protestant one (1530s to 1560s). The Church of England, which everyone was bound by law to obey, usually followed a middle course. So often it would not accept either Catholics on the one hand, or extreme Protestants such as Puritans on the other. This frequently caused friction and drama.

Catholic organisations were dissolved, including, in 1540, the Knights Hospitaller, lords of the manors of Witham and Newland. The manors were bought by Sir John Smith, who was already living at Cressing Temple. Also closed down was the Abbey of St John at Colchester, which had owned 145 acres of land in the west and north of Witham. This was also sold and became the Witham Place estate. In 1567 the new mansion there became the home of Judge John Southcott (who is shown on colour page 5). He was probably not a Catholic himself, but his wife was, and also his descendants. They stayed till the mid 1700s, except for the time in the early 1600s when Witham Place was rented out to the Puritan Dame Katherine Barnardiston.

Making woollen cloth

In the last chapter we heard about fulling, part of the cloth finishing process. In the early 1500s there were several wealthy fullers in Witham. One of them, John Algore, died in 1513. His riverside premises were called 'the Watering'. There was a 'great house' there and large vats and vessels. By this time cloth had replaced raw wool as Britain's main export so it was a particularly good time for the industry. The main products were heavy broadcloths.

The wall of Witham Place in Powershall End. The large mansion built here in the early 1550s was the only entirely brick building in Witham for about 150 years. The only parts remaining are this wall, and a small part of the house which is now known as the 'Barn' and is a meeting room at the Spring Lodge Community Centre. Taken in 2004.

In about 1570 the production of 'New Draperies' began in Witham. These cloths, still woollen, were varied, but mostly very light. So they were suitable for export to countries with warm climates like Spain and Portugal. For the next hundred years or more, north Essex and Suffolk comprised one of the most important industrial regions of England. The centre of Essex production was Colchester, but many other nearby towns took part.

For various reasons, a new 'putting out' system was used. The organisers were the 'clothiers', who could be both prosperous and powerful. They took their wool to different workers in turn, for spinning, carding or combing, weaving and then finishing. Finally the fabric was stretched on tenters, which were frames set out in tenterfields; there were several of these in Witham town centre. The clothiers then sold the cloth to travelling merchants, who took it to markets, especially Leadenhall in London. The first clothier known in Witham was Jerome Garrard, who came to the Moat house, later Moat farm, in the 1570s. He and his descendants became prominent Puritans.

Many of the houses built in Witham during the 1500s and 1600s were later refronted with brick, or rebuilt. But we can still see these three fine houses at 23-27 Bridge Street in their original form. The outer ones probably date from the early 1500s and the central one from later in the same century. The small picture on the right shows a detail from one of the carvings. Taken in the early 1900s and in 2002 respectively.

During this time Witham was transformed by newcomers, as has happened many times in its history. The population of the parish probably doubled between 1550 and 1670, from about 500 to over 1,000. Very many of the new people were coming to work in clothmaking, some from as far away as Nottingham and Northamptonshire. Residents of neighbouring parishes were also given work by Witham clothiers, and the whole area was dominated by the fortunes of the industry. The best times were from about 1600 to 1624. But then England went to war with Spain, which was one of the main destinations for exported cloth, and disaster struck. By 1629 Witham and other nearby parishes were petitioning the House of Commons for help. The clothiers could not recover the money owed them by the merchants, and claimed that they were 'afraid to go home, being unable to pay their workmen or to set them any more at work'. The extreme crisis passed, but fortunes fluctuated for the rest of the century.

Puritans

It was not just in Witham's industrial life that the clothmakers were important. Every year from about 1600 until the outbreak of the Civil War in 1642, a clothier was usually chosen as one of the two churchwardens. This was a very influential post in any parish. Some of the Witham wardens and a considerable number of their fellow-inhabitants espoused Puritan beliefs. They were keen to suppress sins such as adultery and drunkenness, and working or playing games on Sundays. For instance in 1620 they accused Robert Bunny of 'admitting unlawful assemblies into his house upon the Sabbath day, spending their time in drinking, playing and the like in the time of Divine Service'. He was innkeeper at the George (part of which is now the Town Hall).

Puritans were also very hostile to any Catholic leanings. So it was perhaps not surprising that a company of Catholic Irish soldiers who were billeted in Witham should have met with resentment. On St Patrick's day in 1628, they were making merry and dancing 'with swords in their hands'. Then a young boy offended them by tying an Irish cross of red ribbon to the whipping post, and a shoemaker's assistant tied two more to the head and tail of a dog. In the resulting fracas, about thirty people were injured including the Irish captain, who was hit by a shot from a musket as he marched his men down the street.

In 1625 a new young vicar came to Witham. He was Francis Wright, a Yorkshireman. He soon became involved in a whole series of disputes, especially with the Puritans. For instance, churchwarden Robert Garrard refused to kneel during the prayers 'but stands bolt upright in his pew'. Conversely he sat during other parts of the service when he should have been standing. Elizabeth Totteridge took to 'reading aloud the singing psalme' and John Oliver to 'wearing his hat in service time'. All of these matters had particular significance in Church ceremony. The parishioners accused Francis Wright of being 'overtaken with excessive drinking of beer and wine'. They also considered that he used Catholic rituals. The immensely wealthy Dame Katherine Barnardiston of Witham Place encouraged them and contributed to the costs (she is shown on page 5 of the colour section). Her step-sons were the foremost Puritans of Suffolk.

Through her relatives, she helped Thomas Weld, a famous Puritan preacher, to become vicar of Terling, three miles away. Many Witham people started 'gadding' there to hear him instead of going to Wright's services in their own parish church. One of them, Peter Emmens, said that he went to hear 'a good sermon', which he could not get at home. In 1631, Weld left Terling

Witham parish church, where Puritan parishioners used to harass vicar Francis Wright. In 1631 the churchwardens refused to buy him a new bible, prayer book and surplice. When they were asked to whitewash the inside of the church, they did so, but 'blotted out the Creed, the Lord's Prayer and Ten Commandments which were written on the wall'. Taken in the early 1900s.

and fled the country on his way to New England, having been removed from his post by Archbishop Laud, who, with King Charles I, was very hostile to the Puritans. Laud's officials in London also questioned the Witham parishioners.

In 1639 Jerome Greene confessed to giving his vicar 'very foul language in the church yard adding ... he cared not a strawe' for him. Soon afterwards power began to move away from Charles I and towards the Puritans and Parliament, and in August 1642 the Civil War began. Parliament acted against vicars like Francis Wright, who was removed from office and sent to the Fleet prison in London for allegedly 'tempting of women ... to adultery and being a common drunkard' and conducting services whilst drunk.

The Civil War, 1642-1651

There were no battles near Witham during the Civil War. But there were raids on the houses of rich Catholics such as that of lawyer Thomas Bayles in 1642, and of Sir John Southcott in 1648 at the time of the siege of Colchester. Groups of soldiers also passed through sometimes, and afterwards it was said that the floor of the parish church had been damaged 'by reason of the soldiers shutting up there in the late unhappy times'.

Several Witham men went off to fight. Best recorded are the prosperous gentry. One of them was young John Southcott, who joined the Royalists and was personally knighted by King Charles in 1643 after he had captured the commander of Oliver Cromwell's troop. The men who went to fight for Parliament left fewer traces but we do know about Thomas White, who was wounded in the last battle at Worcester in 1651. The magistrates gave him a pension and he became a weaver, but he and his wife Ann died as paupers after the pension was withdrawn in 1660 by new Royalist magistrates.

The Restoration of Charles II, 1660

At the Restoration, many Royalist vicars were sent back to their parishes, and one of them was Witham's Francis Wright. In 1664 the churchwardens wrote a damning report about him. They said for instance that he locked the churchyard to keep his cattle in it, so that parishioners had to climb a gate, even if they were going to a funeral. In addition they said that he claimed the bread and wine of the Communion to be 'the real body and blood of Christ', had been twice convicted of drunkenness, and was 'a frequent swearer'. In the same year he allegedly 'levelled a gun' at John Harris at the vicarage during a dispute about tithes. He was probably deprived of the living in 1666 and he died in poverty in 1668. He must have wished that he had never come to Witham all those years ago in 1625.

New dissenting religious groups had emerged during the Civil War. Visits to Essex by James Parnell and George Fox in 1655 helped to establish the Quakers here. After the Restoration of the monarchy in 1660 their meetings were made illegal. Nevertheless, about one in ten of Witham people were Quakers at their most successful time, during the 1670s (the figure for the country as a whole was only one in a hundred). Several Quakers were arrested at a meeting in Witham in 1664 and sent to Colchester gaol for ten days for not paying their fines. But they were undeterred, and established their own burial ground in Church Street in 1667. Many of them were well respected locally, and sometimes they were appointed as trustees of the charities and overseers of the poor.

Freebournes (now 3 Newland Street, taken in about 1964). Clothier John Freeborne, Witham's first Quaker, lived here. After he died in 1675 it became a farmhouse, as it continued to be until the 1960s. Another Quaker clothier was Robert Barwell, who built a 'great house' on the site later known as the Grove.

2. TUDOR AND STUART WITHAM

Another group in Witham were known as Presbyterians or 'nonconformists'. One of their leaders was George Lisle, who had been rector of neighbouring Rivenhall during the Civil War but lost the post in 1660. There were arrests in 1663 when he spoke in a barn at Witham Place and then in his own home in Chipping Hill. Most of his people also attended the parish church.

In the last years of the century Witham became more settled. Legislation in 1672 allowed the houses of George Lisle and others to be licensed for nonconformist worship (they became the Congregationalists). Jonas Warley became vicar in 1680, staying until his death in 1720, and he partly accepted the nonconformists (though not the Quakers). Even Catholics had a brief period of official acceptance in 1685, when Sir Edward Southcott became a magistrate for three years.

At the end of the 1600s, many of the second generation of Witham Quakers left to join the Church of England. One of them was innkeeper Matthew Nicholls, who even became a churchwarden. He died in 1700, and this is his tombstone. It stands in a prominent position in front of the south door of the parish church. Taken in 1988.

Everyday life in the late 1600s

There were a number of material changes during the 1600s. Buildings were still timber-framed but some now had brick chimneys and glass windows. A few small courts of cottages, such as Collins Lane, were built behind houses in Newland Street. The most distinctive activity was still clothmaking, which temporarily revived in the 1660s, but its character started to change. The clothiers became fewer but perhaps richer, whilst the weavers were poorer and less independent, often living in small cottages in side streets like Mill Lane. A tax list of 1673 included 269 householders in Witham altogether, but 160 of them (60 per cent) were too poor to pay. Some of these were weavers. Looking after the poor had become an important role of the elected parish officials like the overseers, who were always busy.

So were their colleagues, the surveyors of the roads. There was an increase in horse traffic, particularly along the main road through Newland Street. The horses were changed at the inns, and contributing to this was the new postal system which grew up during the 1600s. Witham's postmasters were also innkeepers and they were often criticised. Once the mail was delayed because the servants refused 'to rise out of their beds to forward it'.

In addition the more usual commercial activities of any community continued. Witham's many farms benefited from new developments in fertilisers and crop rotation. Although there were still a number of smallholdings of less than twenty acres (eight hectares), there were more large farms than before (some are shown on colour page 4). There were three large watermills, as well as tanneries, maltings and breweries, usually next to rivers and small streams. The bridge at the bottom of Newland Street was described in 1659 as 'the great bridge adjoining to the two brewhouses at the hither end of Witham'. And a Witham tanner, John Osborne, was accused in 1662 of 'annoying the neighbours by tainting and spoiling the water with his hides'.

Craftsmen's workshops abounded. The most long lasting was the blacksmith's forge which we can still see at Chipping Hill. It has wooden shutters for its shop windows. Many tradesmen produced or prepared their own goods to sell, like the butchers with their slaughterhouses. But draper Samuel Wall, who died in 1673, sold cloth from as far away as Yorkshire and Hamburg, as well as ready-made waistcoats, stockings and socks. It was just before 1700 that retailing in something like its modern form became more common, and Witham's shops were to be an important feature of the succeeding centuries, helped by the patronage of the gentry, particularly the residents of nearby country houses.

Chipping Hill in about 1900. The group of people is in front of the blacksmith's house, which was built in around 1375. Documents tell us that there was a forge here in 1603, but it may well have arrived earlier. During the 1600s one occupant, John Adcock, was also a vet, with 'horse leech books', whilst another, John Greene, produced counterfeit coins.

3. 1700-1815
'A GOOD HANDSOME TOWN'

The best gentry and their mansions

During the 1700s Witham acquired an increasingly genteel image. Some gentry families took up residence in the town, though gentlemen from the surrounding villages continued to contribute to the town's affairs also. One of them was John Strutt of Terling, whose descendants, the Lord Rayleighs, were to lead many local organisations during the 1800s. Usually, the only residents of Witham itself who were really aristocratic were the successive households at the two mansions of Witham Place and the Grove. Some of them had a base in London too, as was common amongst the richer residents of Essex.

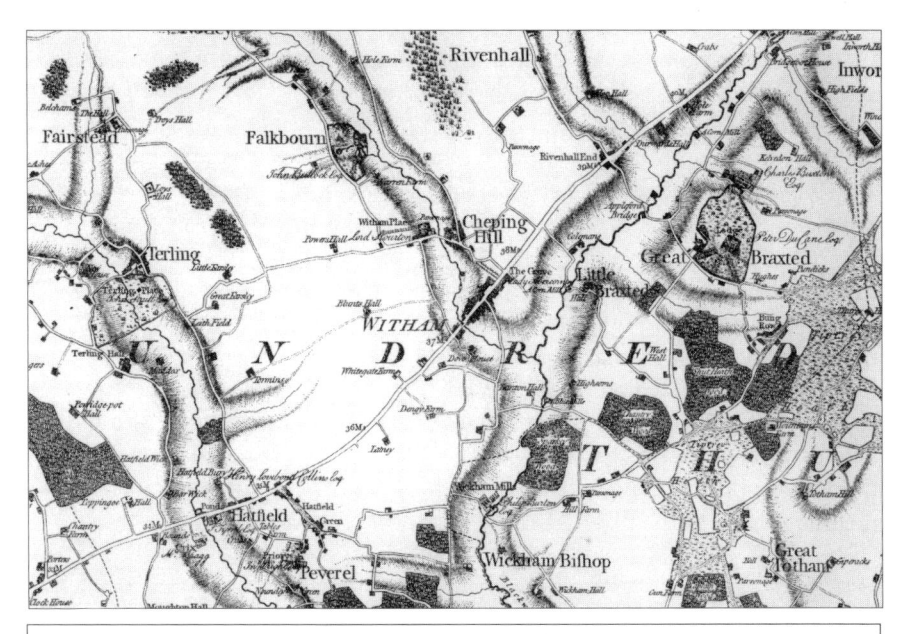

Daniel Defoe said in 1724 that Witham and its neighbourhood had an exceptional number of 'gentlemen of good fortunes'. Many of them lived outside Witham. Some of their country seats are shown on this map of 1777 by Chapman and André. They included Terling Place, Faulkbourne Hall, Braxted Lodge and Hatfield Priory.

At Witham Place in Powershall End there continued to be a succession of Catholic families. Following his Southcott forebears was Sir Edward, who died in 1751. During his time, a traveller described the house as 'a very ancient and excessive pile of building'. Nevertheless the next owner, Lord Stourton, told two youthful converts, Marlow and Mary Sidney, that it was 'a small property'. He provided them and the dozen or so other Catholic families in Witham with an English priest (quite a rarity – most of them came from the continent). Then in the 1790s came the Talbot family, relatives of the Earl of Shrewsbury.

At the Grove in Newland Street, gentleman Robert Barwell began in 1715 to build an ambitious brick mansion. He had previously pulled down his clothier grandfather's 'great house' on the same site, and bought several neighbouring cottages and demolished those too. He enclosed everything with a magnificent brick wall (which is all that survives; part is shown on colour page 17). But by 1719 he had moved to London and was bankrupt 'by reason of losses and misfortunes in trade'. The unfinished building was sold to an Irish peer, Lord Paisley, the 7th Earl of Abercorn. Diarist Daniel Defoe visited the 'pleasant well situated market town' of Witham during his tour of 1724, and noted that the Earl had a 'small but a neat well built new house, and is finishing his Gardens in such a manner as few in that part of England will exceed them'. The family also bought property on the opposite side of the main road and planted a grand avenue of lime trees which survived until the 1920s (now The Avenue; see colour page 7). In the 1760s Essex historian Philip Morant praised the 'plantations of trees and other decorations'.

The Abercorns left in 1782, and the mansion was advertised as 'a suitable abode for a person of the first distinction, or by taking down some part thereof, may be made an exceeding good house for a private gentleman'. Thomas Kynaston from London bought it. He was a lawyer and already owned property in Lincolns Inn and elsewhere. He and his family had their own bath house beside the river Brain – cold water bathing was then a fashionable pursuit. They and the Talbots paid extra Hairpowder Tax so that their children and their butlers could wear wigs as well as themselves.

One mark of success was to be appointed as a magistrate. Very few residents of Witham owned the amount of property necessary for this honour. One of those who did was the rich farmer and landowner William Wright (1719-69). In 1763 he helped to catch the thief of 'a pretty large quantity of broccoli' from the Countess of Abercorn's kitchen garden. His brother John was a

The initials of gentleman William Wright and his wife Mary at Avenue House (4 Newland Street). The drainpipe was needed to take rainwater from behind the parapet of the new brick front. When William died in 1769, local schoolmaster Thomas Allen wrote a eulogistic poem, concluding that 'posterity his merits shall proclaim, and tho' he's dead for e'er shall live his name'. The photo was taken in 2002.

flourishing London coachmaker, who retired to Essex to build a mansion at the Priory in Hatfield Peverel. William and John's success was especially notable because their Witham father was just a cooper (maker of barrels).

The lesser gentry and the military

Witham did have a small but perhaps increasing number of lesser gentlemen or their widows amongst its residents, sometimes only staying a short time. Often they came to take advantage of the proximity to London, and their main properties were elsewhere. One was Thomas Grant (1700-77) who had estates in Yorkshire and Oxfordshire. He lived in Maldon Road for many years, and in 1777 his obituary said that he had been 'possessed of great powers both in body and mind; and in the prime of his life was one of the ablest Mathematicians in this kingdom'.

Prosperous residents were often augmented by travellers and military men. One was Scotsman Robert Scoon who worked for the East India Company. He sailed for Bombay in 1754, an eight-month journey. The stores taken on at the Cape included eighty live sheep. Hazards met by the ship included scurvy, 'hard hearted winds', brandy catching fire, and a near-encounter with the notorious pirate Angria on the Indian coast. Robert stayed in India till he was killed during a battle in 1759.

Meanwhile, in 1756, the Seven Years War with France began, and Witham's John Cleland was made captain of a small sloop called the Merlin, engaged on escort and look-out duties. Almost immediately some of his men ran away. Then in 1757 his ship was captured by the French near Brest. He and his crew of about a hundred were sent back to England in disgrace in another vessel, leaving behind a few men in hospital and a 'Sweed' who joined the French. In 1781 John was promoted to the 'Formidable' with a crew of 600, and in 1783 he and his wife Mary Amelia moved away from the town and sold their furniture, including 'exceedingly good four poster beds' and 'fine goose featherbeds'.

Witham's most prominent soldier of the time was Archibald Douglas, Colonel of the 13th Dragoons in Ireland, who was promoted to Lieutenant General in 1761. For reasons unknown, he and Elizabeth Burchard did not marry until after they had had six children baptised (they had four more afterwards). They lived in the house which preceded the Whitehall (now the library). Archibald was a parish churchwarden and overseer, and spent most of his time in Witham, though when Elizabeth died in 1770 it was after being taken ill in Ireland. Her obituary referred to her 'unfeigned virtue'. Archibald himself died in 1778, said to be 'a gentleman universally respected'.

The Pattissons

Some families managed to join the town's genteel circles by moving up the social ladder. In particular there were the Pattissons. The three Pattisson brothers from the Maldon area arrived in Witham in the 1730s and started buying properties. They were drapers and grocers, and staunch religious dissenters, members of the Congregational church. They had money from their own businesses, and one of them, Jacob, also received an inheritance from his second wife Elizabeth. Her first husband had been John Jackson, a prosperous Witham clothier. The second Jacob Pattisson (1733-1805) called himself a gentleman. He and his wife Elizabeth (a cousin) were cultivated and well-read, and thanks to the interesting family letters which they began to preserve, have been discussed by several historians.

Their elder son Jacob (1758-82) was apprenticed to a surgeon in Colchester, where a jealous husband assaulted him for an improper house-call on his wife and his young lady apprentices. Jacob went on to Edinburgh University in Scotland and became president of the 'medical, speculative and physical' societies all at the same time. He was destined for a glittering medical career but sadly died there in 1782 at the age of 23. His brother, William Henry Ebenezer Pattisson, exchanged many letters during the 1790s with two friends, when they were all articled clerks preparing to be lawyers. One of them was Henry Crabb Robinson of Bury St Edmunds in Suffolk, a relative by marriage who later became an energetic and well-known literary personality. They debated religion and politics, and sympathised with the aims of the French Revolution.

Clergymen

The vicars of Witham at this time were all from extremely rich and well-connected families. There were only four of them during the 140 years from 1680 to 1821, most with glowing memorials in the church. Like many of their colleagues elsewhere, they also had other houses and held other ecclesiastical posts. They were also magistrates. Curates carried out many of the duties; for instance in more than half of the years between 1754 and 1799 the vicars themselves did not officiate at any marriages.

The first, Jonas Warley (vicar 1680-1722), was archdeacon of Colchester. He organised an extensive collection of funds to beautify the parish church in 1704, and left money to local charities when he died. At first his successor George Sayer (vicar 1722-1761), lived here for 'a great part of the year', even though he was also a canon of Durham cathedral. His Sayer relatives were extremely well placed in the Church and the Law. And in 1739 he married Martha Potter, whose father John was Archbishop of Canterbury, an immensely profitable post.

When John died in 1747 he 'amply provided for' Martha and George, who began to spend money on the vicarage. The extensive grounds were given a fashionable new 'natural' style by the renowned landscape gardener Philip

The Old Vicarage in about 1910. As well as having the grounds landscaped, vicar George Sayer improved the house. Essex historian Philip Morant wrote in 1763 that it was 'much enlarged, and greatly (or rather extravagantly) beautified'. Some parts have been demolished since this photo was taken but it is still an imposing building. The garden layout is shown on page 6 of the colour section.

Southcott, son of Sir Edward of Witham Place. Horace Walpole wrote in 1749 that 'what pleased me most in my travels was Dr Sayer's parsonage at Witham ... one of the most charming villas in England. There are sweet meadows falling down a hill, and rising again on t'other side of the prettiest little winding stream you ever saw'. The 'sweet meadows' are now open to all of us as part of the River Walk.

Next came Lilly Butler (vicar 1761-82). He lived at his other parish in Buckinghamshire. His visits to Witham were usually in late summer when he supervised the harvest and replenished his wine cellar. He became insolvent in 1782 and the churchwardens lent him £100 (left by Reverend Warley in 1722 for a charity school). His farming stock and his furniture were auctioned. They included his 'chariot' and two horses, 'exceedingly good' bedsteads, a 'beautiful Wilton carpet', over 'two hundred volumes of books in different languages', a 'large bathing tub', and 'a machine to clean gravel walks'. He went on to become chaplain to the Duke of Buckingham in Ireland and the money was never retrieved.

He was followed by Andrew Downes (vicar 1782-1820), who was the son and grandson of Irish bishops. He was extremely rich – the equivalent of multi-millionaire today. At first he lived away from Witham, and a newspaper advertisement was published to find a tenant for the 'large and convenient' Vicarage. The many inducements on offer included 'beautiful groves', 'choice-fruit trees' and the 'excellent cold-bath' in the grounds. The Downes' son, Richard, was hundreds of pounds in debt and was banished to the army in Canada.

Dissenters

The Congregationalists, otherwise known as Independents, continued to flourish. At first they met in members' houses, then probably in the upper floor of a maltings (now in the Grove precinct), and after that in a building in the Spread Eagle yard. Then in 1714 they bought some land of their own (now the site of the United Reformed Church, their successors). One of their members, Edmund Collins, built a small meeting house or chapel there. He was told to make it timber-framed, of 'hearty oak', underpinned with brick, and with white brick floors in the aisles. The whole was 'to be whitewashed so as will not rub off'. An extra adornment was a sun-dial with gold leaf. To meet maintenance costs and the purchase of coal and candles, the right to sit in the forty-three pews was 'sold' at prices ranging from 2s 6d each for the poorest seat in the gallery to a guinea for the best seat on the ground floor (about £12 and £100 at today's values). In a mysterious episode in 1728, the windows were broken by an unknown hand, and the town crier was paid to seek witnesses. We don't know whether or not he was successful. Extensions were built in about 1760 and in 1795.

The many successful ministers included Reverend Theophilus Lobb in the 1720s. He was also a doctor – he made 'Dr Lobb's Tincture for Family Use' and his publications included a two-volume work about curing fevers. Reverend Charles Case (here 1767-82) ran a boarding school for the gentry and probably also started a charity school for members' children. A description of the chapel in the 1780s describes the choir gathered in the gallery, accompanied by 'a flute, a clarionette, bassoon and bass viol'. It also mentions the free seats provided for the elderly poor, the members who came from a distance eating their lunch in the vestry between services, and the two wardens with long wands to keep order amongst the children in the galleries.

Schools

Church and chapel people played a part in the small boarding schools which were something of a speciality of Witham, especially during the 1760s and after. Nearly twenty different ones were advertised between 1759 and 1800. Some disappeared or changed hands quickly. Usually there would be two or three at any one time, with a peak in the later 1780s when there were often four or five. They traded on the town's genteel image. One of the most long-standing was at the elegant top end of Newland Street, in part of what is now Roslyn House. Mrs Burnett, the wife of the Congregational minister, moved her girls here in 1762, assuring customers that it was 'in an open, airy, part of the town', and 'larger, more commodious, and more pleasantly situated' than her previous place. Her 'Young Ladies' were 'carefully instructed in what is useful and ornamental'. One of the teachers had worked in 'some Genteel Schools about London', and the French teacher 'had her Education in France'. Pupils paid extra for 'Writing, French, Dancing and Musick'.

Reverend and Mrs Burnett moved away to Hull in Yorkshire in 1767, and Anglican clergyman John Caldow turned their building into a boys' school. He taught the more manly subjects of 'English, French, Latin, Greek, Writing, Arithmetic, Book-Keeping, Drawing, & the Use of the Globes, Geography etc', though dancing and music were available as extras. He planned to have twenty pupils, quite a large establishment for the time. In 1790 James Dunn became head and soon moved the boys to what was left of the mansion at Witham Place. He continued there well after 1800, with a hundred pupils in 1811.

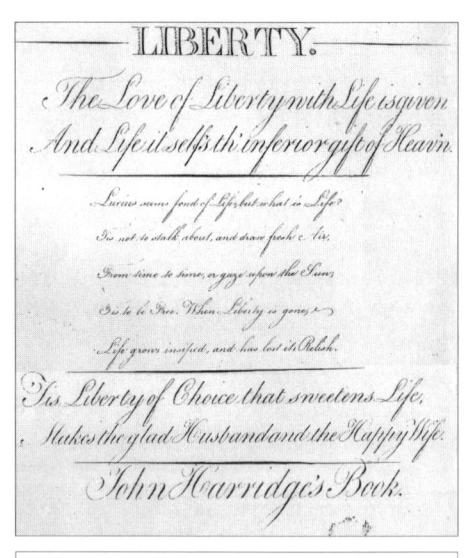

Part of the copy book of six-year-old John Harridge, a pupil at James Dunn's school in 1806. His father Thomas was a Witham wine merchant and brandy dealer. Prosperity in the later 18th century allowed people like him to send their children to such schools, as well as the gentry and aristocrats. Reproduced by courtesy of Essex Record Office (reference T/B 300/1).

Witham Spa and social life

For a time a Spa helped to enhance Witham's reputation for gentility. The spring was in a field north of Powershall End. A recent dowsing survey indicated that the remains of two large structures are hidden underground there (existing houses with 'Spa' names are all later). There had been an unsuccessful attempt to tap the waters in about 1700, and then in November 1735 the business was properly established by a written agreement between four partners. They were Sir Edward and Lady Jane Southcott, Dr James Taverner, and Martin Carter. Sir Edward owned the field, which was part of his Witham Place estate. Dr Taverner, a Catholic like the Southcotts, was the medical man. And Mr Carter was a very rich gentleman and lawyer seeking a good investment. A few years later he had a six-year old 'negro' boy 'belonging' to him at his home (now Avenue House). The lad fell ill, was baptised with the name Scipio Africanus, and died shortly afterwards.

The agreement refers to the 'profits and advantages' to be gained from selling the water, admitting people to the field, and renting out shops and stalls. Expenses included 'wages to servants or dippers', and the purchase of bottles and flasks. Tickets could be obtained at inns in the town, or at the 'Little Room' next to the 'Pump'. The centre-piece was the Assembly Room, or 'Long Room', probably constructed from the remains of the great Hall at New Hall near Boreham. Dr Taverner published a booklet in 1737, stressing that the water was 'of so exceeding volatile a nature' that it could not be transported, however well corked. So invalids needed to 'come to the Spring, and take it upon the Spot'. He also mentioned the 'serene wholesome air'.

I have not found any comments from people who took the Witham waters. But the Sussex man mentioned later as finding Witham 'handsome' wrote that the town was 'universally known on account of the spa, which has two very agreeable walks about it'. Advertisements in the newly founded *Ipswich Journal* tell us about its medical successes and its social life. Visiting patrons could be fetched from their lodgings. During the summer season there were regular gatherings where people could mingle or play cards. The highlights were monthly Assemblies, with a Ball, held in the Long Room.

'Coffee and refreshments' were served at Barnardiston House in Chipping Hill by Jacob Pattisson. In due course he obtained a quarter share in 'the waters', and probably continued to run the Spa after all four of the original partners died (the first being Dr Taverner in December 1747). The

> **WITHAM SPA in ESSEX.**
> THE Mineral Water being now in Perfection, Attendance is given at the Well as usual.
> The next Monthly Assembly will be on Monday the 16th of July; and the Card Assemblies twice a Week.
> N.B. The Monthly Assemblies being kept upon a Subscription, was done only with a Design to exclude improper Company: So that any Person of a genteel Appearance and Behaviour, will, tho' not a Subscriber, find a ready Admittance.

> It took a little while to work out the best admission arrangements for the Spa. To begin with, anyone could buy a ticket for 2s 6d (about half a week's wages for a labourer). Then a subscription was introduced, to ensure 'certainty of meeting good company'. Afterwards a compromise was reached, as shown by this newspaper advertisement of June 1744.

advertisements ceased when Jacob also died in 1754, but a house to let in Terling in 1756 was promoted as being 'about two miles from Witham Spa', showing that the image was still valuable.

And social life continued to flourish. In 1757 a cock fight was advertised in 'a very handsome pit' at the Black Boy (now the Red Lion). More genteel were the concerts, assemblies and balls in the Newland Street inns. One of the promoters was Signor Ghillini Di Asuni. In 1760 he advertised 'a concert of music by the best performers, after which there will be a ball'. An 'elegant and genteel supper for the gentlemen & ladies' was provided. This was at the Red Lion (then at 68 Newland Street). A Mrs Draper gave a recital in 1788, but a diarist recorded afterwards that she had 'so indifferent a voice that in my opinion should never be articulated'. The venue this time was the George, which had a 'spacious Assembly Room, dining parlours of all sizes, elegant bed chambers, wine vaults and beer cellar' (part of it is now the Town Hall).

In 1769 there were home and away cricket matches between the Gentlemen of Witham and the Gentlemen of Kelvedon, each team winning at home. There even seems to have been a theatre briefly, with a pit and a gallery. In 1777 a 'Dramatic Romance' was put on there, 'as performed upwards of fifty nights at the Theatre Royal in Drury-Lane' in London, and also a farce called 'The Wrangling Lovers'. During the 1770s and 1780s there was an annual show called a 'Florist Feast', with a dinner. This was at the Angel Inn on the corner of Maldon Road, and was for the benefit of 'members and others curious in flowers'.

The Great Essex road

In his book of 1737, Dr Taverner wrote that the road from London to Harwich, on the coast, was 'justly reputed one of the finest in England', and that 'stage coaches and the post are every day passing and re-passing through' Witham. The whole of the route was gradually 'turnpiked' between 1695 and 1725, meaning that tolls could be collected by a trust, to help pay for maintenance. Loose gravel was the main road material and the work must have been a losing battle. For instance, the lord of the manor of Newland (a London lawyer) wrote in 1703 of the 'great quantities of cattle' that were driven through Witham from as far away as Norfolk. To him this was a good thing; he obtained permission to hold a cattle market in the town (probably held at first on what is now the western half of the Park, where the cedars are).

Humble travellers on the main road had to walk, unless they could get rides on the carts of the carriers who conveyed an assortment of goods. These took twenty-four hours to cover the forty miles to London. Thomas Read announced in 1769 that his 'stage waggon' would leave the Spread Eagle for London on Tuesdays, returning on Fridays. After he died, his son continued to offer 'proper care and assiduity' to his customers. Nevertheless, a sack of clover seed was lost from his waggon in 1777. Many vehicles came from further afield. In 1809 John Saggart was driving a 'fish machine' through Witham, with fish from the coast, when he was accused of 'wilfully driving over' the legs of another man, who died two months later. The verdict was manslaughter and John was imprisoned for a year.

This iron milepost in the Colchester Road, dating from the 1800s, stands in front of an older stone from the 1700s (which has a 20th century benchmark on it). Taken in 2003. Since then it has suffered a rather garish repainting.. The 37 mile post used to stand in Hatfield Road opposite the Bridge Home but was removed in 1973 (news of its present whereabouts would be welcome). The distance was measured from Aldgate Pump in London.

Soldiers were also frequently on the move and were stationed in Witham at times, probably engaged in policing, including keeping watch for highwaymen. Some had children baptised in the parish church. In 1780 there was a military training camp at nearby Tiptree Heath where Witham's John Wade set up a tavern serving 'dinners, teas, coffee etc.' to 'the Nobility, Gentry and others'.

These 'Nobility and Gentry' also came through Witham itself, and Dr Taverner stressed that the town 'frequently gives entertainment' to prosperous visitors 'from Norfolk, Suffolk, Ipswich, Harwich, Colchester; and is consequently provided of proper accommodations for all sorts of people'. The best-known passer-by was the future Queen Charlotte, who stayed overnight at the Grove in September 1761. Aged seventeen, she was on her way to London by coach from Harwich, after a rough ten-day sea journey from Cuxhaven near Hamburg in Germany. On the voyage she had practised English tunes on the harpsichord. Her host, the Earl of Abercorn, was known for his silence, but he later admitted that she had given him 'a good deal' of trouble. The next day she went on to London, met King George III for the first time, and married him the same evening. Other less exalted 'royal personages' passed through from time to time.

The Grove. When the future Queen Charlotte stayed here in 1761 on the way to her wedding, she consumed a lavish dinner. The first course alone consisted of 'leverets, partridges, carp and soles', brought urgently from Colchester. The chief inhabitants of Witham were allowed to crowd round the door to see her. Taken in about 1905.

3. 1700-1815

The former Blue Posts coaching inn (now 126-28 Newland Street). In 1748 the innkeeper here was 'formerly cook to the Earl of Rochford'. He boasted that he had 'a careful driver'. But in 1777 two of his successor's lads 'wantonly' drove their coach and its four horses into a smaller one at Springfield. They then 'went laughing' through Chelmsford 'in a most indecent manner'. Taken in 1986.

The regular stage coach service was already operative by 1700 but came into its own during the prosperous second half of the century. Eventually this communal form of travel came to be regarded as rather 'common'. In 1758 this reputation led to a stage-coachman being suspected of taking from the Blue Posts 'a middle-sized Spaniel bitch, with large yellowish spots on each side, and yellowish ears, and answers to the name of Phillis'. Phillis's sorrowing owner advertised a reward for her in the newspaper, as did a stagecoach traveller between Ipswich and Witham who in the same year lost 'one shirt, a neckcloth, a cotton cap and sundry drawings and papers, roll'd up in a handkerchief'.

People with more money could hire post-chaises with horses for their own private use at certain inns. They were driven by 'post-boys' (sometimes quite elderly), and on long journeys the horses would be changed en route. The inns had extensive stables. For instance in 1783 the George had accommodation for seventy horses (part of it is now the Town Hall).

One specially important task was carrying the mail, which for much of the 1700s was usually taken on horseback. A local innkeeper would be postmaster, a coveted position. Richard Franks of the Blue Posts lost the job in 1759 to Jeremiah Brown of the George, resulting in a feud. When Jeremiah hired his best horse to Richard in 1766 to take one of Lord Hertford's servants to Ingatestone, the horse died. In court Jeremiah said that Richard was 'more covetous than courteous' and that the rider was 'a monster rather than a man'. The difficulty of supervising horsemen helped the suspected spy John Robinson, who lodged in Witham. He had lived in America for a time, and was arrested in 1756 and accused of secretly sending information and maps about that country to France. Instead of being put in the bags with the mail, his letters had travelled in the post-boys' pockets.

To increase security, the Post Office in London experimented in 1770 with the idea of carrying the mail in coaches on the Harwich run. They adopted a special vehicle designed and built by Witham coachmaker William Perry. This was fourteen years earlier than the date of what is usually said to have been the first English mail coach, on the route from London to Bath in Somerset. Essex's regular system began in 1785, when coaches carried an armed guard and were closely regulated.

Cider, clocks and surgeons

Passers-by and visitors enhanced the economy of Witham. In itself it was still quite a small town, and half of its 300 families were poor (of whom more later). Like other such places, Witham did particularly well in the second half of the century. The busy inns were supplied by local tradesmen such as Peter Hetch, the cider and wine maker. The William Perry who made the mail coach sold a variety of vehicles painted in fashionable colours to 'gentlemen' from his 'new and convenient' workshop. His son continued the business till the 1850s.

Most of the goods sold by craftsmen and shopkeepers were made or prepared by themselves. When Thomas Watts, a 'cabinet and chairmaker', sold his stock in 1773, he had mirrors, tables and chairs, and also 'a large quantity of Mahogany Logs, plank and boards very fine, with walnut-tree faneers,', all 'dry and fit for immediate use'. Another specialist was clockmaker Richard Wright (one of his clocks is on colour page 6). The ambitious retailer would advertise for custom in the newspapers, often using the reflected glory of London. In 1756 Robert Watson stressed that his materials for peruke (wig) making had been approved 'not only in London

3. 1700-1815

Under this building is the arched brick vault where Peter Hetch started making cider and wine during the 1740s (now 123 Newland Street). The cider could be collected at 'the vault door' (visible to the right of the steps). He had 'practic'd making English wines for several years' so that they could 'scarce be discern'd from foreign, by the nicest palate'. Taken in 2004.

but in most capital towns in Great Britain'. They were 'sold in the same terms as the Scotch & other hawkers purchase them in London.' Milliner Mary Darby in 1766 had 'a proper Assistant from London', so 'such ladies as will be so kind as to favour her with their commands, may depend on being served in the neatest and best manner.' And in 1784 leather seller Joseph Matthews advertised 'Gentleman's breeches on the London construction'.

Witham always had several medical men. They were usually 'surgeons' (less reputable than physicians). For instance, Robert Mayhew worked here as early as the 1690s and was known as a doctor, a surgeon and an apothecary. Christopher Mayhew junior, probably Robert's grandson, died young in 1762 with an 'extensive business' in medicine. His widow advertised for a 'clever, ingenious, active Man, that is a good Surgeon and Apothecary, and Man Midwife'. She chose John Heatherley from London (said by a diarist to have a 'mirthful and social turn of mind'). Charles Cottis of Chipping Hill was rather different. He advertised in 1781 that God had given him the talent of using 'simple herbs', so that during the previous twenty years he had cured a variety of ailments. As well as selling his herbal waters from his house, he made visits, for which he charged sixpence a mile (about £2 today).

Witham's 'medical quarter'. A doctor's surgery was first established here in about 1749 by Christopher Mayhew the younger. He was at what is now number 119 (the right hand one of the two tall buildings on the left). One of his successors there sold the business in 1811 to Dr Henry Dixon, who in about 1837 moved along to number 129 (on the right, with bow windows). He took as his partner Alexander Procter, who first lived at the Gables (numbers 125-27, in the middle, with four gables), and then at number 119. In due course Dr Proctor took over, and in 1858 hired a young resident assistant, William Gimson Gimson [sic]. Dr Gimson moved out to the Gables when he married, and then took charge when Dr Procter retired. He died in 1900 whilst helping with an operation at a Witham house. His wife and daughter stayed at the Gables, and his son Dr Karl set up a practice at number 119, where he was joined in 1902 by his brother Edward (Dr Ted). Karl died in 1926. Dr Ted took other partners, moving eventually to number 129. He retired in 1945 after over 40 years, a much loved figure. His partners continued and the practice flourishes at number 129 to this day, having also incorporated the Gables in 1996.

3. 1700-1815

Rebuilding Witham

During the 1700s the centre of Witham was transformed, as its medieval street scene gave way to elegant red Georgian brickwork. We would be shocked if such a great change were to be suggested today. But as a result we have inherited a fascinating variety of buildings. In Newland Street one of the first houses to be changed may have been Batsfords (100 Newland Street), which was probably re-fronted during the 1690s by the prosperous clothier John Jackson. It still looks very striking today, and must have seemed even more so when the rest of the street still retained its medieval plaster. Next we had the mansion at the Grove already mentioned (1715 onwards). Soon afterwards the conversion of ordinary houses to brick gathered momentum. The Pattissons in particular rebuilt or refronted about a dozen houses in Newland street, and financed others with loans. Jacob's own home, built in about 1750, became rather grandly known as Witham

A view down Newland Street, showing some of the fine brick buildings, many of them dating from the 1700s, and most still standing today. At the tall narrow one on the left (now 83), Daniel Whittle Harvey was born in 1786. He was a lawyer, politician and journalist and founded the *Sunday Times* newspaper in 1822. Taken in the 1890s, just before motor vehicles arrived.

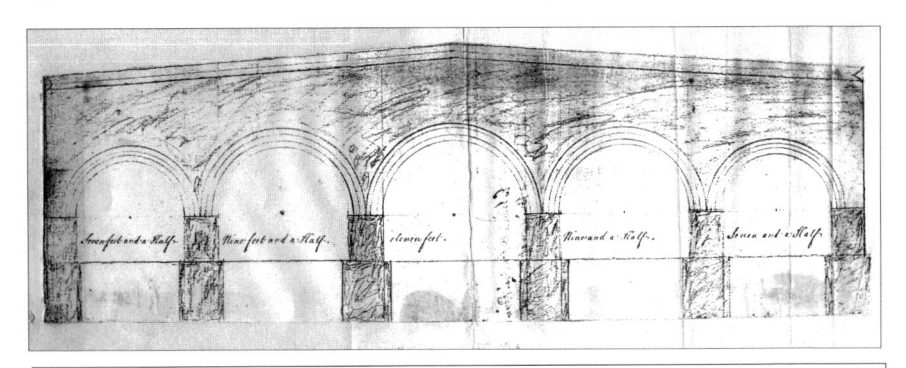

The working drawing for the bridge at the bottom of Chipping Hill. It was designed by bricklayer Samuel Humphreys, with his colleague Charles Malyon. They took just three weeks to build it in August 1770. Most of the other wooden river bridges were also replaced with brick ones during the 1700s. Reproduced by courtesy of Essex Record Office (reference Q/SBb 255/18).

House (57 Newland Street). Sussex man John Collier visited Essex in 1745 and found that Witham was 'a good handsome Town, and has many good houses'. In comparison he found Chelmsford 'indifferent', Colchester 'not very extraordinary' and Harwich 'only a dirty mean place'. In 1768 Philip Morant wrote that 'the Pattissons, eminent shop-keepers here, have of late adorned this place with good brick houses, more than any other persons'.

Apart from High House (for which see walk 3, pages 168-69), the new structures were designed by the owners and in particular by the builders. Local brickmakers and bricklayers and other craftsmen prospered. In 1765 the employees of Witham's carpenters announced that they did not intend to continue work unless they were paid eleven shillings a week (about £45 today). We do not know the reason or the outcome.

Manufacturing and farming

Although cloth making continued, it experienced a general decline and many serious crises. There were a number of weavers until about 1750, especially in Mill Lane, but they were not prosperous enough to pay taxes. Their apprentices were the poor children sent by the parish to learn 'the art, trade or mystery of a weaver'. After the mid-1700s there were only two or three clothiers. The most long established were the two John Darbys (father and son). The father inherited the business from a grandfather in 1731. In 1772 his goods were sold to meet his debts, including looms, packs of yarn 'at different spinning houses in the country' and 'a horse mill' for roughing (raising the nap). These machines, powered by a horse walking round in a circle, caused objections when first introduced because they needed fewer workmen. Finally the loss of exports due to the French Wars virtually closed Essex clothmaking down for good in 1793.

To be noted particularly is the arrival of the Thomasin family in about 1720. They were religious dissenters. The first was Matthew, who made pattens (wooden clogs). His descendants expanded into brush manufacturing, which was to flourish during the 1800s. As explained in the introduction, in some ways they paved the way for the town of today. During the 1700s there were also the usual industries of small country towns like malting, milling, tanning and leatherworking (also known as 'breeches making' – workers' breeches or trousers were made of leather). One curiosity is the 'Coke-oven field', part of the Pattissons' grounds in the 1760s and 1770s. This was earlier than other known coke ovens in Essex. They turned coal into coke and were more usually situated on coalfields or on the coast. It may be that Witham's coke was used in malting, to heat the drying kilns.

Some of the farmers took part in the general improvement of methods

The maltings in Maltings Lane. Originally a 16th-century tannery, it became a maltings in the early 1700s. The brick parts and the tall kiln were added towards the end of the century. Taken in 1984 before conversion into flats. Another 18th century malting is now a shop in the Grove shopping centre.

during the century, particularly the use of fertiliser and the rotation of crops. Agricultural investigator Arthur Young wrote that 'the wheat about Witham was so fine in 1784, that I inquired the preparation'. There was a great demand for wheat and other food for London, especially towards the end of the century. Frequent shortages resulted in high prices. This benefited the farmers in particular, and their lifestyle became considerably more elegant than it had been previously.

The poor

However, these high prices caused great distress to the poor. So far I have shown Witham as a successful and largely untroubled place during the 1700s. But as already mentioned, about half of the town's families were regarded as poor. Even if they were working, wages were low and job security hazardous, especially in winter. So they needed help to prevent them from starving, and money for this was raised by rates levied on the property owners. The organisers were the two elected overseers of the poor and the two churchwardens, who were usually master craftsmen and tradesmen, with a few gentlemen and yeomen.

They built a parish workhouse in 1714, with the intention of saving money by bringing Witham's poor to live and work together. Parish officers from Chelmsford, planning one of their own, came to see it and were impressed. Many of the residents were widows and some were elderly men such as 'old Sharp'. The building was also registered as a 'House of Correction' where 'vagabonds' and 'disorderly persons' could be given punishments such as whipping. The overseers bought fleece wool (including '6 pounds of black wool' in 1720), and the inmates worked at spinning wheels in the 'long working room' in the attic. Two Witham clothiers, William Jackson and Thomas Waterhouse, bought the spun yarn.

Items bought for the workhouse included soap, candles, beef, eggs, beer, turnips, yeast, milk for milk broth, brooms and 'backow' (tobacco). Shoes and clothes were also needed, such as 'a pair of shirts for the widow Long's children', and coffins and burial expenses had to be found. New rules adopted in 1726 included times and menus for meals, the saying of grace, the type of clothes (cheap ones), punishments (deprivation of meals), church attendance, and hours of work (5 am to 7 pm). In 1723 the Witham officials announced that because of new legislation, 'all Persons who take or ask for

The former parish workhouse in Church Street (now divided into cottages, but still known as 'Charity Row'). The long building on the left was purpose built in 1714 by the overseers and churchwardens whose initials are still displayed on it (shown on colour page 20). Some of the bigger cities already had such facilities, but Witham's was one of the earliest in a small town. The builder was Edmund Collins who also put up the Independent meeting house. Drawn in 1918 by Frederick Snell.

weekly relief be sent to the Workhouse'. But in practice, many local people seem to have been helped at home as well throughout the century. In 1727 surgeon Christopher Mayhew was given £8 a year to treat all the poor and supply 'wholesome Medicines of all sorts'.

During the small-pox year of 1724, 114 people were buried in Witham, twice as many as usual. A big step was taken in 1778 when the principal parishioners decided to inoculate the thousand or more poor residents. This was a risky procedure, and afterwards they put an advertisement in the local newspaper to point out that only seven people had died as a result (four of them were babies and one was over seventy). Witham also kept a 'pest house' for infectious parishioners, situated where the Victoria Cottages now stand in Maltings Lane.

At difficult times the poor sometimes tried to take matters into their own hands. In 1772 Witham residents joined a widespread campaign of stopping waggons and seizing the food so they could sell it cheaply or give it away. One newspaper report said that 'Last night a carcase butcher's cart was stopped at Witham, and this day the meat is to be sold at three-pence per pound. Five more are expected in the morning, and the moment they arrive they will share the same fate'. Miller Robert Bretnall of Powershall End was one of the Essex men who advertised for information about 'disorderly people' who had gathered 'in a riotous manner, armed with bludgeons', and harassed millers and farmers to sell their wheat more cheaply. In 1777 the members of the Witham 'Association for the apprehending and convicting of Horse Stealers' discussed extending its interests to the detection of sheep-stealing and other crimes.

By the 1780s the situation was aggravated by the virtual disappearance of cloth making and particularly spinning. The custom of hiring farmworkers for a year at a time was also in decline. Winter was always worst. A local newspaper reported in February 1784 that 'the inhabitants of Witham have collected about £50 to distribute amongst the poor of that parish in bread and coals; an example worthy of imitation' (about £3,500 today). However, more detailed evidence survives for other nearby towns, and suggests that treatment of the poor in this period could often be very harsh.

Meanwhile the spiritual and moral welfare of the poor was becoming a matter of concern to the Churches. In addition to the Congregationalists' school, by 1790 there was a busy Sunday School and part-time Day School provided by the worshippers at the parish church. There was also a 'poor man, a Papist, who keeps a school – children of every persuasion are taken at a very early age to learn to read.'

The French Wars, 1793-1815: the poor

The plight of the poor was aggravated by the conflict after the French Revolution which became the Napoleonic War. The rapid national population increase of the time was reflected in Witham; where the number of inhabitants increased by half between 1780 and 1810, to about 2,300 (500 families). But the resultant rise in rate income was more than wiped out by inflation. And whilst wages rose, food prices increased even more. 1794 and 1795 were very difficult, with poor harvests aggravated by more small pox and another inoculation programme. 1801 was even worse and bread was rationed. By then, the product of a penny rate in real terms was only half what it had been before the War, so that the rates had to be nearly trebled to cover the extra expenses, which included a three-fold increase in the number of 'casual poor' needing temporary help. Later in the War many of these people had been transferred to the list of people having to receive regular 'weekly payments' with little hope of improvement.

Notices were posted at each end of Newland Street in 1805 to warn off beggars, but it was reported that Irish vagrants looking for farm work were still

Part of a declaration made at Witham in 1801. Bread rationing was also proposed. The aim was 'to alleviate, by every means in our power, the burthens of the Country in general, and more especially the distresses of the Poor'. The King had issued a proclamation about shortages and high prices during the War. Reproduced by courtesy of Essex Record Office (reference D/P 30/8/16).

'infesting' the town. In 1807 the parish gave an extra £5 to the governor to run the workhouse 'on account of dearness of provisions', and in 1811 he had £10 'on account of the high price of flour'.

The French Wars, 1793-1815: the wars

In 1797-98, it was feared that Napoleon would invade Essex (we now know that Kent was his target). Every parish was ordered to be ready to assist the troops in defending the county. Sixteen waggons, each with four horses, were promised from Witham, mostly by the farmers, and twelve carts, each with two horses, mostly by the tradesmen. Five 'conductors' were to guide them. In addition there were 150 men 'willing to act as Pioneers or Labourers'. A separate list showed the 'implements they can bring', which were twenty axes, six pick-axes, ten spades, six shovels, two bill-hooks and eleven saws. Many of them, like John Bickmore with his spade, could only bring one item. At first it was planned to lay the countryside waste to impede the invading enemy, but when the lists were revised in 1801 this aspect was abandoned.

Like many other places, Witham also formed a part-time armed Volunteer Corps for local protection. A meeting at the Blue Posts in 1798 agreed that it should have between sixty and eighty men. The 'Peace of Amiens' of 1802 gave a year's respite but on the resumption of fighting in May 1803 they re-formed on a more official basis. In that year they exercised for twenty days, but in 1813 it was only five – the danger lessened after the Battle of Trafalgar in 1805. The Witham corps had buglers instead of the more usual drummers. One of them was sixteen-year old James Dace, later organist and parish clerk (he appears again in the next chapter, with his equally musical son (page 73)).

In addition there was a statutory body called the militia, who usually served in Britain. They were normally part time, but became full-time during war. A number of men from each parish were recruited by ballot. The parishes often gave money for substitutes from other parishes to go instead – in 1802, the Witham overseers paid £80 altogether to send seven of them (about £4,000 at today's money). They also maintained the militia men's families.

Meanwhile, many regular soldiers from Witham were fighting around the world. We know most about the ones who were injured or ill and discharged with a pension. For instance Private Charles Keatly sailed for Lisbon in

Portugal with the 13th Light Dragoons in 1810 for the Peninsular War, and had been rendered 'deaf and worn out' by 1814. In the same conflict was Sergeant William Swain of the Coldstream Guards, a shoemaker in civilian life. He had enlisted when he was sixteen in 1807, and was badly injured in the face at the Battle of Bayonne in France in 1813, but was not discharged until 1837 when he was 'worn out by age and length of service'.

And at least two Witham men survived the battle of Waterloo in Belgium which brought the Napoleonic War to an end in June 1815. One was Sergeant John Egar, of the 59th foot, who had joined the army at 16 and was still only 21, and the other was a 38-year old private, Thomas Lancaster of the 11th Light Dragoons. A year later Thomas had his arm badly broken by a 'kick from his horse' in France. After being discharged in 1819 he went to Birmingham, married, and had three daughters. As we will see in the next chapter, his widow Mary Ann fell on hard times after he died.

Soldiers from the time of the Napoleonic War. Several Witham men were in the army then, and at least two fought and survived at the Battle of Waterloo.

4. 1815-1901
'A RADICAL PLACE', OR
'A RESPECTABLE LITTLE TOWN' ?

In December 1815 the Prince Regent made one of his regular visits to the Blue Posts inn. One resident noted that these were always 'right royal drunken' occasions. Nevertheless, 'the loyal inhabitants saluted his Royal Highness with the old English tune of 'God Save the King'. His brother was here too, and visited Captain Nicholas Tomlinson, who was living opposite after an eventful naval career during the War. The Captain's house was 'brilliantly illuminated' (now 129 Newland Street, the surgery). The Prince paid for 'a handsome treat for all, of which the poorer classes were allowed to partake'.

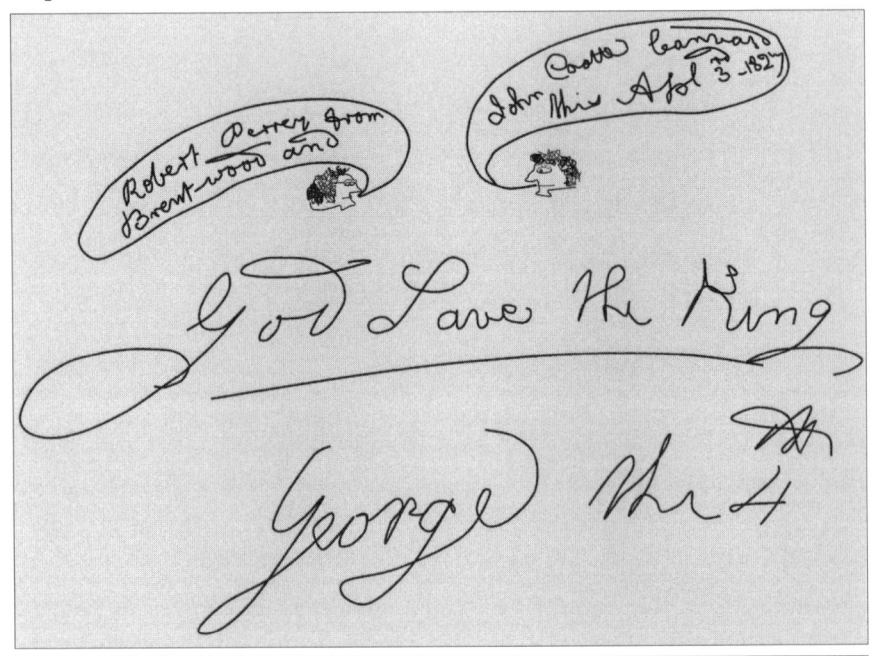

Two patriotic men in 1827. They wrote this in pencil on wooden wall panelling at Barnardiston House in Chipping Hill. After they had 'canvas'd' the wall, wallpaper would have been pasted onto the canvas. Upholsterer John 'Cootte' (Coote) lived across the road in Church Street until 1881, and became a prominent auctioneer and estate agent.

The Witham Fires, 1828-1829

The end of the War did not improve the life of these 'poorer classes'. By 1820, when the Prince Regent became George IV, they were suffering from unemployment and the effects of inflation. In some parts of Essex, labourers protested by rioting and machine-breaking. But arson was quite rare at that time – the offence still carried the death penalty. So it was a shock when two suspicious fires broke out in Witham on 5th November 1828. One of them was in John Crump's barn at Freebournes farm in Newland Street; he was an overseer of the poor so was potentially unpopular. Crowds ran through the darkness to watch. At first fireworks were blamed, but soon the finger of suspicion pointed at local labourers. The newspapers published long reports, the victims offered rewards, farmers and gentry held meetings and investigations, and there was great concern all over Essex. A new improved fire engine was ordered for the parish.

In February 1829, after a period of great anxiety and the outbreak of several more fires, a sixteen-year old farm boy called James Cook was interrogated about the most recent conflagration, at Olivers farm in Maldon Road, where he worked. He was sent to the new gaol in Springfield Road in Chelmsford to await trial. His father had died two years previously, so James was the only bread-winner for his ailing mother and five younger children. Whilst he was in custody there were two more fires, and farmer William Hutley of Powershall received a threatening letter. Nevertheless at the Assize court in March the jurors found James guilty. They asked for him to be treated leniently (as did the victim, farmer William Green). But the judge sentenced him to death as 'a severe example' to others. Further pleas were to no avail and he was hanged a fortnight later. The local newspaper published an illustration of the event (shown on the next page).

Three weeks after the hanging, a youth called Edmund Potto was arrested on suspicion of causing seven of the fires, and of sending the threatening letter. He was a nineteen-year old apprentice tailor. When he was put into custody the fires stopped. He had influential relatives, because his aunt Jane was the wife of James Thomasin, who owned Witham's flourishing brush works. The family paid for a lawyer and many witnesses to claim that Edmund was insane, and therefore should not be considered responsible for the crimes. The proceedings took all day instead of the usual twenty minutes or so, and earned a full page report in the newspaper. After taking the unusual step of leaving the court-room, the jury declared him innocent. They said that there

THE AWFUL FATE OF AN INCENDIARY.

The hanging of James Cook, aged 16, on 27 March 1829 outside Chelmsford prison. This is a newspaper illustration. The fire that he was alleged to have started at Olivers farm, south of Witham, is also shown. This was the only hanging in Essex in that year and it attracted a large crowd. The Witham fires continued while James was in custody, so it is probable that he was innocent. In 1993 a new wood near Olivers farm was named after him by Witham Town Council.

was insufficient evidence, and that they had not been influenced by the suggestion of insanity. This verdict was 'received with the greatest astonishment by a crowded court'. Spectators felt that the jurors were influenced by the 'cruel hanging of the little boy', James Cook.

Next morning the court re-assembled, and the judge declared the jury's verdict 'unintelligible'. He was Mr Justice Park, well known for thinking that jurors were 'mere idiots'. Edmund was sentenced to transportation for life for sending the threatening letter. In 1830 he went in a convict ship to New South Wales, where he worked on a large new estate at Segenhoe (he died eleven years later) (see colour page 9). Witham farmers held a celebration at which the 'utmost hilarity' prevailed. Late in 1830 the 'Captain Swing' protests by Kent farmworkers began, and spread to the whole of south-east England, but according to vicar John Newman 'there were no Burnings or Riots in Witham Hundred in 1830 and 1831'. Over seventy years later, in 1907, the local council discussed the fate of the fire engine which had been bought in 1828. There was a suggestion that it should be 'put in a glass case as a curiosity'. But they decided to sell it for scrap for £3 (about £200 today).

The poor before 1834

In 1834 Witham's parish officers answered a Government questionnaire. They wrote that there were 1,600 'poor people' in the town (well over half the population). They amended this to 'labouring people', and finally put 'working class'. This made sense; anyone who was working class was poor.

Most of the people who could not work through illness or disability were still receiving a weekly allowance at home. Only about twenty very frail people were in the workhouse. Special problems were dealt with sympathetically – in 1818 William Coney was sent to an institution for the blind, and Joseph Hills to the Bethlem asylum in London. However, the able-bodied poor presented an eternal dilemma. Perhaps they weren't earning enough to survive, or perhaps they couldn't find any work at all. There was said to be a 'vast number' of unemployed in Witham in 1818. But the ratepayers wanted to spend less, not more, and they managed to halve the amount of relief paid out between 1822 and 1834. They did this by setting up a special committee called a Select Vestry. Its members met every week, and interviewed the hundred or so people who queued up to ask for help.

In 1822 they allowed 'the wife of Thomas Trew' twelve shillings 'to go for one month to bathe in the Sea', but such generosity was very unusual. In 1824 it was decided to send all the pauper girls between the ages of ten and sixteen to work in the Morses' silk factory. This was a forbidding place in Hatfield Peverel with a 'lodging house' for forty or fifty children, where the girls were often ill treated and some tried to run away. Most paupers were well known to the Vestry members or their friends. So when Benjamin Sayer said he was sick, Dr Tomkin advised that he was not. And when John Pavelin and others asked for help, farmer William Hutley of Powershall said he had offered them work.

People who weren't polite enough to the committee were sent away empty handed. In 1822 Bloss Branwhite was 'insolent' after emerging from one of several visits to prison for poaching, theft, or not supporting his family. A few months later he 'promised to be good for the future if the Vestry would forgive him', but his resolution failed several times more. In 1830 he came out from 31 days solitary confinement in the new Convict Gaol in Chelmsford, and the clerk noted sympathetically that 'he looked very bad and he said the punishment was dreadfully severe', so they gave him a shilling. He never reformed, though. In 1838, when he was about 50, the

Witham's poor people lived in tiny cottages. These ones in Mill Lane look pleasant enough until one realises that there were five of them, and that each consisted of one room about 10 ft x 15 ft (3m x 4½), with steps leading out of it into an attic. Also that they had no water or drains and were just across the road from a very smelly tannery. Taken in 1914. They were demolished in the 1920s. © Crown copyright NMR.

Witham parish constable met him walking away from Chantry Wood with an oak plank on his shoulder. He disarmingly told magistrate William Pattisson that 'It is no use to deny it, for I did it certainly'. For this he was transported to New South Wales and then to Norfolk Island in the Pacific, 'a place of the severest punishment short of death'. He returned to England later.

The Union Workhouse and the poor after 1834

A new Poor Law was introduced in 1834, as part of the Government's plan to spend even less money. Nothing was to be paid to people living at home. Instead, everyone who didn't have enough to live on would have to go into a workhouse (this approach had been tried sometimes before but hadn't lasted). So in 1835 Witham's Vestry Clerk, Robert Bretnall of Spring Lodge, wrote to the widowed Mary Ann Lancaster in Birmingham that 'The new Poor Law Bill is in operation here and no relief can be given you out of the workhouse. Hoping you will see better days'. She was weak and asthmatic, and had three daughters. Her late husband Thomas was one of the Witham men who had fought at the battle of Waterloo in 1815.

4. 1815-1901

The new Poor Law Unions were combinations of parishes, with shared workhouses, and run by elected Boards of Guardians. The Witham Union, under the chairmanship of Lord Rayleigh of Terling, had seventeen parishes in its care. At first the old workhouses at Coggeshall and Witham continued in use, but with renewed severity – for instance 'old married people' were separated. In 1836 seventeen-year old John Castle spent a fortnight at the Witham workhouse. He wore a uniform, worked on dusty machines for turning old carpets into flock beds, and, with others, falsely claimed to be a nonconformist so that the Sunday walk to church would be longer and more interesting – it would take them down to Newland Street instead of just across the road.

In March 1837 the Board decided that a completely new workhouse was needed for the whole Union. They built a towering prison-like brick building in Hatfield Road, on what was then the edge of Witham. Of course all the materials had to be brought by horse and cart, including about a quarter of a

The entrance to the Witham Union workhouse, which was completed in 1838-39 to hold 350 people. The young architects were George Gilbert Scott and William Moffatt of London. The Witham Board of Guardians were not happy with them, and complained that they took too long, charged too much, and didn't visit often enough. Later, George became very famous. His best-known works are the Albert Memorial and St Pancras station in London.

The photo was taken in 2002 during a ceremony to commemorate the imminent closing of the Bridge Hospital, a more recent user of the building.

million bricks. In late 1838 or early 1839 the paupers from all the Union's parishes were moved here, and were not allowed out without permission. Witham tradesmen supplied such necessities as coal, brushes, coffins, food, beer, shoes and stockings. At Christmas the parishioners subscribed to give all the inmates 'beef and plum pudding'. The old Church Street property was turned into cottages, still known colloquially today as 'Charity Row'.

When the census was taken in 1841, there were 131 inmates. Half were children under fifteen, who often, like the four Chignell sisters, all under ten, had no parents with them. Many others were elderly. One, Hannah Dudley, was ninety. This was in June, when the able-bodied would be out working in the fields. It was different in winter. In December 1840 Witham's Dr Dixon wrote:

> Cold and snowy today and most outdoor labour on the land suspended, and it will be needful for the poor to suspend eating, for the Guardians of this Union relieve nobody but their salaried officers and the inmates of their bastille.

In 1850 one of the inmates was Sarah Calcraft, mother of William, England's public executioner.

The policy of putting all the paupers into workhouses was not adhered to for long. Already by 1850 the Witham Union had twice as many people being helped at home instead (in later years there were often about five times as many). In summer 1858 the inmates were only the 'debilitated' elderly people, or the 'destitute', like unmarried mother Mary Aldous, whose baby was born in the workhouse. Amongst the people being given relief outside instead were four young girls known as 'Ager's orphans', who were put out to domestic service, and about thirty young Witham families where the wage-earner was 'sick', like the Pavelins of Trafalgar Square in Maldon Road.

Keeping the pauper families at home meant that the wives and children could help bring in money. Even children lucky enough to go to school had to work. The six-week school 'holiday' always began when the harvest was ready, but gleaning often continued into the autumn, when children would also be absent for tasks such as 'picking up stones' and 'picking up acorns'. In addition the girls regularly had to 'carry the washing home done by their mothers', or to 'help Mother cleaning up for Easter'. After about 1860 pea-picking began to dominate the family year, and did so for nearly a hundred years afterwards. Education became compulsory in 1870 but many little girls were away from the National School in July 1876 because there was 'more

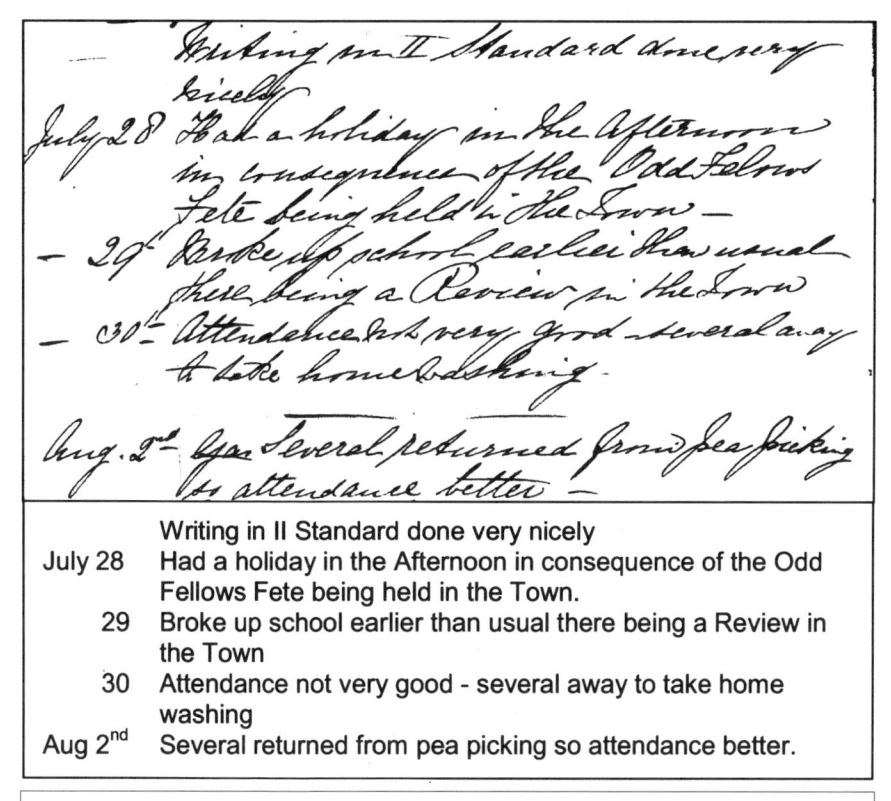

	Writing in II Standard done very nicely
July 28	Had a holiday in the Afternoon in consequence of the Odd Fellows Fete being held in the Town.
29	Broke up school earlier than usual there being a Review in the Town
30	Attendance not very good - several away to take home washing
Aug 2nd	Several returned from pea picking so attendance better.

An extract from the school log book of the Girls' National School in 1869 (with a transcript). Reproduced by courtesy of Essex Record Office (reference E/ML 74/1).

pea-picking than has been known for a long time'. They did disappear for treats as well, such as celebrations of Royal events, the 'Oddfellows fete', the 'Witham fair', and visits by circuses and 'Wombwald's Menagerie'. A special event was the annual Schools anniversary 'feast', which as early as 1855 had taken 200 children to Harwich so that many experienced both a railway train and the seaside for the first time.

The staff of the workhouse were often troublesome, and in 1879 the Guardians accused the Master and Matron of drunkenness, 'falsehood', absence from duty, wasting food, and overbearing conduct. In the following year Witham Union was dissolved and merged with Braintree during a general trend towards larger units. Since 1880 the Witham building, 'the Bridge', has been owned in turn by several organisations caring for disadvantaged people; it closed in March 2003 to be turned into flats.

The Railway, 1840s

'Railway mania' approached Witham during the 1830s. The first entirely mechanical steam passenger line had opened between Manchester and Liverpool in 1830. The Eastern Counties Railway Company endured many troubles whilst constructing its line from London towards East Anglia. But by 1840 it had reached Brentwood, twenty miles before Witham, and local people started going there in horse-drawn coaches to join the trains.

Soon afterwards the works reached Witham itself. Tall new brick viaducts and embankments appeared in the river meadows, and ancient objects were found whilst cutting through the old earthworks. The station was 'small but in every respect well-adapted' and the adjacent bridge 'elicited the admiration of eminent judges of bridge building'. In summer 1841 there were about fifty navvies living in Witham, causing some apprehension. The railway company provided a policeman, William Bird, and claimed that he was always 'instantly obeyed'. The men worked night and day and it was dangerous. At least three of them were killed here (including a 19-year old Witham lad from Collins Lane), and more in neighbouring parishes – at Kelvedon a whole viaduct collapsed.

At last, on 27 February 1843, the directors and shareholders crowded onto two flag-bedecked trains for an inaugural journey from Shoreditch in east London to a dinner at Colchester. An expectant crowd gathered at Witham to see them pass, but were disappointed. After various problems the important travellers only reached Mountnessing, and returned to London 'wet, hungry and in no very pleasant temper' (the earliest carriages had no roofs). Next day the company's general meeting took place under something of a cloud.

However, the second attempt on 29 March 'passed off with considerable eclat'. The celebratory train paused at Witham, where 'it appeared that all the population had turned out, both sides of the line being thronged four or five deep for a considerable distance', whilst an orchestra played. The musicians then joined the train and entertained the passengers all the way to Colchester. Within a fortnight, Dr Dixon was writing that:

> the effect of the Rail-road here is sensibly felt in this Town. Noticed more particularly by the absence of the Coaches with the exception of one Coach (the Colchester Wellington). We see nothing now but a single <u>half</u> omnibus something like a bread cart, plying up and down

the Town to catch a lame or stray passenger for the Trains at the Station at Chipping Hill.

At about the same time, local poet Charles Clark wrote 'I was at Chipping Hill Witham ... and stopt to see some of the trains – saw <u>four</u>. I did not have a ride – nor have I as yet'. He expected that even the surviving Wellington coach would 'go to pot', and wondered whether a new 'Aerial Steam Carriage' by William Henson might in due course supersede the trains (it did not fly, though a smaller model may have done).

In 1848 branch lines were opened to Maldon and Braintree. There were six wooden viaducts on the way to Maldon, including one at Witham near Sauls bridge (another at Wickham Bishops is now the only one surviving in the country). In 1849 the magazine 'Punch' wrote:

Witham railway station became a 'junction' in 1848 with the opening of the Braintree and Maldon lines. In the following year this drawing appeared with an article about Witham in the new satirical magazine 'Punch', which often mocked the railways.

> We believe the Directors think of advertising for a sort of human three-in-one to fill the situation at Witham, his duties being to turn the points, ring the bell, and work the telegraph. We understand that an individual who squints is always preferred on this line, for the faculty of looking two ways at once is likely to be useful to him in the discharge of his duty.

EASTERN COUNTIES RAILWAY.

NOTICE IS HEREBY GIVEN,

THAT THIS RAILWAY IS OPENED FOR TRAFFIC, FROM LONDON TO COLCHESTER, THROUGHOUT,

— AND THAT THE TRAINS RUN AS FOLLOW :—

DOWN TRAINS.—LONDON TO BRENTWOOD, CHELMSFORD, COLCHESTER, &c.
Every Day (except Sundays).

USUAL DEPARTURE FROM, OR ARRIVAL AT,

	London	Mile-end	Stratford	Forest Gate	Ilford	Romford	Brentwood	Chelmsford	Witham	Kelvedon	Colchester
MORNING	30 m. p. 8	26 m. to 9	*	....	....	5 m. to 9	10 m. p. 9	10 m. to 10	20 m. p. 10	29 m. p. 10	5 m. p. 11
AFTERNOON	11 o'clock	....	10 m. p. 11	....	18 m. p. 11	28 m. p. 11	17 m. to 12	23 m. p. 12	53 m. p. 12	2 m. p. 1	22 m. to 2
"	2 o'clock	4 m. p. 2	....	....	18 m. p. 2	28 m. p. 2	17 m. to 3	23 m. p. 3	....	....	....
"	3 o'clock	....	....	....	....	24 m. p. 3	21 m. to 4	19 m. p. 4	49 m. p. 4	58 m. p. 4	26 m. to 6
"	13 m. p. 4	....	25 m. p. 4	29 m. p. 4	35 m. p. 4	15 m. to 5	5 o'clock	20 m. to 5	....	....	....
"	5 o'clock	....	....	....	....	24 m. p. 5	21 m. to 6	19 m. p. 6	49 m. p. 6	58 m. p. 6	26 m. to 8
"	30 m. p. 6	....	20 m. to 7	....	12 m. to 7	1 m. to 7	14 m. p. 7	....	....	....	....

* This Train will take up and set down Passengers at Stratford on Wednesdays only.

UP TRAINS.—COLCHESTER, CHELMSFORD, BRENTWOOD, &c. TO LONDON.
Every Day (except Sundays).

	Colchester	Kelvedon	Witham	Chelmsford	Brentwood	Romford	Ilford	Forest Gate	Stratford	Mile-end	London
MORNING	....	....	....	5 m. p. 8	15 m. to 9	9 o'clock	11 m. p. 9	....	19 m. p. 9	....	29 m. p. 9

An early railway timetable. The single fare from Witham to London ranged from 5s 6d (third class) to 9s 6d (first class), the equivalent of about £16 to £28 today. The journey took an hour and fifty minutes. Even the speediest horse-drawn coaches had taken about 4½ hours, with considerable discomfort and very few passengers on each vehicle.

The complications of the junction resulted in regular accidents in subsequent years, especially to railway workers. Several were fatal.

New opportunities soon made up for the loss of employment in the coaching trade, and horse power was still required to get around the rest of the town and the countryside. The Perrys' extensive and long-established coachmaking business in Newland Street had already run out of money by 1830 so it suited them well to become a 'railway office' and 'omnibus proprietor and booking office'. The number of people in Witham working on the railway increased steadily, from twenty in 1851 to ninety in 1901 (including thirteen signalmen and twenty porters). Some of them were softly-spoken Suffolk men from further up the line, but Witham people benefited too. Railway employment was much valued as 'a job for life'.

It is difficult for us to imagine the magical impact of the first steam trains. Those who could afford it took advantage immediately. Robert Bretnall went to London every two months or so to stock up with luxuries such as 'the very best black tea' and 'a spotted shirt'. He went to Chelmsford on market days, and on Christmas Eve 1847 'came home by the Train that should have been at Chelmsford at 4 o'clock but did not arrive till past 5 o'clock owing to its great weight with two powerful Engines & as reported more than 800 Passengers'. Excursion trains for special events at reduced prices encouraged poorer people to travel also.

For the carriage of goods the effect was even greater. A horse-drawn waggon used to take at least twenty-four hours to reach London from Witham, and dozens of them would have been needed for the amount of coal or fertiliser that a train could carry. When the branch line reached the coast at Maldon the price of coal in Witham and Braintree dropped considerably. And as Dr Dixon anticipated, the line opened 'other sources of trade not at present contemplated'. The railway goods yard at Witham was a large and flourishing place for over a century, where factory owners, craftsmen, shopkeepers and individuals sent or collected their goods and parcels.

The telegraph

The railway company used the newly invented telegraph. Messages were amazingly conveyed by sending Morse code along wires. In 1870 the private telegraph systems were taken over by the Post Office. So in that year Witham's postmistress, Hannah Garrett, added the sending and receiving of telegrams to her many duties. Her family had run the Witham establishment since before 1800. When she retired in 1885 a larger place was opened. Fourteen-year old William Oxbrow joined the staff in 1890 and delivered the telegrams on a penny-farthing bicycle (he was later a champion cyclist). It was often the Post Office staff who first heard about important national events like the Relief of Mafeking in 1900, when they sent out another cyclist to spread the news.

Tanning, gas and coke, and brushes and drills

There were still several traditional industries in Witham, mostly connected to local agriculture. The largest was now tanning and fellmongering. This entailed turning animal skins into leather, an arduous and messy task. After the railway came, the number of tannery workers increased, and there were often about thirty of them during the rest of the century. Many of them lived near the tannery in Mill Lane, backing onto the river. This was set up by James Matthews in the early 1800s. His family had been fellmongers for fifty years previously, and his successors kept the business going until the 1960s.

A few yards away, local shareholders opened a Gas and Coke works in 1835. The gasometer and other ironwork came from Neath in South Wales, probably by sea. In November the lighting of the first twenty-six 'brilliant' street lamps was celebrated with a brass band and a dinner at the works. There were already eighty private indoor lamps. For Queen Victoria's Coronation in 1838 the Post Office was illuminated with a crown and a star 'in gas', and there was the customary parade, eating and sports. The same decorations were brought out for her marriage in 1840. The gas supply was extended to Chipping Hill in 1847.

Specialised industries were few. A small silk factory behind the Spread Eagle lasted only a few years during the early 1840s. The Thomasins' brush works and yard off Newland Street was the most important place. It had expanded from Matthew Thomasin's patten-making of the early 1700s, and now also made mops and brushes. The most important raw material, bristle from wild boars, was imported from Russia, and the products were despatched far and wide.

There were about twenty brushworkers in 1829, and fifty by 1841. It was skilled work. The tramping system, discussed later (page 77), meant that they mostly came from other parts of the country. In 1841 four out of every five of them had been born outside Essex (compared to only one in every seventy of the farmworkers). The strange accents, tarry smells, and self-sufficient welfare system must have made the brush yard a mysterious place to local residents. But by 1851 the tramping system was waning and half the workers were Essex men, with a third born in Witham.

The arrival of the railway in 1843 probably increased the profits. After James Thomasin died in 1845, his son George took over, buying more properties and helping the nonconformist cause in local debates. Appointing Samuel Spooner as manager and 'commercial traveller', he moved his own family away from the yard into the imposing Roslyn House at the good end of the street. He died in his fifties in 1868, after trying to 'doctor himself upon the homeopathic system'. Shops closed for his funeral and over fifty men and boys from the brush yard joined the procession. One of them, Thomas Farrow, had worked there for 55 years.

George's assets were worth nearly £45,000 (about £2 million at today's values) in addition to land and buildings. His young son James was set to be a stockbroker, so his widow Mary persuaded some of her sister's family, the

4. 1815-1901

```
Hogs' ditto
Dutch Hogs' stiff for Cloth or Carpet
Carpet Banister Brushes, hair and whisk
Dust Brushes
Ditto best, for Chimney Sweepers
Turk's Heads and Pastry Cooks
Lynn Heads, or Scrubs
Nailed Scrubs, or Boat Brushes
Bass and Cane ditto
Weavers' Brushes
Hearth ditto, common-white, mahogany-
   stained, black-japanned, black and gold,
   red and gold and mahogany
Bed Brushes
Ladies' Dusters, plain-japanned, and black
   and gold
Cowmouth Scrubbing Brushes, all sizes
Fancy ditto, various shapes
Ditto with solid backs
Dairy Brushes, common and best
Hard Shoe ditto
Shining ditto
Blacking ditto
Improved Shoe ditto
Roach-back, and spread-face best Shoe
   ditto, hard, shining, and blacking
Stove ditto, flat and roach, tufted or ended
Ditto handled various
```

Thomasins' brush works. Above left is part of a long list of items made and sold in 1849. An even more detailed list from a similar company shows that in those days there were special brushes for cleaning everything imaginable, from window ledges to horses, and from celery to railway carriages. Above right is George Thomasin, owner of the works after 1845. He described himself as a 'gentlemen' when he completed the 1861 census forms, but his neighbour Joseph Howell Blood, the registrar, wrote him down as 'brush manufacturer' instead. George has posthumously had the last laugh – his great-great grandson, Mark Thomasin Foster, was High Sheriff of Essex from 2003-04.

Adnams, to come from Berkshire and run the factory with Spooner. They closed it after three years, in 1871. The young men George and Ernest Adnams left their father in Witham and went to Southwold on the Suffolk coast to take over a brewery. George was restless and moved to South Africa, where he drowned (or, in some versions, was eaten by a crocodile). But Ernest received a handsome loan from his aunt Mary Thomasin out of her late husband's brushmaking profits to enable the Southwold brewery to survive. So the Adnams ales which are so famous today owe their existence to the old Witham brushworks.

The other main special factory was Smyths', making seed drills (horse drawn machines for sowing seeds) (see colour page 10). They arrived in about 1845 to take over the extensive premises of the old Blue Posts inn. Their main works at Peasenhall in Suffolk were then many miles from a railway, so the Witham branch used the new main line to serve the extensive export market. The dozen or so skilled workers, including blacksmiths, wheelwrights and painters, came with their families from Suffolk with manager Peter Hannar. To begin with he lived in part of the old inn. The works continued until he died in 1894.

Farming

Until the 1870s about a quarter of the men in Witham were farmworkers. In Church Street the proportion was a half and in Powershall End it was three-quarters. They and their families were often the poorest people in the parish. Only about half had anything like a permanent job, the rest only being needed at busy times. In mid-century the Hubbard family of Victoria Cottages often survived on turnips, and John Lapwood, shown on the facing page, later recalled his life from those times to writer Rider Haggard in a well-known interview that was later published in the book *Rural England*. John was born in 1823 and brought up on Blue Mills Hill:

> He stated for that for months at a time he had existed upon nothing but a diet of bread and onions, washed down, when he was lucky, with a little small-beer. These onions he ate until they took the skin off the roof of his mouth, blistering it to whiteness ... They had no tea, but his wife imitated the appearance of that beverage by soaking a burnt crust of bread in boiling water. ... He became so feeble that the reek of the muck which it was his duty to turn, made him sick and faint ... I asked if his children, of whom there were eight, lived on onions also. He answered no; they had generally a little cheese and butter in the house, but he could not put it into his own stomach when they were hungry and cried for food.

William Hutley, John's employer, was one of the most successful farmers in Essex. He had about 1,500 acres altogether, about 500 of them in Witham. He was called to London in 1848 as a witness to the Select Committee on Agricultural Customs, where he described his 'very great' improvements. He used new types of feed, drainage, and artificial fertiliser, including chalk and star-fish imported by sea from Kent to his own wharf on the river Crouch. A friend said that his methods 'excited much attention', and his farms were 'visited by men from all parts of England and elsewhere'. Enthusiasts also thronged to Tiptree, five miles away, to look at the controversial modernised farm of Alderman Mechi (formerly a successful razor maker in London).

4. 1815-1901

John and Ann Lapwood at their home in Blunts Hall Road, where they spent the whole of their married life. John was interviewed by writer Rider Haggard in 1901. He worked at William Hutley's flourishing Powers Hall farm, over a mile away.

Farm machinery was expensive, especially the new steam driven equipment, and there was good business to be had in hiring it out. For instance, John Randall moved to Witham from Suffolk in about 1860 and became a 'proprietor of agricultural machines' at Cuppers farm. His family later moved to Church Street and continued until the 1930s. Farm sizes varied over time, but after the 1840s there were usually four with more than 250 acres, of which two had over 500 acres and nearly thirty permanent workers each. The eight or nine farmers were important men. They held debates at their Agricultural Society, founded in 1845, and ran the Labourers Friend Society, which held contests for workers, particularly in ploughing. A special honour was hosting the Essex Show in 1863. Over 400 animals, numerous displays of farm implements, and throngs of people, gathered in Witham House grounds (now the Park and cricket ground). The lavish decorations included an arch erected by the Smyths' drill makers. One writer thought the Witham show was the best ever, and described the invasion of the 'usually quiet, and always respectable little town' by a 'congregation of men and beasts'. There was a grand dinner for 200 gentlemen in a barn at Freebournes farm.

Peculiars, Congregationalists and the like

Perhaps a third of the population of Witham attended non-conformist churches, and so were known as 'dissenters'. Many of them were important tradesmen. The smaller groups had only a few members, often people who came with the industries. But they were augmented by worshippers from nearby parishes, and they played an important part in 'disreputable' but significant movements like Chartism and the Co-operative Society.

Thus in 1840 there were ten Baptist families and three or four Quaker ones. Methodism was late arriving in Essex, though John Wesley did pause in Witham 'for refreshment' in 1785. Hatfield Peverel, three miles away, had a Wesleyan Methodist meeting place by the 1820s, and it was supported by Witham's James Church, who came from Kent, and Peter Hannar from Suffolk, managers of the gas works and the drill factory respectively. Peter and his wife Susan said that other churches were:
> not quite so plain and not quite so willing to be counted singular and not quite so willing to stoop so low, as to go out into the highways and hedges and compel the Poor and needy, and outcasts of society, to come into the fold of Christ.

In 1851 another Methodist, Daniel South of Powershall End, described

Some of the nonconformists' buildings of the 19th century (1) Quaker meeting house, Maldon Road, built 1801-02. (2) Gospel Standard Baptist chapel, Maldon Road, built 1828. (3) Congregational church, Newland Street, built 1837-1840, probably designed by James Fenton (the only one of the four still used for its original purpose). (4) Methodist chapel, Guithavon Street, designed by Charles Pertwee, opened 1863. All taken 1981 to 1982.

himself to a census taker as a 'Rank Dissenter labourer', and his two sons as 'Church Labourers'. Surprisingly, the Primitive Methodists, a more working-class sect, only came for a year or two.

The evangelical Essex group called the Peculiar People, also known then as the New Lights, rented a cottage in Church Street in 1869, and then about four years later took over the Quaker meeting house in Maldon Road. Their first Witham leader, farmworker William Horsnell, is said to have lost his job because of his beliefs and spent a winter with his family in the workhouse.

But the Peculiars flourished and eventually built a new Evangelical chapel in Guithavon Valley in 1932.

The largest dissenting group were still the Congregationalists. The prosperous Samuel Shaen of Hatfield Peverel was a member. In 1829 he was one of the first men in the country to take advantage of a new law allowing dissenters to be magistrates. In 1837 they built a new school in Maldon Road for 'labourers, mechanics and indigent people' (now the Parkside Youth Centre), and started the rebuilding of their church in Newland Street in imposing white brick, to hold 800 people.

William Henry Pattisson

We left William Henry Pattisson as a radical law student in the last chapter. He became a very respected Witham solicitor with influential friends and visitors from the cultural and literary world. He and his family had long been

WITHAM IN AN UPROAR!

'TWAS the Fifth of November, and dark was the night,
For nought save a star and a squib gave a light;
When the gay lads of Witham determined to try
To light-up a fire, and commem'rate Old Guy.
Their sport thus resolved on was destined to meet
A strong opposition, from some in the street;
Whose names—to be lib'ral—I wish not to write,
But perhaps you'll detect them by metaphors light.
First,—*Closefist*, the Lawyer, no fire would allow,— ×*Pattisson*
His wife was afraid it would end in a row;
Her coach, too, she fear'd, would be soil'd with the smoke,
And it to repaint would indeed be no joke.
His house, 'tis well known, is the best in the town,
And should it catch fire 'twould perhaps be burnt down:
'Tis certain that *Closefist* was quite in a rage—
He declaim'd, then he paused, then he threat'ned the cage!
Next, *Pigtail*, the Grocer, came ARM'D—and declared, †*Butler*
To disperse them at once he was fully prepared:

The first part of a poem written in 1819, by lawyer James Daniel. At that time solicitor William Pattisson was still a religious dissenter, but obviously doing well. The handwritten names were added in 1841 by Charles Clark, a satirical writer and publisher from nearby Great Totham. Bonfire night was always rowdy in Witham. Reproduced by courtesy of Essex Record Office (reference D/DU 668/5).

enthusiastic members of the Congregational church. But in 1826 the deacons there told him to stay away until he had removed a 'stigma' which had been cast on his 'moral character' by a 'public rumour'. He and his wife Hannah promptly joined the Church of England instead. Several recent historians have studied the family, and thought that the disgrace must have been financial or political. However, research by my friend Maureen Scollan has shown that a different story was known to Thomas Noon Talfourd, a friend of Charles Dickens and a relative of the Pattissons by marriage. He claimed that William had 'wronged' a 'fair' unnamed lady, and wondered whether he would marry her after Hannah died in 1828 (he did not). William's son and daughter-in-law were tragically drowned on honeymoon in 1832, and the family provided a lavish memorial in their newly adopted parish church.

The Church of England and the Reverend John Bramston

The parish church was at Chipping Hill, nearly a mile from the town centre where most people lived. In February 1840 a survey by its worshippers revealed the effect of this location. Charles Jackson complained that 'when there is so much to do, walking so far takes up so much time'. And whenever the weather was wet James Woodyards' family chose the Congregational church instead. Furthermore, Mrs Cooper had originally gone to the latter just because it was nearer, but now she liked it better. The vicar, Reverend John Newman, began collecting donations for an additional church, but sadly he was ill and died in April 1840.

The Bishop of London said that he considered Witham to be 'a very important parish', and appointed Reverend John Bramston, from a rich Essex family, to the vacant post. The new vicar eagerly took up the building

Vicar John Bramston, sketched by his wife Clarissa. When he came to Witham in 1840 she said he was 'much tired and depressed' about the success of rival denominations. In December he 'severely lectured' his church clerk, James Dace, for letting his son (also James) play the 'Serophine' (an organ rather like a harmonium) at the opening of the new Congregational church (Dace's music shops still survive in Chelmsford). Reproduced by courtesy of Essex Record Office (reference D/DLu 14/18).

plans, and a committee discussed sites, styles, architects, and dedications at length throughout 1840 and early 1841. In the end William Pattisson provided some land cheaply. To reach it, the new Guithavon Street was laid out, which had the advantage of giving an imposing view of his Newland Street house and opening up more of his land for development.

The committee rejected two architects who would have made the church famous, had they known it. One was William Tite, who soon afterwards designed the Royal Exchange in London and later became Sir William. The other was the young George Gilbert Scott, who was out of favour for taking so long to build the workhouse. The choice was John Brown of Norwich.

It was decided to build Church Schools next door with room for nearly three hundred children. White bricks were ordered from Copford, and red ones from Witham's Sarah Elmy and her son William. They operated a brick kiln in Maltings Lane as well as a flourishing plumbing business. At first Lord Rayleigh declined to lay the two foundation stones, but he changed his mind after the Bishop decided to attend. On the appointed day in September 1841 a long procession wound its way on foot and by carriage from the parish church, and his lordship was watched by an 'immense concourse of

Guithavon Street, soon after the completion in 1842 of the new Anglican church of All Saints (which was closed in the 1960s and is now the Catholic church). On the right are the new National Schools, with smoke from the fires issuing from the chimneys. The drawing is by James Kellaway Colling, whose illustrations of architectural details are now much sought after.

spectators'. The fourteen workmen were given dinner at the White Hart and there were two hundred buns for the children.

The new All Saints church was completed in the following year – Mrs Bramston wrote that the consecration service 'passed off most happily'. However, she was rather concerned about 'the echo', and other problems soon followed. The ceiling starting to fall in, and Mr Brown was called back to explain himself. The building was still regarded as 'dangerous' in 1860, when substantial alterations and repairs were necessary.

Despite this successful building programme, it took some time for Reverend Bramston to be accepted in Witham. In his early days he was involved in widely publicised disputes about the church rates and the burial of dissenters which even troubled the Bishop. Also many parishioners found his services to be too 'High Church' or even Catholic. Dissenter Dr Dixon wrote that 'some people never mend, we shall see if he does'. But when Bramston left thirty years later, Dixon described him as 'the best man of his order', with a 'well-earned character', 'rarely giving offence'. And Samuel T Davies said that he had exercised 'almost unbounded influence'. He occupied many positions of authority in the town and the county.

Catholics

In 1800, Witham's Catholics started worshipping at the house called 'Stourton' in Powershall End, and in 1851 they built a new church on the Colchester Road. Cardinal Wiseman, the Roman Catholic Archbishop of Westminster, came to open it in the presence of the ex-king of Portugal (probably here in honour of Witham's Portuguese priest, Joseph da Silva Tavarez). Copies of an English translation of the Latin service failed to arrive in time, but nevertheless, some of the townspeople looked on with friendly interest. However, Catholics were still disapproved of by many. The Cardinal was described as a 'fox in a henroost' by Reverend Henry Du Cane and as 'a yellow, fat, bloaty disagreeable looking man' by Dr Dixon. On 5th November his effigy was paraded in Newland Street and thrown on the bonfire, alongside one figure 'dressed as the devil' and another representing vicar John Bramston. Guy Fawkes night is of course anti-Catholic in origin. More sober debates on church ritual for years. After one discussion on the subject in 1891, a local newspaper announced that 'other letters have reached us on Church matters at Witham, but we are getting a little tired of the subject'.

Charity and self-help

Poor relief was supplemented by charity, much of it organised by the churches. As one Witham vicar said, it was a:
> common thing among the poorer sort, for the Husband and Wife to frequent different places of worship, in order to keep friends of every kind, and even the same person will go both to Church and to Meeting for the same motive.

The parish church administered most of the older charities, including the 17th-century legacy of Dame Katherine Barnardiston which was now used for bread and coal. Churchmen and women led special projects like soup kitchens. Much of the money collected weekly at services was for similar purposes. In 1873, £70 of it went on food for '838 different cases of sickness or urgent necessity', £20 on blankets and fabric for '96 poor families', and more on individual items like 'a sewing machine for a sick girl'.

'Ladies' were particularly active in charitable work. They ran the savings clubs which expanded after Reverend John Bramston arrived in 1840. Miss Jane Luard (sister of William, later Admiral), would sometimes spend a whole day auditing the accounts. The most important was the Clothing Club, for which the town was eventually divided into twenty districts, each with a lady collector who went every week to the poorer houses to collect 'a penny or more' as savings. They were officially called District Visitors, but were often known as 'pence ladies' by those whom they visited. Some wealthier residents added a little extra to the funds. At times there were over 350 poor members (out of 750 households in the town). In 1842 eight of them were banned because they had 'misconducted themselves', and it was also ruled that no-one should be allowed to join 'who is in the habit of wearing artificial flowers'. The poor did not actually get their money back; instead they were given tickets annually to 'spend' in local shops. Afterwards they had to queue up and show their new clothes and shoes to the ladies for approval. This system continued into the 1920s.

In contrast, local Friendly Societies were run by their members, whose contributions entitled them to sick pay and other benefits. In 1858 Samuel T Davies gave a lecture about the history of the Oddfellows to the Witham branch, of which he was secretary, and it was published as a pamphlet. He wrote engagingly that 'it was written during brief intervals of daily labour, and therefore may be expected to bear marks of evident imperfection'.

4. 1815-1901

On the right, with the gables, is the Spread Eagle. Three of Witham's five Friendly Societies were already meeting here when registration was introduced in 1794. Most of the small societies disappeared during the 1800s but were replaced by branches of larger ones. Taken in the early 1900s; also shows the White Hart and the Angel in the background.

The Witham branch of the Brushmakers Society was particularly active. The national Society was in effect a pioneer of trade unionism, which was then illegal. Its members followed a 1,200 mile tramping route round the country, looking for work. Witham was the first stop out of London and the local branch would help travellers and newcomers. They met first at the White Hart and later at the Swan. Local deputations went to meetings in London. On one such occasion in 1826, 'the eyes of the Trade were on Witham', because our branch had made new proposals about sick pay. The Society paid for some members to emigrate to America to find work, and Witham's James Mount was probably one of them.

Chartists and reformers

Although many of society's struggles were fought out through the churches, secular issues were not ignored. For instance, there was a group of Chartist sympathisers in Witham from the early days of the movement in the 1830s. The radical proposals of the Chartists included universal male suffrage and the secret ballot. Two prominent Witham members were boot and shoemakers. One was Charles Fish, a Baptist, who denounced the 'infamous proceedings' of politicians. The other was George Pluck of Collins Lane. In 1847 he and his wife Emma named their baby son 'Jesse Fergus O'Connor

Pluck', after a national Chartist hero. In 1861 they entered his full name on the census. Amongst the real Fergus O'Connor's projects was the Chartist Co-operative Land Company, aiming to set workers up in cottages with land. There were twenty-five subscribers from Witham, mostly young single men, from all religious denominations. Many of them were labourers but there were also six brushworkers.

An interesting episode in October 1852 also raised the question of the vote. As ratepayers, the tenants of most properties, including numerous farmworkers and a few women, could vote in elections for local bodies such as the Guardians. Farmer William Hutley now proposed that for smaller houses, both the rates and the votes should fall on the owners instead. A big parish meeting was preceded by several days of 'excitement and consequent bustle'. Hutley's supporters consisted overwhelmingly of farmworkers, and he was accused of 'packing' the meeting with them. He was opposed by an alliance of tradesmen, craftsmen, professionals, and brushworkers. Amidst 'cheers, laughter and confusion', there were speeches on both sides from several working men who rarely attended such events. After a continuation of the poll (in public) on another day, Hutley's proposal was rejected. In a poster its opponents had urged people to pay their rates and so keep their votes, declaring that 'today determines whether the poor shall be riden over rough-shod, or whether they shall remain free !!'

Other reforming causes were actively supported by Witham's middle class, especially Congregationalists like Thomas Butler, a rich grocer and draper. In 1832 he chaired a lively meeting of all the Essex committees concerned with Parliamentary reform, at the Saracen's Head in Chelmsford. In the same month a lecture was given at Witham's White Hart to explain why 'Negro Slavery' should be abolished.

Respectable mid-Victorian life

Even non-political townspeople took an active interest in the world around them, particularly through the Witham Literary Institution. It was founded in November 1844, had premises in Newland Street with a well-stocked library, and survived for forty-six years. 'Party politics and controversial theology' were excluded, though it was sometimes alleged that it was dominated by nonconformists. The monthly lectures were heard by 'large and highly respectable' audiences, including women. One was about 'The Moral and

Intellectual Influence of Women on Society' by a Mrs Balfour. A lecturer on 'Mesmerism' failed to hypnotise any members. In 1865 they had a visit from a future Nobel prize winner, Lord Rayleigh's 23-year old son John William Strutt, from neighbouring Terling. He spoke about measuring the distance of the sun from the earth, and the opportunities to be obtained from transits of Venus in the years 1874, 1882 and the far distant days of 2004 (it was on June 8; the next will be in 2012).

A special public meeting was held at the Institution in 1850 to hear about plans for the spectacular Great Exhibition to be held in the following year in London at the Crystal Palace in Hyde Park. In due course, Witham people joined the thousands who thronged to see its exotic inventions and displays. Adding to the spectacle were bearded visiting foreigners (Englishmen at this time were clean-shaven). Local applicants for space had included the Smyths with their seed drills and Robert Harrington with a special clock.

However, only Cornelius Walford seems to have been permitted to exhibit. He was a hairdresser and naturalist, and displayed fifteen varieties of stuffed bird, including three different owls, in a rather remote gallery. His son had been secretary of the local application committee. This was Cornelius junior, who went on to become a well-known but argumentative insurance expert. He wrote on other topics including shorthand, Canada, and the histories of fairs and of famines. He had a high reputation in America, which he visited in 1861 during the Civil War (it was rumoured that he was arrested for speaking against the Northern Government). On a later trip he was welcomed in a speech by novelist Mark Twain.

Samuel T Davies, another versatile man, drafted a guide book for Witham in 1869, writing that during the previous thirty years there had been a 'very fine catalogue of town improvements, showing unmistakable vitality'. There were 3,000 people – similar to a large village like Kelvedon today, but much more crowded together. The tradition of gentility continued, and the annual Witham Ball in January at the White Hart attracted distinguished gentlemen and their wives from all over the county. For a time there was also a 'Tradesman's Ball'.

Cricket, a gentlemen's game, was increasing in popularity and the Witham club was very successful, playing in the grounds of Witham House (now the Park and cricket ground). In 1868 there was the unique excitement of a visit from the first Australian touring team, all aborigines, who according to the

> **GRAND GALA AT WITHAM, ESSEX.**
> THE
> **AUSTRALIAN ABORIGINES**
> HAVE BEEN ENGAGED TO COME TO
> **WITHAM**
> On **MONDAY & TUESDAY, SEPTEMBER**
> 14th and 15th, 1868,'
> WHEN
> **A CRICKET MATCH**
> AND VARIOUS
> AUSTRALIAN & ENGLISH ATHLETIC SPORTS,
> Including Flat and Hurdle Races, Jumping, Throwing
> the Boomerang, Sham Fight, Kangaroo Rats, &c., &c.,
> WILL TAKE PLACE
> On the Grounds of R. PARTRIDGE, Esq.
> For further particulars see hand-bills, which will
> shortly be issued.
> ___
> **TO PUBLICANS & OTHERS.**
> GRAND GALA AT WITHAM, ESSEX,
> 14th and 15th September, 1868.
> **THE AUSTRALIAN ABORIGINES.**
> TENDERS for supplying the LUNCHEON for the
> CRICKETERS BOTH DAYS, and for HIRING
> GROUND for the ERECTION of REFRESHMENT
> BOOTHS on the above occasion, will be received on
> or before the 1st of September, 1868.
> Applications, in writing, for the above Tenders to be
> addressed to C. Stevens, Esq., Witham, Essex, where
> a Plan of the Ground may be seen and any information
> afforded.

Adverts for the visit to Witham of the very first Australian touring cricket team, in September 1868. The aborigines beat the local team handsomely. Afterwards a display of 'native sports', including boomerang throwing, was attended by between 4,000 and 5,000 people. A special grand stand had been constructed, and 'many carriages of the local gentry' were 'drawn up on the ground'.

local newspaper were 'humorous, somewhat artful, and likely to deceive the batsman'. Years later the great W G Grace played here, scoring very few runs but taking fifteen wickets.

Jacob Howell Pattisson

By the time the aborigines visited it, Witham House no longer belonged to the Pattissons. The reasons show a darker side to Witham life. During the 1850s the family had been represented by William's surviving son, lawyer Jacob Howell Pattisson, once a carefree younger brother (pictured on colour page 8). He held a very trusted position in the county, looking after many people's money, though in 1852 he did have an unfortunate experience at a Witham Building Society meeting. Some of the audience cheered when he lost a public argument with his 24-year old former clerk, Cornelius Walford junior (mentioned earlier). The newspaper couldn't publish all the details for fear of libel.

Then in June 1859 Dr Dixon wrote 'A frightful disaster has occurred at Witham. Mr Pattisson has left home in consequence of pecuniary difficulties and it turns out that he is much in Debt'. We now know that he had been living beyond his means for many years, and that two days earlier he had been asked by a judge to produce accounts for a Witham lady's will. An advert in *The Times* described him as 'very thin' and offered a reward of £25 for his discovery. The sheriff spent four days auctioning the contents of the family home, built by his great-grandfather a hundred years earlier. They included two pianos, silver plate, four-poster beds, a Constable painting, two thousand books, a cellar of wine, two carriages and three horses.

Fortunately Jacob's wife Charlotte, a sister of Captain William Luard (later Admiral), was 'a lady of prompt decision and activity'. She rented a house at Tonbridge in Kent for herself and their thirteen surviving children and Jacob eventually re-appeared there. He reluctantly resigned from the Athenaeum club in London, his second home for many decades. In April 1864 he was found trying to commit suicide for a second time, on the railway line at Hampstead in London. A few weeks later he wrote to ask for a loan from his father's old friend Crabb Robinson. The latter, now ninety years old, had supported the family emotionally and financially during their troubles after some initial doubts.

The Empire and foreign parts

One of Jacob's sons went to New Zealand in 1865 to try his luck as a sheep farmer (with the help of £200 from Robinson). Many other young men emigrated in happier circumstances. For instance in 1852 a farmer's son, Samuel Crump, set out for Australia with his wife Jemima and six children. They were in 'high spirits at their prospects', in spite of the disapproval of Jemima's parents, the Bretnalls. 'Exciting' letters from others had showed 'the increasing prosperity of the country as much perhaps from active farming habits as from this picking up of Gold'.

Many military men also became semi-permanent emigrants. Two of Witham's most distinguished were William Garnham Luard, and David Hawkes VC. William was born at Witham Lodge (son of William the magistrate). He captained sailing ships all over the world in places such as North Wantong and Fort Tycocktow, and fought against the 'Chin-a-Poo' in the wars about Britain's exports of opium from India into China. Witham's townspeople followed his career enthusiastically, and saw more of him after he married Charlotte Du Cane in 1858 and took land-based posts. In 1866 he displayed his 'Japanese curiosities' at the Literary Institution, and a group visited him when he was head of Sheerness dockyard in 1873. He met them at Southend pier and took them across the Thames by steamer. They toured the *Great Eastern*, Brunel's enormous ocean liner. Luard became president of the Royal Naval College at Greenwich in 1882, retired as an Admiral in 1885 and was knighted in 1897. In later life he was an active Liberal. He was one of only six naval officers whose career reached from the reign of William IV (1830-37) to George V (1910-36). It is hard to believe that the kindly bearded figure of later photographs had such a dashing career (see page 93).

David Hawkes, Witham's only holder of the Victoria Cross, was brought up in one of these three small weatherboarded cottages in Powershall End. His parents were William, a farmworker, and Sarah. Sarah died in 1839, and in the following year, when David was eighteen, a recruiting party from the Rifle Brigade visited Witham, and he and five other young men enlisted. He served for many years in Canada before going to India where he won his medal. The photograph was taken in 1914 – the cottages have since been demolished (they stood about where number 51 is now). © Crown copyright NMR.

Private David Hawkes is the only Witham person to have been awarded the Victoria Cross. After he enlisted in the Rifle Brigade in 1840, he first joined an eleven-day march to Wales, where tempers where still running high after the famous Chartist rising at Newport. Then in 1841 a two-month voyage took him to Canada, starting in the cold of Nova Scotia.

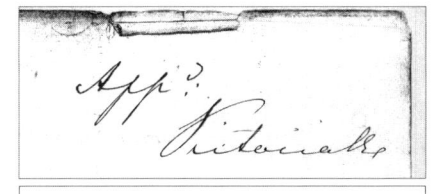

Queen Victoria's signature in December 1859, on the document approving the newly created award of the Victoria Cross to David Hawkes and others.

He received good conduct pay for a time, but spent his last year in prison for desertion whilst guarding the border with America. Returning to England in 1852, he took the 104-day 'passage to India' in 1857. There British soldiers were fighting against the 'Indian Mutiny'. Another Witham man in India recalled surviving on 'half pint of water per day to wash and drink' and losing most of his colleagues to cholera. David was awarded the Victoria Cross in March 1858 during the siege of Lucknow and died at Fyzabad in August (the fighting at Lucknow is shown on colour page 9). After some delay and confusion, his medal was posted to his elderly father William in Witham. Two years later William fell on hard times and was moved into the Witham Union Workhouse with his second wife Elizabeth. They both died in 1862. The medal had little intrinsic value to start with, being made of bronze, but was sold in London in 1919 for £78 (about £2,000 at today's values). We don't know how it got there or where it is now.

Water, drains and health

In mid-century Witham was still without mains water and sewerage. By then it was known that such conditions could cause cholera. After 128 Witham ratepayers submitted a petition, the Government sent Edward Cresy to investigate. He was a respected architect and author, who as a younger man had travelled Britain and Europe making drawings of historic buildings. In contrast, his work as an inspector must have been dispiriting. He arrived in the 'biting cold' days of January 1849 and announced that 'he saw no reason why Witham, so beautifully situated, should not be as well drained as any place in the kingdom'. He spent three days walking the streets and back yards, seeing things which the more genteel inhabitants usually avoided. A representative of the *Chelmsford Chronicle* went with him, and also a few prosperous parishioners.

His report is full of adjectives like 'polluted', 'very offensive', 'filthy', 'foetid', 'disgusting', 'pestilential', 'unwholesome', 'horrible', and 'deplorable'. Even where there were cess-pools they overflowed, often into yards full of houses. Behind Charles Barwell's butcher's shop there were piles of offal and manure with 'pigs gloating' on them. Mr Cresy told the reporter this 'was enough to poison a whole neighbourhood'. Finally the party went through the fields to Chipping Hill. They could smell it from 'some little distance'. At least in the town centre most people had access to a well, but not on 'the Hill', where water had to be carried from the river – a few bigger houses had pumps but they were 'kept private'. Mr Cresy wrote that it was 'lamentable' to see the inhabitants 'begging a commodity so important for health and cleanliness'.

The effects of this squalor were not only unpleasant but lethal. During the 1840s, one third of the burials in the parish churchyard were children under five years old, and one seventh were babies under a year old. Mr Cresy found that the expectation of life in Witham was five years less than in West Ham, a crowded and by no means healthy parish on the edge of London.

As a result, Witham was allowed to have its own Local Board of Health in 1852, with nine elected members. They began to plan a public water supply and drainage system, but in 1855 were petitioned by 94 ratepayers demanding that no more money should be spent. The petitioners' leader was Dr Thomas Tomkin, who ran a 'lunatic asylum' at the Retreat in Maldon Road. The plans were abandoned. Then in December 1867 a very serious and widely publicised typhoid epidemic broke out three miles away in Terling. Witham's Dr William Gimson Gimson [sic] distinguished himself, and the nursing was organised by one of Captain William Luard's sisters, Mary Ann (who afterwards founded a county-wide Church nursing agency). Nevertheless nearly fifty people died. A report was scathing about Terling, with its terrible health and diet, its inbreeding and low intellect.

The 'filthiness' of Witham itself was also mentioned, and two noisy public meetings were held. One speaker said that bad health 'was not on account of the necessity of drainage, but it was a visitation from the Almighty', who might disapprove of human interference. But this time the Local Board members stood their ground and agreed to borrow £6,000 to provide both water and sewerage, which were completed in 1869. In due course most of the water came from a spring in one of Lord Rayleigh's fields near Blunts Hall. As noted by some parishioners, this worryingly gave his lordship the power to cut Witham off if he wished..

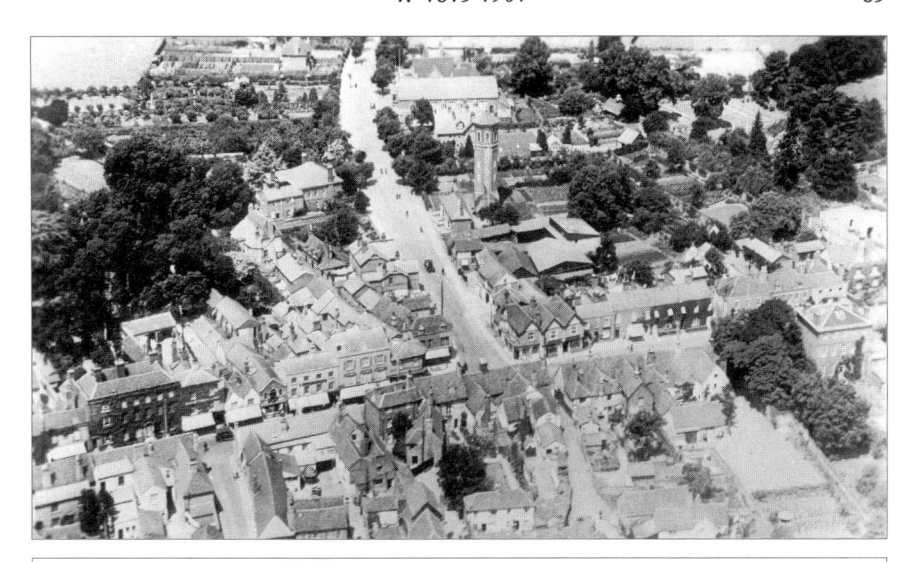

Collingwood Road and the red brick water tower. Both were constructed in 1869 during the provision of mains water and drainage, after many years of resistance from the ratepayers. 'The Tomtit', Witham's short-lived scurrilous newspaper, was supportive of the scheme, publishing a 'Song of the Drainage' in eight verses. Taken in the early 1930s.

There was still a long way to go before Witham was healthy. Outbreaks of disease continued to occur regularly. Chipping Hill did not have drains until 1884, and some places, like Powershall End, had to wait much longer. Most older houses weren't connected to them anyway. Pigs were still in evidence in the late 1870s. One in Newland Street had an unusually clean sty, but had 'rooted holes' into an adjoining house. And seven people slept in one bedroom at William Nicholls' tiny damp cottage by the river in Mill Lane. At a meeting in 1894, postman George Robjent said that working people's houses 'were in such a state that affluent people would disdain to stable their horses in them'. He represented the Co-op, of which more later.

New houses and factories

Many buildings dating from about 1810 till the 1860s had white, grey or yellow bricks. Some were very fine, but others had cheap mottled London stocks. Amongst the earliest of the latter were the sixteen small cottages of the grandly named Trafalgar Square in Maldon Road, built by plumber, glazier and brickmaker Benjamin Elmy in the late 1820s.

Small houses in Chalks Road, built 1869-78 of grey London stock bricks by John Chalk. Similar houses had been appearing since the 1820s, and were encouraged by the removal of the brick tax in 1850. Taken in about 1930. The royal portrait painter Richard Stone was born at number 9 in 1951. Another such group is 'Chipping Hill Terrace' (100-134 Church Street, built 1850s).

Most such building was in fairly small groups until in 1883 the sale of Temples farm near the station (the site of the old earthworks), paved the way for a larger estate. Between 1841 and 1901 Witham's housing stock increased by one third (from about 600 to 800), and nearly half this growth took place after 1883. In Temples farm's twenty-two acres about eighty varied plots were provided. The railway divided the site, and the sale catalogue stressed that it only took seventy minutes to reach London by express train. The new houses included the relatively humble dwellings of Braintree Road, which soon became a favourite of railwaymen, and the grander ones at the top of Avenue Road. They were put up by individual builders and tradesmen over a period of twenty years. Most are distinguishable by their red brick, often with grey trimmings and sometimes adorned with names and dates.

Half were built by the enterprising Joseph Smith of Moat Farm. From humble origins, he came to Witham from Great Leighs in the 1870s. On one of the plots he put his 'steam joinery works, sawing, planing and moulding

4. 1815-1901

mills'. He liked to decorate his houses with special bricks and chimneys made by James Brown of Moulsham in Chelmsford, often moulded into flower and leaf patterns (see colour page 17). Amongst his other Witham buildings were the three lavish Medina Villas in Newland Street which didn't sell at first – they were too grand. He was a 'staunch Liberal', and a deacon of the

Joseph Smith (left), a very successful Witham builder. At his funeral in 1919, he was said to have been a 'tender, sympathetic and kindly man, who loved to do good without a blare of trumpets'. His son Joseph Ernest (right) continued the business, and his grandsons, including Leslie (centre) became well-known local farmers. Taken in about 1900.

Congregational church for over forty years. When he was made a magistrate at the age of 73, it was said that if his political views had been different, he would have achieved the honour much earlier.

The station area also began to attract new industrial and warehousing buildings, near the busy railway goods yard. During the 1880s, maltster Charles Harrison Gray set up the Station Maltings (its successor still stands, said to be the largest in Europe). And in 1891 George Taber brought his seed business there from neighbouring Rivenhall. Soon afterwards his women pea sorters, many of whom worked at home, went on strike about their wages. This was only three years after the famous match girls' strike in London. They told a reporter that pea sorting was their only way of earning any money in the winter. In 1894 George had a large new warehouse built by Joseph Smith at the bend in Avenue Road (it burnt down in 1953). His former partner Thomas Cullen also came to Witham in the 1890s, and went on to put up similarly handsome buildings in White Horse Lane. By 1901 there was a thriving export trade, and about twenty men and ten women worked in the seed and pea warehouses, with many more working at home.

Trouble on the farms

Farmer Thomas Beadel of Howbridge Hall said in 1867 that workers had started to leave for London and the 'manufacturing districts'. Wages were better there, and soon afterwards, the National Agricultural Labourers' Union (NALU), started encouraging such movement. The Union's Essex activities were launched in 1872 by its charismatic leader, Joseph Arch. He addressed several gatherings including one at Witham's Congregational church. In the audience was Abraham Whybrew, a farmworker and a preacher for the Peculiar People – he could still recall the drama as an old man in the 1930s.

In April 1874 'some of the finest peasantry of the Eastern Counties' converged on Witham railway station, singing Union songs. They were travelling to Tilbury docks to join a ship for Queensland. A leader wrote:
> It was a remarkable day ... It looked as if the Royal Family must be expected at Witham, for every available space was filled by people come to see some 200 working folks leave the country. Cheer after cheer came from the onlookers ... for miles ... ploughmen stood still and waved their hats.

Church Street, where many of Witham's farmworkers lived, including Abraham Fryatt, who became branch secretary of the National Agricultural Labourers' Union in the 1870s. He had recently obtained a job on the railway, but amongst his many relatives there were still boys who were starting work on farms at the usual age of ten. Taken in about 1905.

The situation was aggravated by the deep agricultural depression that started in the mid 1870s, and between 1871 and 1881 the number of farmworkers in the parish decreased from about 225 to 175. The resultant decline in the total population was probably the first for several centuries.

Men who did not move away were encouraged to demand higher wages, and Witham became an important Union centre. One local member said that farmers treated their workers as 'something less than men'. In 1876 NALU's Vice President, George Mason Ball, became one of the Essex organisers and came to live here. He often attended between five and ten public meetings a week over a wide area, walking from one to another. Strikes in Witham in 1877 and 1891 achieved some modest gains locally – in 1891 the men came to a strike meeting with their scythes in their hands. Encouragement was also obtained from the extension of the vote in 1884 to include farmworkers, who had been largely excluded from the previous electoral reforms of 1867. In 1901 when labourer John Lapwood was talking to Rider Haggard about his hard life, he said 'Things is better now' (see page 68).

The Co-op, 1887

Abraham Whybrew, who heard Joseph Arch in 1872, had a son Stanley, who became manager of the Co-op shop in the 1920s (I once had the privilege of meeting him). The co-operative system in Britain had been initiated by the Rochdale Pioneers' Society in 1844. In December 1886 a letter was circulated in Witham entitled 'Unity is Strength', after which 72 working men contributed sixpence each (about £1.50 in today's money) to start a local Co-operative Society. At a public meeting in January 1887 postman George Robjent took the chair, and announced to cheers that he hoped the Queen's Golden Jubilee year would see 'the commencement of a new era in the history of the working men of Witham'. The new committee often met in the schoolroom of the Baptist chapel, and the first President was Alfred Sayer, an elderly bootmaker who was a Baptist deacon. The other Committee members also worked in small industries or crafts, with one or two railwaymen.

Some difficulty might have been expected in obtaining a shop, due to opposition from rival tradesmen, but George Adnams helped. He was much the most prosperous Committee man, and allowed the Society to rent a property from the estate of his late brother-in-law, George Thomasin, the brushmaker and fellow Congregationalist. The shop opened in July 1887 and a celebratory tea in October was attended by over 200 people. A public meeting a year later was addressed by the Hon Charles Strutt, one of Lord Rayleigh's brothers. He was cheered when he said some people would call the co-operative system Socialism, but that 'if Socialism meant putting wealth or money in more hands without hurting any one, then he was a bit of a Socialist'. Not many other Essex Co-ops received support like this from their rich neighbours.

The shop moved to larger premises in 1896. The society continued to expand and its social events became highlights of the town's year, especially the annual 'treat', when there was a procession, tea and games. By the end of the century some of the committee members like hairdresser John Hogben and carpenter James Hubbard were putting their organisational experience to use in elected bodies like the School Board and the Urban District Council, both set up in 1894. The vociferous Mr Hogben sadly died of influenza in 1899 at the age of forty-one, but James Hubbard continued in public life for many years. The activities of such people were sometimes unsettling for the better-off people who ran the town.

4. 1815-1901

The first shop of the Witham Co-op (now 85 Newland Street). This Christmas card was sent to Charles Hubbard, a committee member, in 1909, by which time the shop had moved to larger premises further down the street. James Hubbard (Charles' second cousin) had helped to found the Witham Society in 1887, and in 1895 became one of the first Urban District Councillors, standing as a 'working men's' candidate.

A fair in Newland Street in about 1870. The picture was reproduced in a newspaper article in 1931, whose author recognised a shooting gallery in the foreground and a boxing booth on the left. He recalled that 'at night the booths were illuminated by naphtha flares. Cakes and gingerbread found ready purchasers. Itinerant pedlars disposed of their wares. As the evening wore on the public houses became full'.

The Victorians' last word

The poorer people had long enjoyed Witham's annual fairs, on the Friday and Saturday of Whitsun week in Newland Street, and on the 4th and 5th of June on the green at Chipping Hill. However, in 1891 the magistrates applied to have the fairs abolished. Police Superintendent George Allen was consulted, and admitted that 'during the last five years no cases of disorder or immorality have been discovered'. But he objected to 'the obstructions caused by shooting galleries, swinging boats, and cocoa nut shies, all of which are very dangerous, and they are generally attended by gypsies'. Furthermore, 'the respectable part' was held in private and it was 'only the low element who stand in the street'. A notice from Whitehall was posted around the town by George Wood the town crier. No-one had the temerity to write to London in support of the fairs, and they were abolished.

5. 1901-1945
PARADISE IN CRESSING ROAD

An eventful start to the century

In October 1905, Witham people looked back in time as they celebrated the centenary of the Battle of Trafalgar with their own Admiral Sir William Luard. There were decorations, a procession, and speeches, and everyone sang 'Rule Britannia'. Shortly afterwards there was an unwitting look forward, when a young unknown viola-player called Frank Bridge came to play in a string quartet. Later he became a well-known composer, and taught Benjamin Britten. The well-attended concert was at the new Public Hall in Collingwood Road, which had become a lively place since it was built in 1894.

A family group at Witham Lodge for the Golden Wedding of Admiral Sir William Luard and Lady Luard on 7 April 1908. On either side of the couple are their eight daughters, and two of their three sons. Two years later the Admiral died after an accident, at the age of 90. This was only ten days after the death of King Edward VII, so the mourning was doubly heart-felt. Reproduced by courtesy of Essex Record Office (reference D/DLu 104).

The first years of the 20th century in Witham were notable for dramatic events, several of them tragic. On 1 September 1905 an express train heading for Cromer crashed into the station. Eleven people were killed including a baby from Great Baddow with his mother, and foreman porter Josiah Doole of Chalks Road. Death and injury on our railway were quite frequent occurrences, but not on this scale. The signalmen were rewarded for preventing a worse disaster (see colour page 11). Then in February 1910 fire destroyed the Constitutional Club in Newland Street (which bore the town clock). The fire engine performed badly (a new one was purchased in 1911 in honour of George V's coronation). In May 1910 Admiral Luard died after falling from his horse and trap near the Swan, and striking a telegraph pole. On a brighter note, in June the Essex Agricultural Show was held in Witham for the first time since 1863 and was a great success – there were still several farms in the parish. In April 1912 there was another reminder of mortality – a collection was made at the parish church for the Titanic disaster fund.

Novelty

Some of the many innovations of this time were introduced by the Witham Urban District Council (hereafter referred to as 'the Council'). Like other UDCs it began work in 1895, superseding the Local Board of Health. It soon had a wide range of powers and obligations. In 1900 its nine members began to look after the new Recreation Ground or Park in Maldon Road. Most of the purchase money came from an anonymous donation of £1,000 to commemorate Queen Victoria's Diamond Jubilee of 1897 (worth over £60,000 today). The benefactor was later revealed as Tom Motion who lived with his brother at Faulkbourne Hall. His great-great nephew is Andrew, the present Poet Laureate. The land was formerly the Pattissons' garden and still has many beautiful trees.

In 1903-04 the councillors improved the water supply at considerable expense, with new artesian wells and a second water tower (on the road to Cressing). In 1904 Witham became the first small council in Essex to have its own library, donated by the defunct Witham Literary Institution and said to

> On the facing page, contrasting photographs of Arthur R Brown's yard in about 1908 (it is now 97 Newland Street; the last of his surviving buildings there were demolished in 2004). As we can see, he was still making horse-drawn vehicles at that time, but the notices at the entrance also offered repairs to 'Motor Cars', and 'Aeroplanes and flying ships built to order'. When his son anxiously asked what would happen if anyone asked for a plane, Arthur assured him 'I'd find out how it's done'.

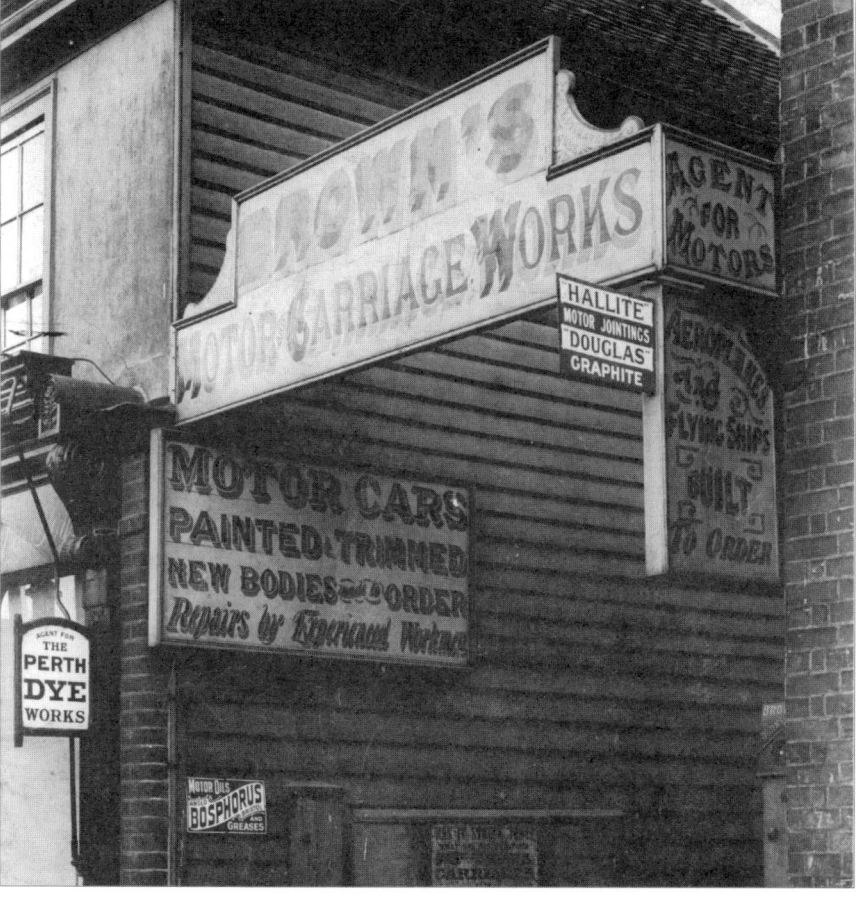

5. 1901-1945

be very popular. Also at this time, two different examples of community life were founded. One was the Bowls Club, which celebrated its centenary in 2004. The other was a branch of the Brotherhood, a Christian movement dedicated to helping the poorer residents.

London had a telephone exchange in 1879, and a company planned a system for Witham in 1889 but did not proceed. In 1897 Edward M Blyth installed his own phone line on 30 foot poles between his shop in Newland Street and his mills in Guithavon Valley. Then in 1905 the National Telephone Company opened a Witham exchange, and Mr Blyth was one of the twelve inaugural subscribers. Another was the doctors' surgery in Newland Street, whose number was Witham 8 (it is still the same today, with some extra digits in front). At the town post office the old telegraph equipment was symbolically moved upstairs to make room for the new exchange and call office. The National Telephone Company was taken over by the Post Office in 1912.

The arrival of motor cars was even more noticeable. In 1899, a newspaper referred to the 'Hippopotami on wheels' that were beginning to terrorise the Essex countryside. Even when they were standing still, their 'horrible noise', 'offensive smell' and bright colour frightened nearby horses. And when they raced along, sometimes at 20 mph, they were intolerable. But they were good for business, and Witham's carriage builders and bicycle agents rushed to learn new skills. As well as Arthur R Brown's yard, illustrated on the previous page, Glover brothers' cycle and motor works flourished, and for a time they actually assembled their own cars and motorcycles. One establishment still displays their name today.

When in 1904 vehicles had to be registered, three of Witham's young men already had their own. Proud owners built 'motor houses' and washing spaces in their gardens. Motoring was an adventure. In 1911 Harry Smith was chauffeur to Mr W B Gladstone at Braxted Park (the former Prime Minister's nephew). He was driving into Witham with the gardener's wife beside him, when they met a herd of bullocks, and collided with one. In avoiding another beast Harry drove up the bank and damaged an axle. In February 1913 a speed limit of 10 mph was introduced in Newland Street and Bridge Street but it was often ignored – many towns and villages on the London road had no such restriction. Later in 1913 the Witham police set a 'trap' on a measured furlong (about 200 metres), and caught dozens of people 'speeding' – many had no speedometer.

Motorbikes were also popular. Seventeen-year old Leonard Cullen used his machine to help his father Thomas, the seed merchant, as well as for fun. Later he set up his own motor business. It was a motorcyclist that was tragically killed in 1917 in Witham's first fatal road accident. He was Captain Edward Kay-Shuttleworth, grandson of the famous Victorian reformer. He sped round a corner on the wrong side of the road and was impaled on the shafts of a greengrocer's cart (where Cressing Road meets Rickstones Road – it was open country then).

Witham was less eager to adopt electricity. Some larger towns had a supply before 1900, and in 1897 Joseph Kuner set up a generator at the Crown in Guithavon Street and advertised an 'Electric Light Company for Witham'. He was said to have many orders, but left as suddenly as he had arrived. Girling's of Maldon and Crompton's of Chelmsford both proposed electricity operations here in 1912, but neither scheme proceeded. So for the time being Witham's energy requirements continued to come from the old gas works (still directed by local men until they reluctantly gave in to a take-over by the British Gas Company in the early 1930s).

Pinkham's glove factory and the Liberals

Pinkham's, also known for a time as the National Glove Company, made a great contribution to employment, especially for women. However, it had only small beginnings. What really brought William Pinkham to Witham was politics – he was a professional agent for the Liberals. When he arrived in about 1904, some townspeople told him that he was 'not wanted'. He organised the campaign for the 1906 General Election, and because he noticed some wrongly counted votes, his candidate narrowly defeated the Conservative MP, Hon Charles Strutt of Blunts Hall. This reflected a national upheaval.

William and his wife Rebecca had come from the flourishing glove industry of Great Torrington in Devon. So they began making gloves at home in Witham. Before long several girls were helping, and in 1912 they had a new factory built (said to be the first new glove works in Britain for seventy years). Soon afterwards, hostile flyposters amended the recruiting notice outside to read 'Girls Wanted – For the White Slave Traffic'. By then William and his Liberal colleagues had obtained nearly half the seats on the rather conservative Witham Council. He resigned as agent in 1915 to

When the Pinkhams decided to expand their glove-making business in 1912, there was some opposition. But fellow Liberal Joseph Smith sold them some land and built this factory for them near the station. The photo is of an early works outing and includes in front (left to right) Leslie (Bert) (son), William, Curly the dog, and Rebecca (also see page 12 of the colour section).

concentrate on the business, by which time he felt it was possible for a Liberal to 'hold up his head' in the town.

Women and ladies

Much of women's paid work went unrecorded by official statistics. Nevertheless, in 1901, a third of Witham's women told the census takers that they had a job or a position. Half of them were domestic servants. Three-quarters of the latter, 230 in all, were living with the family they worked for. Most of them were in ones and twos, but there were fifteen houses with three or more servants. A stockbroker living at the Grove had eight, whilst the Luards at Witham Lodge had seven. Witham girls also went away into service; Ellen Hubbard was a housemaid to the civil servants who lived at the Foreign Office in Whitehall in London.

Another fifty women were washerwomen or charwomen, working from home. Thus the widowed Sarah Coe and her two daughters of Hatfield Road were 'laundresses'. A very few girls might find shop work, but this was still mostly a man's job. When Pinkham's glove factory started to grow, the work there, although gruelling, gave another option.

Women could vote in elections for local bodies if they lived in houses of sufficient rateable value, and this included some poorer women, though they were rarely able to become really involved in the town's affairs. The Co-op did have a female committee member from 1890 to 1902. She was Mrs Amy Bloomfield, born in Suffolk and wife of a tan-yard worker. Another of my heroines is Mrs Clara Jane Hubbard. She was also from a labouring family and she lived in the very poorest part of town, but she had two £5 shares in the Gas Company. So for three years, until she died in 1913, she went to its general meetings. She was the only poor person there and the only woman. Perhaps it helped her confidence that she had been to London in her youth to be a piano teacher near Bond Street; her neighbours had included an Italian actress and a lady artist.

Middle-class women who were widowed or single often became dressmakers and milliners. One of them was Miss Elizabeth Smith, a basketmaker's daughter, who worked for fifty years at the top of Collingwood Road, starting in the 1880s, with a high-class clientele. For many decades before 1900 there had been about sixty women in this trade, a surprisingly large number. Their married sisters had less need to work and might spend time in community endeavours, particularly if they had a servant or two. For instance, the women of the

In the early 1900s, domestic service was the only option for most poorer girls when they left school at thirteen. This is Minnie Fisher in her maid's uniform in about 1910, at her home (now 30 Church Street, part of 'Charity Row'). Her father Charles was a farmworker.

Congregational church ran a branch of the YWCA, whose members debated in 1894 'are we better than our grandmothers, i.e. is the present better than the past' (the majority said yes). In Church of England organisations, such women were rather more likely to be making tea under the direction of the prosperous 'ladies'.

These ladies' role in charitable work continued. Amongst them were Admiral Luard's many daughters. They trained in nursing or social work, or organised local events. In 1890 Alice ran a soup kitchen, and in 1894 she set up an early charity shop – a 'depot for the sale of anything that has been put aside as worthless', to the 'poorest classes'. The poor became rather less dependent on charity after the Old Age Pensions Act of 1908 and the National Insurance Act of 1911. At a meeting in the Public Hall to explain the latter, there was a young civil servant from London – he was Clement Attlee, who became Labour Prime Minister in 1945. But the Braintree workhouse continued to be the fall-back solution to poverty until 1929. People who were unable to walk there were 'carried off in a jolting cart'. So there was still scope for the Misses Luard to go round on foot or cycle, offering help and advice (the latter not always welcome!). They continued to be tireless in their devotion to Witham's organisations and to the Church well into the 1930s.

Women could serve on Local Government bodies and when education was re-organised in 1903, the County Council appointed Alice and Edith Luard as school managers. In 1905 Edith's name was drawn out of the hat to be chairman at the Council School, but she declined the honour. The Boards of Poor Law Guardians were regarded as male-oriented and boorish, and it was said that the old Witham Guardians (disbanded in 1880) used to 'fight like fun'. But their successors, the Braintree Union, had a woman member as early as 1895. Miss Margaret Tabor from Bocking, a Liberal, joined them in 1913. She was a suffragist like her better known sister Clara Rackham, and when she first arrived, Witham's Captain Abrey expressed a fear that the meeting might be 'blown up'.

He seemed less anxious about his neighbour Miss Susannah Vaux. She became a Guardian in the same year, with the help of the Conservatives, and was thus the first woman from Witham to serve on an elected body (she was unopposed). She was born in India in 1858, where her father supervised the building of the Bengal railway, but had been brought to England as a baby to live with relatives. After training as a nurse, she was matron at the Birmingham Eye Hospital. Like lady Guardians elsewhere, she was never chosen for committees which dealt with finance. But she did become chairman of the two which were concerned with children, and the local newspaper noted the importance of the few lady Guardians, with their 'kind hearts' and 'anxious care for the women and children'.

In the early 1900s, women were still not allowed to vote in elections for parliament. In 1911 a group of Conservatives held a crowded meeting at the Public Hall where Lady Rayleigh of Terling announced that her husband, also present, supported her in thinking that women householders should be given the vote. On the other hand, Witham's vicar Canon Ingles said he didn't agree at all, and nor did any of the nine women in his household! There were also two well known national speakers – Mrs Selina Cooper, a former Lancashire mill worker, and Mrs Betty Balfour.

In July 1913 a 'pilgrimage' of 'non-militant suffragists' marching from East Anglia to London paused in Witham for an open-air meeting, again chaired by Lady Rayleigh. It was 'very orderly' in spite of some heckling along the lines of 'You're trying to wear the trousers'. It was not until 1918 that some women gained the parliamentary vote, and not until 1928 that they all did.

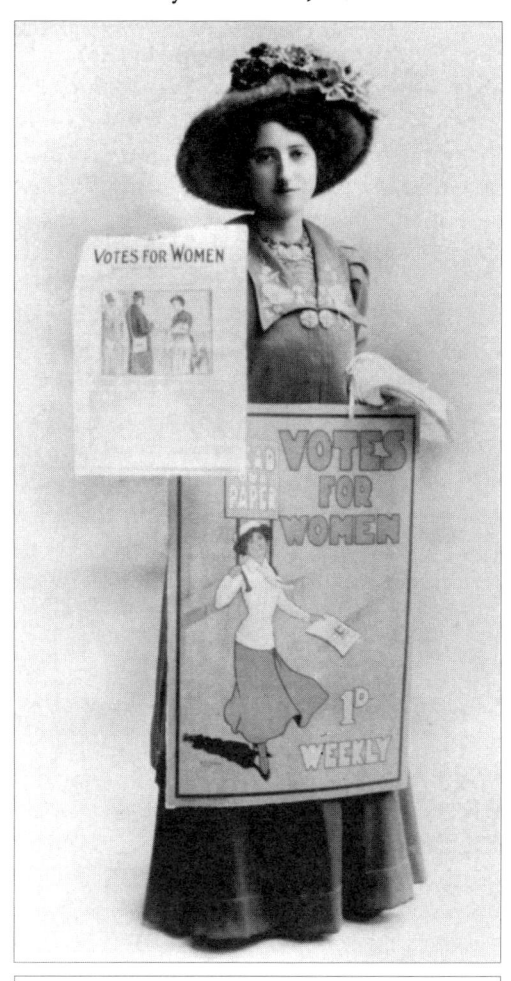

Grace Chappelow, a suffragette from neighbouring Hatfield Peverel. She was arrested at a riot in London in 1911, together with two hundred others including Mrs Constance Lytton. Their tactics were denounced on the following day by Constance's sister, Betty Balfour, speaking at a meeting about women's suffrage in Witham Public Hall.

Health and houses

Witham's health had improved. By the 1920s less than one in twenty of the people who died were children under five, compared to one in three during the 1840s. But there were serious illnesses that we don't have in England today – during an emergency in 1911, tents were hired for isolating typhoid patients. And housing was very slow to change. In the last chapter we left many residents living in tiny privately rented cottages. In 1907 another Government health inspector came, and noted the damp and crowded 'courts, alleys and yards'. Although it was forty years since mains water and drains had been provided, about one in eight of the houses still only had water from wells, and drainage into cess pools or ditches. And many of the people who were on the mains were sharing a cold tap and a 'filthy' and poorly flushed toilet in the yard with their neighbours. Hot water systems and baths were a rare luxury confined to the big houses.

Public housing was eventually to be the solution, but only after a long struggle. In 1911 the Council drew up plans for some new 'workmen's cottages' under the limited powers that were then available. However, Bell Field in Braintree Road, the site they chose, was charity property, and the resultant legal complications were still holding up the scheme when the First World War intervened.

The First World War, 1914-1918

War was declared on 4 August 1914, and Lieutenant Auriol Round of Avenue House went immediately to fight in France with the Essex Regiment. Three weeks later he was brought back to London wounded, and died of tetanus on 5 September. Most of Witham's inhabitants watched as his funeral procession made its way sadly to All Saints churchyard. It gave reality to the schoolboys' new 'War Map' at the National School – they had marked the position of the armies in red and black sealing wax. Two of Auriol's brothers also lost their lives in the War.

On 4 September a meeting at the Public Hall considered Lord Kitchener's call for recruits, after the Town Band had played 'patriotic airs' in the streets. The vicar, Canon David Ingles, announced that the War was 'a visitation sent from God'. He wanted 'all the single men from 19 to 35 years clean out of Witham parish'. A few weeks later his only son was killed in France.

A band from the Royal Army Medical Corps (1st South Midland Field Ambulance), coming down Collingwood Road for Church parade on 11 April 1915. As we can see, local boys appreciated the spectacle – they also enjoyed watching the training exercises in local fields.

By then, hundreds of soldiers with strange Midlands accents were filling Witham. The 1st/7th Battalion of the Royal Warwickshire Regiment was the first of several units to be sent here whilst training, including the 2nd/7th Warwicks in spring 1915 and the 2nd/9th Royal Scots in spring 1916. There were nearly 2,000 men sometimes, doubling the adult population. Camps in the Avenue fields and in Maldon Road filled with horses, vehicles, tents and equipment, and the roads were busy with the noise of men, guns, waggons, and lorries. Mounted soldiers billeted in Hatfield Peverel were sent on imaginative exercises – one entailed retrieving stolen Christmas rations from 'the notorious Mahomet Alli Khan' who was hiding in the 'Danbury jungles'.

Some of the men in Witham lived 'rough' in empty buildings but most were billeted with families. The knock on the door announced an officer come to view your house – then the allotted number of soldiers would tramp in with their kit. There were some stresses and strains. It was irksome to the councillors that the military horses were given precious water from the mains, when consumption in the town had already risen by nearly a half. But every cloud has a silver lining. James Goodey, who ran the water works, successfully asked for a pay rise in 1915 because of increased work. He was

64 years old and had earned the same wage for the previous 33 years. And when the soldiers' rations and a small allowance arrived, the eyes of Witham people were opened to another world. The joints of meat and the large tins of jam were remembered for decades afterwards. So when Captain Abrey visited Chipping Hill School in October 1914, he 'found all the children looking well, in fact quite surprised ... and put it down to the troops'. Mrs Alice Dazley of Maldon Road called her baby son Warwick to commemorate the regiment (he died but his name was handed on to another new brother). Local businesses flourished too. Army horses were shoed at Alice Brockes' blacksmith's shop in Newland Street, and Stanley Tyrell mended army boots at Chipping Hill.

The troops and the locals vied to entertain each other, particularly in the new YMCA hut built in July 1915. The soldiers revealed many talents including dancing, playing cards, reciting and preaching. Some could sing, others played the organ, the bagpipes or the euphonium. The Scots who arrived in 1916 had a band which gave stirring outdoor concerts. When a regiment was leaving for the front, there were poignant farewell events and church services. In 1915 one of the Warwicks' soldiers wrote back from France to his former hosts that 'you cannot realise what it is like'.

Fifty Special Constables were recruited from the older men (no women). They were to inspect 'vulnerable points' and to question people who 'look like foreigners or suspicious persons'. Hairdresser William Dibben was very good at patrolling the streets because he had a bulldog, but was fined in 1915 for not attending drill evenings, and resigned. The residents were also warned to keep alert. They reported the 'somewhat suspicious movements' of a German Jewish lawyer, Leo Weil, who was staying in Church Street with his English wife's relatives, the Deans. Some people continued to spurn the Dean family themselves even after the War, in spite of the fact that John Dean fought in France with the Essex Yeomanry (some of the drawings from his diary are shown on page 107). At nearby Great Totham, a spies' lookout tower was reported on a house (Ruffins) being built by pioneering art nouveau architect Arthur Mackmurdo. The police decided 'there is no reason to suspect [him] of espionage, he is believed to be an Englishman'. In the same parish, an alleged wireless installation was found to consist of poles for nets round a cherry tree. In September 1915, motor cars were suspected of signalling to enemy aircraft with their headlights in eastern Essex. A special watch was kept but the results were 'nil'. In the same year a local committee was appointed to prepare for German invasion.

INVASION.

DEFENCE OF THE REALM.

Witham District Emergency Committee.

SPECIAL DIRECTIONS TO CIVIL POPULATION.

Invasion though possible, is somewhat improbable. It will be notified by the Military Authority through the Police, and from them, to the Headmen of the Parishes, their Aids, and the Special Constables.

The Signal of Invasion will be the continuous ringing of the Church or other alarm bells, on which the Headmen, Aids, and Special Constables will proceed to a central spot, already agreed upon, to make final arrangements.

Their duty will be to assist people into waggons, carts, and other vehicles; point out the route to the drivers; direct them at the cross roads; regulate the traffic; suppress panic; supervise the removal and slaughter of cattle; destroy supplies; collect implements; and carry out other duties already laid down by the Authorities.

N.B.—(Information on these and other points can be obtained through Members of the Local Committees).

People will proceed at once to places pointed out by Special Constables, who will provide conveyances, as far as they are able, for the infirm, old, women and children (in the order named).

No Large Packages may be taken. People are advised to take with them their money and jewels.

Food for 48 hours, an extra blanket or two, warm clothing and thick boots.

Main Roads will be used by the Military, Bye-roads by the Civilians.

Police will assist Special Constables where Military or Main Roads have to be used.

Fire Arms must not be used or carried by civilians on any pretence whatever. After cattle have been destroyed the fire arms should be destroyed, buried, or otherwise safely disposed of.

Cattle. Farmers should slaughter, or cause to be slaughtered, their own cattle which are not driven away, on receiving an order to do so from the Police Authority, who will arrange the compensation to be paid.

Branding should be done by means of scissors or pitch-brand in letters 2 or 3 inches long on the near hind quarter and in addition to PRIVATE MARKS those of ⚡ signifying WITHAM.

Entire Horses and other valuable MALE STOCK to be moved first, milking cows last, lambing ewes not at all, pigs to be destroyed.

Motors, vehicles and horses of military value must be taken to Chelmsford to be available for the General Officer Commanding as soon as possible after they have conveyed people to their destination in Oxfordshire, (twenty-four hours is the given time).

Spades, picks, axes, &c. must be deposited at places in each parish as directed by the Headman through his Aids and Special Constables.

N.B.—Aids and Special Constables will be known by White Armlets marked W (red).

Stores of Paraffin and Petrol which cannot be moved, must be poured off.

Depots of food will be provided at intervals on the road to Oxfordshire by Emergency Committees, and every assistance that can be reasonably expected will be given by these Committees and their assistants.

Refugees are exhorted to obey such directions as they may receive from time to time, and to avoid panic as much as possible.

GOD SAVE THE KING.

Richard Poole, Printer, High Street, Maldon.

In 1915 a committee began to plan the escape of Witham's residents into Oxfordshire if the Germans invaded. This was part of a county-wide scheme. The route for our refugees led past Blunts Hall into the back lanes, passing a food depot at Terling. The main routes were left clear for the military. A hundred of these notices were kept in readiness but never used. Reproduced by courtesy of Essex Record Office (reference L/P 3/6).

Much of the effort mentioned has been male. But as more men joined the forces, some women were given unusual jobs – Gladys Brewster drove Ardley's bakers' cart and actually wore trousers. In 1916 councillors appointed their first female staff member when Mrs Millie Mens, wife of a haulage contractor, became rate collector. Some employers were resistant to this development. When it was proposed that women should work on farms, Philip Hutley of Powershall feared that 'agriculture would go to the wall'. Nevertheless, this scheme was successful in the Witham area. In 1917, novelist Virginia Woolf noted that her young cousin, another Virginia, was milking cows for Lord Rayleigh at Terling Place. The girl really preferred horses, 'but she couldn't get horses, and she's very fond of cows'.

Most members of the Witham VAD, the Voluntary Aid Detachment, were ladies. Like others, it was formed before the War. They used to practise First Aid in the Doctor Gimsons' garden – one of their victims later recollected being accidentally dropped in a gooseberry bush there. They joined the British Red Cross's huge war effort, meeting wounded soldiers on passing trains, and giving them refreshments such as hot bovril and sandwiches. There was also an active 'Work Depot' where over 10,000 garments were made.

The largest endeavour was the Red Cross Hospital, with 34 beds, in a wing of the Bridge Home. 700 soldiers in turn stayed there for treatment of minor injuries. The visiting medical officer was Dr Karl Gimson (his brother Dr Ted was in the army). But otherwise it was run by women. The Commandant (first Mary Gimson and then Charlotte Pattisson) organised everything including the finances. The Matron supervised the small number of trained nurses and all the VAD helpers. Some Witham ladies also went to other hospitals, including two or three to France. Lilian Luard, one of the Admiral's daughters, spent a year at Calais and Le Treport.

To return finally to Witham's own soldiers. Efforts at recruitment increased through 1915, while killing continued on the Western front, and also in Gallipoli where four Witham soldiers died. In early 1916, compulsory conscription was introduced for the first time ever. This hit small businesses. Local Tribunals heard appeals and William Pinkham asked to keep his son Bert to look after the complex machinery at the glove factory – he had been specially trained in Germany. But he had to go. Several men from the Peculiar People's chapel were pacifists and were given non-combatant work, though some of the Tribunal members were hostile to them. In March 1917

John Douglas Dean of Church Street made these drawings in his diary during the First World War. He was with the Essex Yeomanry in France and Belgium. Their most valiant action was a dismounted bayonet charge at Frezenberg ridge in 13 May 1915 during the Second Battle of Ypres; they recaptured the front line trenches. 69 out of 302 were killed including the Commanding Officer. John received a special commendation for his role as a stretcher bearer. He wrote that he 'went up & down the line bringing the wounded down, saw some awful sights & blood flying ... once a shell fell in front of us putting 2 men out, thought every minute my turn next, cannot describe the full details of that day'.

The funeral of Charlie Sneezum, aged 22, at All Saints. He died in October 1915 after being injured at the battle of Loos. The Town band played the Dead March. Five months later his brother George (aged 24) was killed. George's fiancée Lily wrote to the family 'All our letters were of the future even his last letter for I never once thought of him getting killed, I don't know why I did not'.

Albert Thompson, headmaster of the Boys National School, left for the army, and his wife Kate took over his work – the school inspector noted approvingly that she was 'a strong disciplinarian'.

The most devastating slaughter began in 1916. Over three quarters of the men named on Witham's war memorial were killed after March of that year. We lost eleven on the Somme in 1916, when the guns could be heard in Essex, seven at Arras in Spring 1917 (including Charlie Driver of Mill Lane, a popular singer), fifteen at Passchendaele and Ypres in late 1917, and fifteen in the German spring offensive of 1918. The three Chaplin brothers were all killed after September 1917. Then on 11 November 1918 a soldier in Newland Street heard at Afford's shop about the armistice. He wrote to his father 'Flags are flying from every house: boys are marching round the streets with flags'. In the evening there was the customary bonfire in the main street, 'the greatest seen for many years' (see also page 164).

There had been many hardships at home that I have not had space to describe, such as the fear of Zeppelins and enemy aircraft, the darkened streets, the shortages and later the rationing. But they must have seemed petty compared to the slaughter. More than a third of Witham's thousand men had gone to fight, many had been injured, and about seventy had been killed. In addition, Congregational Minister David Picton died at home in 1916 when a Scots officer was showing him a hand grenade and it exploded. In 1919 Percy Laurence of the Grove gave land for a War Memorial, money was raised, and the opening ceremony was held in November 1920. The Laurences were the last survivors of the rich and benevolent military families who had formerly played such a large part in the life of the town.

1919 was a boom year for the country but a disturbed one for labour relations, with a well-known miners' strike. In October there was a national walkout of railway workers, in which Witham joined. Nearly one in ten of the men in the town worked for the railway company by this time. Most lived close together near the station – a tightly-knit and influential group. In the following year the largest farmworkers' rally ever seen in Essex was held in a Witham field to demand higher wages. Over 10,000 men from all over the county came by train and coach, many of them marching along with four brass bands.

'Auld Lang Syne' at the closing of the Red Cross Hospital on 28 February 1919, with VADs in uniform. The helpers ranged from Mrs Caroline Chaplin (in the white dress), who 'scrubbed' the hospital for nine hours a week, to Miss Constance Round who nursed for 4,783 hours altogether between 1914 and 1919. Mrs Chaplin had three sons killed in the War and Miss Round lost three brothers.

Pinkham's again

In March 1919 two-thirds of the girls at Pinkham's glove factory walked out and began 'dancing up the High Street', demanding better wages and conditions. Some went as far as Sudbury in Suffolk to collect money for their cause. The dispute continued for several weeks, with the support of Workers' Union representatives from Chelmsford (including Miss Florence Saward who later, as Mrs Balaam, became a Witham magistrate). Rallies and meetings were held, and Union organiser Lieutenant Pollard said that he had 'faced machine guns' and so was not afraid of William Pinkham. The vicar, Canon Francis Galpin, offered to mediate, but the result is not clear.

By 1924 there were about 150 people at the glove factory, mostly women, producing 24,000 gloves a week, and a branch at Chelmsford. There were also many home workers, so the total employed probably reached 500. William's son Leslie (Bert), was secretary of one of the national glovemakers' organisations, and in 1930 presented a casket of special gloves to Queen Mary. He took over after William died in 1938. The building was doubled in size in 1948, but after several crises it closed in 1965.

Crittall's window factory

The arrival of Francis Crittall's new factory was the most important event of inter-war Witham. His first works at Braintree had been making innovative metal windows for several decades, but space there was limited and badly laid out. The sympathetic Witham Co-op was happy to sell him an eleven-acre field in 1917 and the factory began work in 1919-20, designed for mass production with modern tools and equipment. Like the glove factory before it, it was unpopular with some of the better-off residents. At first it made metal furniture, but soon switched to specialise in the new 'standard' metal windows (previously they had been made to order).

In late 1921 the post-war boom faltered. The workers were often on short-time and the company even fell behind with paying its gas bill. A boost to morale came at the end of 1923 when Valentine Crittall, the 'guv'nor's' son, briefly became a Member of Parliament (the constituency's first Labour MP). Then in 1924 new Government assistance for house building brought a great demand for windows. They were also supplied to prestigious commercial projects. The company set up agencies and subsidiaries from China to Brazil,

5. 1901-1945

A lorry-load of windows outside Crittall's Witham factory in the 1950s. This frontage, in Braintree Road, was added in 1937 to provide a new loading bay and social club. By that time there were often about 400 people employed in the factory, many earning more than twice as much as they had done previously as labourers. It was very hard work, but, as was often said, 'Crittall's made Witham' (there are more pictures on colour page 13).

and became the largest metal window maker in the world. Workers came to Essex from Wales, Scotland, and the north, where older industries were still in difficulties. In 1924 a works was built for British Oxygen next door, whilst in the following year a separate lead glazing factory was set up temporarily in the old maltings in Maltings Lane. It mostly employed young women – there is a picture of some of them on page 185.

At the end of 1925 a 'huge' extension to the Witham works was completed at a cost of £75,000 (the equivalent of about £2¼ million today). It was 150 yards across (125 metres), with its own railway sidings. 4,000 people gathered in it for a rally in February 1926. They arrived on special trains to hear a speech about rural poverty by the charismatic and controversial Ramsay Macdonald (the first Labour Prime Minister), and his colleague Ellen Wilkinson.

Houses at Crittall's 'garden village' at Silver End, founded in 1926. The family used noted architects and the startling white flat-roofed modern style was controversial, but a local newspaper reporter predicted in 1930 that it would be 'in vogue' by 1950. He was on the right lines; the village is now protected as a Conservation Area. Taken in 1966.

On his way to Witham, Mr Macdonald had visited Silver End, three miles to the north. There he planted an oak tree at the site of the company's proposed 'new garden village and model factory'. The tree was destroyed by an unknown vandal in 1933, but Silver End itself grew apace, an exciting project helped by small weekly investments from employees. Eventually it had nearly 600 houses and 2,000 people, with a village hall, a leafy park, shops, and a department store. The factory there made small parts, so was suited to disabled workers, particularly ex-servicemen. A close association developed between Witham and Silver End, and Crittall's provided a regular bus service connecting them. In 1933 the village, together with the rest of Rivenhall parish, was put into an enlarged Witham Urban District.

The benevolent principles of Silver End also operated in the Witham factory, with such facilities as a medical service, a dentist, and a barber. A social club and canteen were started. The brass band played regularly in the Park, and by 1929 Crittall's football team had attracted 'all the local talent', so the town club was temporarily suspended.

5. 1901-1945

The General Strike and the Great Depression

Crittall's did well during the mid 1920s, and production quadrupled between 1924 and 1928. However, there was strife elsewhere. During the General Strike of May 1926, Crittall's Witham workers were permitted by the Trade Unions to make a financial contribution instead of taking part, because their work was so essential to housing. But all the town's many railway workers walked out except the foreman (who was later presented with a china cabinet and a silver teapot by season ticket holders). Captain L F Bevington was put in charge of the volunteers who went to fill the breach. Railwaymen spoke at a rally in Newland Street defending their position.

The Great Depression began in the late 1920s, and in May 1929 the head of the Boys' National School wrote that 'the child population is declining here owing to reductions of staff at Messrs Crittall's'. Following the collapse on the New York Stock Exchange on 'Black Friday' in October, some men were sacked and others put on short time. There was a disastrous slump in Christmas spending, after which many shops stood empty for several years. After a slight recovery in 1930, the following three years at the factory were dire, with more dismissals, a three-day week, and wage cuts. George Hayes recalled later that Valentine Crittall told his men that 'I'm afraid if we carry on we'll have to reduce the wages'. As George said, 'of course we agreed and everybody clapped him'. Some people thought Crittall's could not survive.

In the winter of 1930 to 1931, the unemployed were given special assistance by many organisations including the British Legion, the Brotherhood and the churches. Some speakers at a public meeting in January thought that these efforts were adequate, and Miss Edith Luard said that it was 'a tremendous drop for a man who had a wife and children ... earning over £3 per week to come down to 28 shillings dole, but what of the agricultural labourer ... only earning 30s a week less health insurance' (£3, Crittall's normal wage, is worth about £125 today, and 28s about £60). Nevertheless it was agreed to set up a special 'Distress' or 'Relief' committee, with a donation from Valentine Crittall, under the chairmanship of William Pinkham. In the following winter Pinkham's glove factory closed for six months, and was only reprieved by the restoration of import duties on competing foreign goods. In spring 1932 schoolteachers complained that the Park in Maldon Road was 'monopolised by the unemployed, whose afternoon football disrupted the children's games sessions'. The men also spent some of their leisure hours catching rats on the Council's refuse dump, once killing 127 rats in one week.

In April 1932 the troubles were reflected in the Council elections, said to be so heated that they resembled a General Election. William Pinkham lost his seat after 21 years service. As chairman of the Council and the Distress fund, he had become associated with the unpopular means test which restricted unemployment benefit. The Communist-inspired 'Workers' movement' opposed him, choosing labourer John Mawdsley as their candidate. His spirited but unsuccessful campaign was led by his brother-in-law Albert Poulter, later a much-loved writer of Witham history.

Other protests in 1932 included a 'hunger march' by 2,000 people to the local workhouse at Braintree, and the resignation of two Witham magistrates from the Public Assistance Committee. One was Mrs Florence Balaam of Silver End, who as Miss Saward had helped with the strike at the glove factory in 1919. In autumn 1932-33, Witham clergymen combined to set up a soup kitchen at Church House. It was said to be a 'real boon' and was helped by donations of food from local shops.

That winter a revived Distress Committee spent over £300 (the equivalent of about £17,000 today). Any householders who could afford it subscribed 2d a week. The National School was asked about 'boys with bad boots' but there were 'only a few'. In December solicitor Gerald Bright sent twenty-five wild rabbits to the Labour Exchange, to be given to the men with the largest families. Finally, Crittall's began to recover in 1935 with renewed house building.

Progress

In spite of the economic gloom, the 1920s and 1930s saw the wider application to ordinary life of many earlier inventions, particularly in communications. The Council purchased a Gestetner duplicator in 1926 – until then the minutes had been written by hand. Gradually, more telephone subscribers joined the original twelve of 1905. There were 82 in 1926 and 169 in 1934. In 1932, many of the phones rang all together one night, due to a 'slight defect'. By then, many shopkeepers had phones as well as the factories and professionals who had taken up the earliest lines. For instance the number Witham 66 was given to Albert Mondy the ironmonger in about 1926 – Mondy's shop still has it. But private phones were still rare. Even in 1937 fewer than one in twenty of Witham households had them. In the Council estate in Cressing Road only one house had its own phone, and the subscriber, who had a carting business, was regarded with awe. But the public could make calls from the Post Office, and a separate coin-operated box was put up in the town centre in about 1930.

Early phone lines were sometimes used to transmit music and drama. But wireless broadcasting as we know it today began here in Essex in the 1920s. After experiments in Chelmsford in 1920, Marconi's radio station 2MT opened in 1922 at Writtle. Peter Eckersley, its gifted director, engineer, and announcer, lived at Batsfords in Newland Street until leaving for London in 1923 to become the controversial first chief engineer of the new BBC.

At first Witham people would gather in public places to hear broadcasts, but personal radios soon caught on. In 1925 Charlie Rumsey fixed his aerial to a tree in the Park behind his house. The self-taught 'wireless doctor' Edgar Sainty set up in business in Albert Road (shown on page 143), and also had his own short-wave station talking to the far corners of the world. In 1932 he visited his old school in Guithavon Street to play a music broadcast to the boys. The headmaster later acquired his own wireless – selected pupils listened to it on special occasions like the launch of the Queen Mary in 1934.

Tommy the Gas Company horse, at the works after winning a first prize at Tolleshunt D'Arcy show in 1920. He was bought for £150 in March 1918 (about £3,700 in today's money – it was war-time and horses were scarce). His predecessor, costing £100, and uninsured, had died after three months. In front is James Croxall the manager and behind is Arthur Capon, the coal carter.

Candles, oil lamps and open ranges were still common in the 1930s for light and heat and cooking. But better-off residents had gas lighting, and some used gas cookers and fires. The gas supply and the price were often threatened by failing coal deliveries, due to economic problems and industrial disputes. A few factories and farms had individual electric generators – in 1914 Robert Wakelin of Freebournes farm had put wires along the street to light up his sister's house in Collingwood Road. Similarly in 1919 William Pinkham supplied his house from his glove factory.

The most public struggle over energy concerned street lighting. The 104 gas lamps, turned on and off by the lamplighter, were owned by the Council who bought gas from the Witham Gas Company. There were often arguments, in spite of the fact that many of the councillors and Company directors were friends, and a few people served on both bodies. In 1890 there had been plans to run the lamps on oil, but ratepayers successfully protested. During the early 1900s the lights had only been illuminated on winter evenings (with several days unlit altogether at the time of every full moon). When they came back into use after the First World War, only half were lit. During emergencies this number was reduced further, and in autumn 1921 the streets were in darkness for over two months during a breakdown in negotiations.

The initials of the East Anglian Electric Supply Company on a switching station in Cut Throat Lane (taken in January 2004; n explosion in October 2004 has resulted in substantial alterations). The company had first brought electricity to Witham in 1927. The supply was rather chancy at first. It failed one Sunday in 1929, silencing the newly electrified organ bellows at All Saints Church (luckily a hurried search found the old handle).

Meanwhile, the Council had started to consider using electricity instead. They decided that it was time to 'make a stand' against the Gas Company's demands, and in 1920 they were about to engage a Suffolk electricity firm when the latter ran short of money. In 1925 it resurfaced as the East Anglian Electric Supply Company, and two years later brought power into Witham from Braintree, set up an office, and started laying mains. In 1929 the Council finally gave it the honour of lighting some of Newland Street, and in 1931 many other parts of the town were also taken into the scheme. Soon afterwards the new National

Grid helped to regularise the supply. However, demand for domestic gas for cooking continued to grow, and a number of houses in the town were still lit with gas until well after the Second World War.

More motors

Private cars remained a luxury for some time, but motor buses reached Witham in 1918, and public and commercial bodies started to move towards motorisation as soon as the First World War was over. In September 1919 the Council was presented with its own 20 hp Ford ambulance by the Hon Charles Strutt, so it was no longer necessary for patients be carried in a hired horse ambulance.

During the 1930s many of the tradesmen stabled their horses for the last time, and bought vans instead for their extensive delivery rounds. One of them was baker Edward Palmer – these two photos show his roundsman Arthur Shelley with his horse in the yard of 83 Newland Street on its last working day, and posing proudly with his new van soon afterwards.

A year later he gave money to pay for poorer patients to use it. In the same year Glovers started to advertise farm tractors, and the Witham Cartage and Coal Company bought a three-ton lorry and offered to carry out furniture removals with it.

There were many hazards. In 1919 a lorry load of ladies' corsets caught fire in the main street. In the same year the County Surveyor's chauffeur was hurt by stones shattering his windscreen in Newland Street – tarmac was not put down until 1922, when the workmen were paid extra because of the damage to their boots.

In 1930, boys in nearby villages had to fetch petrol for their new school bus before it could bring them into Witham. And in 1932 one of Hicks' buses was attacked and damaged by an elephant which was walking with a circus from Witham station to Silver End.

It was not only elephants that felt vulnerable, but also horses, cyclists, and pedestrians. When a frightened Council horse ran through the town in 1919 the 'pea buyer' who stopped it demanded a reward and was given ten shillings. In 1934 a milkman's tricycle from Freebournes was knocked flying by a car and three gallons poured out from his delivery can. The *Braintree and Witham Times* was launched in 1929, and its editor suggested abolishing horse traffic altogether. He also complained that the law favoured pedestrians over motorists.

In 1930 the Council replaced the fire engine bought in 1911 – pulled by horses and pumped by steam – with a new Morris motor. The pioneering ambulance of 1919 was vibrating badly, even when tested with three sacks of corn in it by a councillor who was a miller, so a new one was bought in 1933. The horse-drawn 'scavenging' carts gave way to a dustbin lorry in 1935, after a new young Sanitary Inspector arrived. At first he himself had to travel to his inspections at all hours on foot and by bus, even in the countryside, which did not please him – his previous job was in West London.

The 'Great Essex road' again

The arrival of the motor meant that Witham's historic position on the London road, the A12, re-asserted itself after the relative peace of the railway age. In the early years it was possible to stand in an empty Newland Street waiting for a car to appear. But during the railwaymen's strike of 1919 there was a foretaste of things to come when amazing convoys of lorries poured through. Between 1904 and the late 1920s the annual number of new registrations in Essex increased twenty-fold, and then doubled again by 1939. Under a new Road Traffic Act, town speed limits for cars were standardised at 30 mph in 1932. Some Witham people tried unsuccessfully to keep their 10 mph limit.

The Act also introduced many new offences. As a result of this and the increased traffic, Witham's police and magistrates were overwhelmed by careless drivers from distant parts without lights, brakes or licences. Often

5. 1901-1945 119

Drivers pouring down Newland Street in about 1930. They were probably returning to London after a day at the seaside – there was no by-pass in those days. Taken from an upstairs window at the Croxall family's house next to the gas works (now the site of the Mill Lane car park).

they were still too fast as well. In 1931 the Bolivian driver of a Mercedes 'cut in' on another car at 70 mph when approaching from Kelvedon. The two later got out and threatened each other in front of an appreciative (and racist) crowd. The chairman of the bench called the culprit a 'road hog', and fined him £20 (the equivalent of £1,000 today).

The flow was reinforced by cheerful weekend motorists and charabancs, heading to and from the seaside. In 1924 the Council was troubled by the 'great and increasing number' of them which stopped in Newland Street, where they caused 'a nuisance' because of the absence of a public toilet (the minute-taker was too polite to give any more details). Problems with finding a site and funds delayed this facility, but it was eventually built in 1929 in Maldon Road. On Whit Monday 1930 'an extraordinary volume of traffic poured through Witham' and on the same day in 1933 it was estimated that 1,000 cars an hour were passing. For comparison, during today's weekday rush-hour there are about 1,000 cars an hour on Hatfield Road (the old A12), and over 4,000 on the by-pass (the 'new' A12).

As the 1930s went on, safety did improve somewhat with innovations like compulsory driving tests, and the installation of facilities like parking places, bus stops, and pedestrian crossings with the new belisha beacons. In 1935 traffic lights were placed at the Maldon Road junction (though motorists

OVERTAKING ON THE WITHAM CATHOLIC BRIDGE MAY MEAN IMPRISONMENT. —*Official.*

New notices on the Catholic bridge seem to be having little effect in September 1937, to judge from this newspaper photo. The magistrates were beginning to think about gaol sentences for erring motorists. One day in July they had spent ten hours, in two shifts, 'hearing complaints against users of the Kings Highway'.

IRON AGE, ROMANS, AND SAXONS, see pages 8-11

A representation of the Roman Temple at Ivy Chimneys (©Essex County Council). By the fourth century it was probably used as a Christian church, but it was demolished before 400 AD, and the site may have returned to pagan use.

A 19th century view of the earthworks at Witham. They were started in the Iron Age and enlarged in 913 AD. A railway viaduct now crosses this view. The artist was William Henry Bartlett (1809-1854), a prolific 'topographical draughtsman' both at home and abroad. The publisher, George Virtue (c 1793-1868) issued over 20,000 engravings during his career.

CHIPPING HILL, see pages 10-15, and 150-159

Above. An air photo of Chipping Hill taken in 1988. This was the centre of Witham for over five hundred years, from Saxon times until about 1200 A.D. The photo shows the parish church, and the green which was the old market place. Crossing diagonally from the bottom right is Church Street, formerly the road to Cressing and also known as Hog End.

Left. Timbers blackened with soot from medieval open fires – the original house was open to the roof. Three arms of a four-sided 'crown post' are visible. This is the blacksmith's house in Chipping Hill, dating from about 1375. The bricks are much later. The photo was taken during restoration in 1974. See also pages 28 and 155.

NEWLAND STREET, see pages 15-19, and 160-180 3

Newland Street (also known as High Street). The Templars set it out as a new town in about 1200, after which it became the main commercial centre of the parish. Over time, some of their long half-acre plots have been divided into even narrower strips, whilst others have been combined into wider ones. Above is an air photo taken in 1988, looking north. Below is a view looking north-east in about 1904, showing the wide central part of the street, originally the market place.

4   MANOR HOUSES, see pages 12-13 and 183

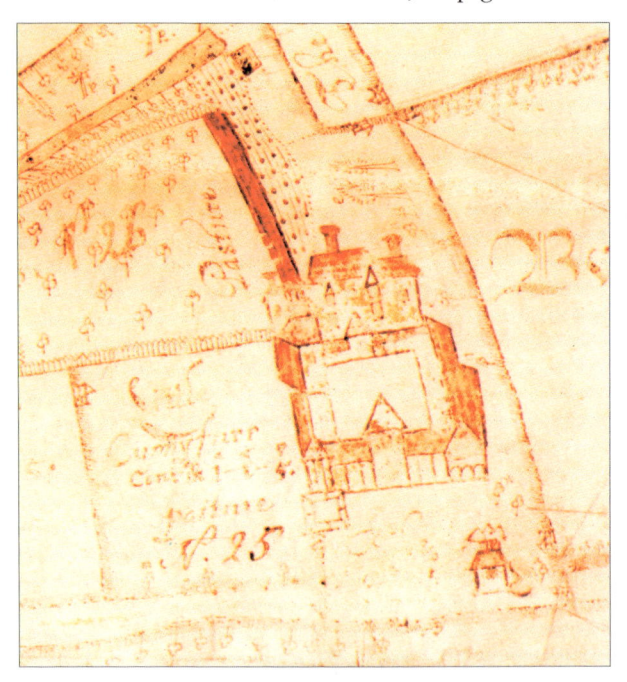

Left. The manor house of Powershall, from a map drawn in 1657. It was one of the largest farms in Witham, with about 375 acres (150 hectares). When Thomas Chipperfield died there in 1680, his many possessions included six leather chairs in the parlour, and he had thirty horses, mares and colts in his yard. Today there remain two of the barns on the right, and a much altered house at the back. Reproduced by courtesy of Essex Record Office (Accession A10763).

Right. The manor house of Howbridge Hall, built in about 1580. In the early 1920s a variety of antique features were added to the interior, obtained from demolished houses elsewhere. The result earned an article in the magazine *Country Life* in 1924. Taken in about 1960.

TUDOR AND STUART WITHAM, see pages 20-28

Left. A painting of John Southcott wearing his judge's robes. He lived at the mansion of Witham Place in Powershall End from 1567 to 1585. His descendants, who were Roman Catholics, owned it until the 1780s, and often lived there. There is a fine monument in the parish church bearing the recumbent images of him and his wife Elizabeth (see page 21).

Right. Dame Katherine Barnardiston, on her memorial in Kedington church, Suffolk. She rented Witham Place from the Southcott family. She helped the Witham Puritans' campaign against their vicar Francis Wright. When she died in 1633 she left money for Witham's vicar to buy mourning clothes, but he could only have it if he was not 'Mr Wright that now is vicar' (see pages 24-25).

Left. A map of the grounds of the vicarage in 1762. They had been landscaped by Philip Southcott, son of Sir Edward Southcott of Witham Place. The work was commissioned by vicar George Sayer and his wife Martha, who was the daughter of a prosperous Archbishop of Canterbury. (see pages 33-35 and 158). Glebe Crescent and Ebenezer Close are now situated on what was Great Field, Bramston Green is on Bath Field, and Chipping Dell on Home Field. The Meadow has been made into the River Walk. So nowadays children play in the spring that was part of the 'cascade', and the remains of the bath are buried in undergrowth. Reproduced by courtesy of Essex Record Office (D/P 30/3/5).

Below. The brass dial of a small grandfather clock assembled by Richard Wright of Witham in about 1780. His son and grandson continued the business until the 1840s (see pages 42 and 164.).

THE 1700s (2), see pages 29-53

This avenue belonged to the mansion at the Grove, on the other side of Newland Street, and was planted for the Earl of Abercorn (see page 30). In 1724, diarist Daniel Defoe, finding the gardens nearly complete, wrote 'few in that part of England will exceed them'. Taken about 1900. The trees were cut down in the 1920s to build houses in The Avenue.

Some of the elegant houses built during the 1700s, looking down Newland Street (High Street) from the top (east). This was the grandest end of the town centre. The two large buildings are High House on the left (see pages 168-69) and Avenue House on the right (see pages 30-31 and 171). The engraving dates from 1832 the two sides of the street do not match each other very well, if compared to the real view. The trees on the right are in the gardens near the Avenue (see above). The artist, George B Campion (1796-1870), was better known as a water-colour painter. Another of George Virtue's publications.

8 THE PATTISSONS, see pages 32-33, 72-73, 80-81, and 122

The young brothers William Henry and Jacob Howell Pattisson. When the famous Thomas Lawrence painted this portrait in 1811-17, the family was at the height of its social and financial success. But tragedy followed. William was drowned on his honeymoon in 1832, and Jacob left town in debt in 1859. The painting was sold at Christie's in 1860 and made 200 guineas (about £10,000 today) (Polesden Lacey, The MacEwan Collection, The National Trust / NTPL).

The small picture shows a Peek Frean biscuit tin made in the 1930s, which I purchased online from a shop in Iowa, USA..

THE EMPIRE

The Segenhoe valley in New South Wales, to which Edmund Potto was transported in 1829 for sending a threatening letter at the time of the 'Witham fires'. It is likely that he started the fires too, but the jury found him not guilty on that charge, probably to save him from being hanged like James Cook earlier in the year (see pages 55-56).

The 'siege of Lucknow' in March 1858 during the Indian Mutiny, as imagined in a painting by Cecil C P Lawson. It was here near the bridge that Witham's David Hawkes won the Victoria Cross for his bravery in rescuing a fellow-soldier under fire, when he himself was already badly wounded. He died at Fyzabad in August of the same year. The location of his grave is not known. (see pages 82-83).

THE SMYTHS' DRILL FACTORY, see pages 67-68

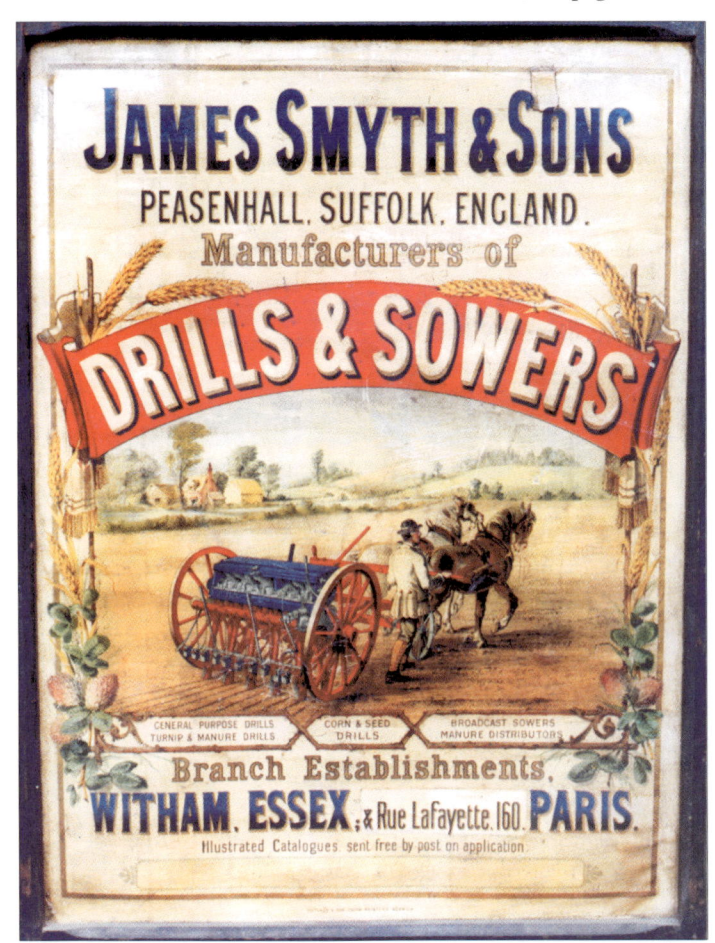

Smyths' seed drills were made in Witham and Peasenhall and sent far and wide, particularly to the company's depot in Paris, which served the rest of Europe and also Russia. Special types of drill were also made for Africa. On the left is an advertisement from the 1870s.

Below is a photo taken in 2002 of a drill made in Witham in 1860. It was bought by a farmer at Orsett in 1862, and is still on the same farm and with the same family today.

THE RAILWAY, see pages 62-65, 94, and 141-142   11

Right. Part of a certificate given to signalman Ben Sainty in 1905 after the Cromer express crashed into Witham station. He and his colleagues Thomas Bannister and Fred Parrish were each honoured with one of these certificates and 'a purse of gold' from the passengers, for stopping another train that was approaching from Kelvedon.

Below. A new station was built in 1906, and its skilful construction can still be admired today. This view shows it in the 1950s, looking towards Colchester, with an express heading for Liverpool Street in the centre, a Braintree train on the left, and the maltings on the right. It was painted by Malcolm Root from information provided by Mr R Smith.

12   PINKHAM'S GLOVE FACTORY, see pages 97-98 and 110

William and Rebecca Pinkham started making gloves at home at 4 Albert Road (far left) in about 1901, when William came as the Liberal agent. Soon they moved to 13 and 14 (near left); they lived in 14 and girls made gloves in 13. In 1912 they built a factory in Chipping Hill where many more were employed (below, in 1983, now the site of Templemead flats). After an extension in 1948, they closed in 1965. At the bottom, a bag and some gloves.

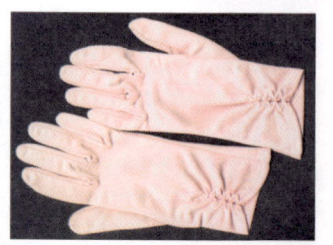

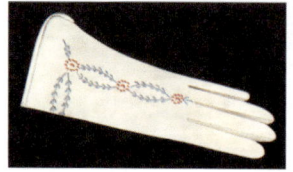

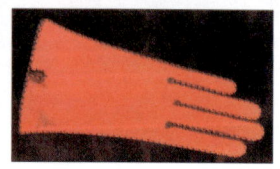

CRITTALL'S WINDOW FACTORY, see pages 110-112   13

Crittall's metal window factory at Witham opened in 1919-20, and made a tremendous difference to the town. It closed in 1990, and the remaining workers were moved to Braintree. At the top, the Braintree Road frontage. Next the view across part of the roof towards the parish church. The rest of the photos were taken inside the factory after it closed.

14 THE 1920s and 1930s, see pages 110-130

More features of the 1920s and 1930s, as seen in later photos.
(1) In 1921, one in five of the men in the parish still worked in farming (taken near Silver End about 1960).
(2) The first Council houses, 17-27 Cressing Road, completed in 1923. (see pages 121-124)
(3) The Whitehall cinema, opened in 1928 (now the library) (pages 127 and 172).
(4) Chain stores became more common – the Home and Colonial arrived in the late 1920s. These traffic lights came in 1935, and for several years they were Witham's only set. These buildings facing the top of Maldon Road were demolished in about 1966.
(5) Through traffic at 'the most dangerous corner in Witham', by the red brick gas manager's house (now site of Mill Lane car park) (pages 66 and 115-16 for gas, 118-121) for traffic (taken in about 1960).
(6) The statue of Dorothy L Sayers, the novelist, playwright and theologian, who lived in Witham from the early 1930s till her death in 1957 (page 126).

THE SECOND WORLD WAR; see pages 130-139 15

An emplacement in Chess Lane for a Second World War 'spigot mortar' gun (also known as a 'Blacker Bombard' after its inventor). The guns, issued to the Home Guard in 1942, would rotate on the stainless steel spindle, with the men standing in a pit round the edge. This is one of three which can still be seen in strategic positions along the old Maldon railway line, forming the biggest surviving group known in Essex.

In September 1941, over 250 Witham premises were found to have iron railings, gates or chains which were eligible to be taken away for war-time salvage. However, they all remained standing because of a long dispute between the Urban District Council and the Government about the details. For instance, the Council wanted to leave behind all the cast-iron gates in Chipping Hill like these at Oaklands (no.37), and just take the railings.

16   LOOK FOR IRONWORK – see the walks, pages 140-182

(1) and **(2)** More railings – this gatepost and nameplate are at 20-26 Newland Street and date from 1876. There were two Davey brothers from Witham who helped James Paxman set up his engineering firm in Colchester; one of them left in 1871. Three sets of their railings survive in Witham, more than the total known elsewhere (see pages 172, 176 and 182). **(3)** Coal holes (at the first houses built in Guithavon Street, in 1843, see page 177). **(4)** Foot scrapers (this, at 129 Newland Street, has lost its scraper). **(5)** Wall letter boxes (mostly late Victorian, small 'C' type, with 6 inch aperture, makers name at bottom – this one was installed in 1894, see page 176). **(6)** and **(7)** Railway station structure (from careful rebuild of 1906, see page 141). **(8)** Oddities like this 1930s vase at a garage (corner of Avenue Road). **(9)** Man-hole covers (earliest surviving in roads probably from the 1920s, e.g. this by Ham Baker in Kings Chase). **(10)** Fittings for shop blinds, many now disused, these probably from the 1950s (made by J Dean of Putney), at 149-51 Newland Street.

LOOK CLOSELY AT BRICKS (1) – see the walks, pages 140-182   17

For this page and the next two, I am extremely grateful to Pat Ryan for generous help and advice from her wealth of knowledge. **(1)** Medieval bricks, possibly imported (parish church, see pages 156-58). **(2)** 'Rolled' corners at Batsfords perhaps about 1690. (Batsfords, 100 Newland Street, pages 45 and 180). **(3)** Shaped bricks, early 1700s (Grove wall, pages 30 and 170). **(4)** and **(5)** 'Pressure marks', caused by one row of new-made bricks resting on another whilst drying diagonal ones usually about 1670 to 1815 (Roslyn House, pages 171-72), horizontal ones late 1700s onwards (37 Chipping Hill, page 154). **(6)** 'False pointing' – real joints disguised, neater ones added on top (Town Hall, page 166). **(7)** Moulded bricks made by James Brown of Moulsham, used by Joseph Smith (pages 86-88), 1880s onwards, despised by some then as 'cheap ornamentation' (Collingwood House). **(8)** Blue 'bull-nosed' (rounded) bricks, 1906 (railway station, page 141). **(9)** Across the bottom, more from James Brown. **(a)** numbered extracts from his catalogue **(b)** same numbers on builder's drawings **(c)** the results today ('Oaklands', 37 Chipping Hill, p.154).

18 LOOK FOR BRICK BUILDINGS (1) – see the walks, pages 140-182

This page and the one facing show brick buildings from four different periods and styles. In each case, the left hand picture is an example of the 'best' style, and the right hand one shows the more everyday one. More thanks to Pat Ryan for help with these.

About 1695 to 1750. Red and black. In panels for 'best' (on the front of 'Totscott', 11 Church Street). 'Chequered' for the rest (on the side of Roslyn House, 16 Newland Street, with a newer white brick front added later).

About 1740 to 1810. Red, with fine porches and windows (87 Newland Street). Several new brick bridges were built too (Chipping Hill bridge, see page 46).

LOOK FOR BRICK BUILDINGS (2) – see the walks, pages 140-182

About 1800 to 1870. White, grey, or yellow, varied types and qualities of brick. Left, 'Recess' (14 Chipping Hill, see page 154), built early 1840s. Above, 35-37 Church Street, built 1860 for farmworkers by the Hutleys of Powershall (page 156).

About 1860 to 1914. Often red, with white trimmings (a 'streaky bacon' effect), sometimes vice versa. Left, Warwick House (48 Collingwood Road), built in 1910 for the Heddles, who had a shop here (see page 146). Above, 25-31 Church Street, built in 1895 for shopkeeper John Wadley to rent to tenants.

20 LOOK FOR ODDMENTS – see the walks, pages 140-182

(1) and **(2)** Original street names and door numbers, fixed by Witham Urban District Council in 1914 and 1922 respectively. Not many survive. **(3)** and **(4)** Names and dates. These are in Church Street (on the old workhouse, see pages 48-50), and in Bridge Street (page 182). **(5)** Tombstones. This, for the first of the well-known Pattissons, is at the United Reformed Church (pages 32-33). **(6)** People doing interesting things like preparing a new telephone pole in Guithavon Street. **(7)** The poles themselves, with owner (GPO on this old one in Chipping Hill, page 152), length (36 feet), girth (M for medium), and date (1957). Later ones instead have BT, and their length in metres, plus a line three metres from the bottom, and a code for the origin of the pine tree most are Scots or Norwegian. Note that in contrast, lettering on electric poles seems to make no sense. **(8)** Finally, Ordnance Survey bench marks, for fixing levels when mapping. Not used much now because of satellite technology, but several survive; this one is at the corner of Guithavon Street and Newland Street (page 177)

kept ignoring them, and warning notices had to be put up). But the town's vigilance continued. In 1938 a Hertfordshire motorist remarked that the severity of Witham police was 'well-known from Lands End to John O'Groats'.

Businesses welcomed the passers-by, just as they had during the 18th century. Cafés were set up, and Harold Cook's shop produced pork pies for the 'hamper trade' – Winston Churchill is said to have been a customer. When the County Council planned a by-pass in 1935, traders petitioned against it because of the potential damage to their livelihood (their complaints reached the pages of *The Times* newspaper). It was not built until 1964.

Flight

In 1932 an aerodrome was built at Broomfield ten miles away. A group from the Council went to the opening ceremony and rode in a 'ten-seater airliner' which must have been an amazing experience – they found that Witham looked 'splendid' from the air. Equally exciting was the impromptu arrival in 1933 of a small two-seater plane in a field next to Witham town centre. The pilot had been sent from Colchester to give rides to some friends of a friend. He chose his own landing place – it was where the Sports Centre now stands in Bridge Street. An enthusiastic crowd clustered round to watch the take-offs and landings, and he looped the loop several times over Guithavon Road. Police Constable Jordan was not pleased and the pilot was later fined £5 (about £200 in today's money).

Living and housing

After the First World War, shortages meant that private builders could not build enough houses for 'heroes to live in'. The pioneering Housing Act of 1919 put the duty onto local authorities and offered a state subsidy for the first time. Witham's councillors embarked on two extremely difficult years making arrangements to build. At last in 1921 they were ready to start twelve houses in Cressing Road in the north of the town. But in August, before a brick had been laid, the Government withdrew support (the subsidies had proved costly and there had been a severe economic downturn). An impassioned protest by new railwayman councillor Ebenezer Smith was to no avail. When he had been elected in the previous year as the first Labour

Miss Charlotte Alice Pattisson on a donkey cart in about 1907. To the right are her sister, friend and servants, in front of their house at Pelican Cottage, 16 Collingwood Road. She came to Witham in about 1900 and became Witham's first female councillor in 1922. Her grandfather was Jacob Howell Pattisson (for whom see pages 80-81).

member, he had felt very unwelcome, but later he became the leader of the Council's campaign for better housing (Ebenezer Close is named after him). The Council started again on its own, and finally in October 1923 completed the first six council houses (17-27 Cressing Road, see colour page 14).

They were mostly designed by the councillors, and it was their first 'lady councillor' Miss Charlotte Pattisson who suggested 'rough casting' some of them to provide variety. She had been elected in 1922, when she defeated two other contenders including a well-known local farmer. The Women's Institute had campaigned for lady candidates and she was helped by the Witham branch (founded in 1919, four years after the national body). One of her Council colleagues said on welcoming her that, 'ladies were taking a tremendous part in national matters'. She was fortunate to be put onto the Housing Committee, which was becoming increasingly important. She had run the Red Cross Hospital during the second part of the First World War, and was a popular organiser of the local Boy Scouts.

5. 1901-1945

Continuing the housing programme was a struggle. The lurching national and local economy often made it hard to find tenants who could afford the rents. The arrival of Crittall's factory in 1919-20, and its intermittent growth thereafter, provided a welcome boost. But in the dire times of 1931 the firm tried to entice Council tenants into its own houses at Silver End (it was also said to favour Silver End residents for jobs at Witham). The greatest trial was the ebb and flow of national policy. New legislation and regulations appeared constantly. Civil servants visited Witham to urge less or more expenditure according to the times.

In due course some government help again became available, and small groups of houses were added to the first estate, in the Cressing, Rickstones and Cross Road area. At last by 1932 over 150 houses had been completed. This was a revolutionary development for the town, and a vibrant community grew up there (there was hardly any traffic then). As one resident said later, 'they thought they'd woken up in paradise'.

The necessarily stringent economies meant that there were no baths in the first few houses. Then for a time the baths were upstairs but the hot water was downstairs. The councillors' dilemma was that the rents were still beyond many people, and they were embarrassed in 1927 when their own dustcart driver said he could not afford a Council house. In the same year it was found that one of the builders (from Brentwood) was incompetent and some of his houses were damp. And in 1936 the Council Clerk and

Barbara Rice (right) at home in Cressing Road in about 1929, with Lionel, Sheila and Alan Stoneham. On the left are bricks waiting for new houses to be built in 'The Gap', which became Cross Road. The houses in this area were commissioned by the Council from several different builders, hence the variety of names on the manhole covers still visible in the gardens.

a civil servant had a secret discussion about the 'dullness' of the more recent buildings, designed by the Council's own Surveyor. But in 1937 another ambitious scheme was begun in the Church Street area on the other side of the railway line. Part of it was built on former Church property, or glebeland, which explains the name of Glebe Crescent.

Such was the demand for accommodation that in 1930 Witham still had most of its slums, as the old unhealthy houses had become known. Two councillors had been sent out with Dr Ted Gimson in 1919 to survey them and had been 'disgusted', finding about 150 unfit. Dealing with them was another long and tortuous process. Finally the Housing Acts of 1930 and 1935 brought more procedures, more subsidies, and more civil servants bemoaning the 'magnitude' of the problem in Witham.

Landlords could be ordered to close substandard houses, or carry out repairs, but some were uncooperative and councillors were divided about how to respond. In 1929 Councillor Ebenezer Smith wanted his colleagues to display on these decrepit cottages in Guithavon Valley 'the name of every owner and the rent that was being charged'.

Demolition became the order of the day. The friendly but notorious Trafalgar Square in Maldon Road bit the dust in 1937-38. It had figured prominently in a survey of overcrowding in 1932 – its houses had two bedrooms but often only one was fit to sleep in, and some of the families had four or five children. Compulsory 'Clearance Orders' were issued for about 140 Witham houses between 1935 and 1939, and others were demolished by landlords after being declared unfit. The people who lost their homes were all entitled to be provided with new ones, so more Council houses were built at the far end of Powershall End for the purpose. In addition a newly introduced system of rebates helped the tenants with their rents if necessary.

The councillors used other new ideas too. In 1929 they began an unusual but popular scheme, building to sell. A £10 deposit and repayment on 'easy terms' secured one of the forty-four houses on former allotments in the Millbridge Road area. They were said to be 'a distinct acquisition to the town'. In addition, grants were paid for about sixty of the houses put up by private builders. The best-known private estate was in the Avenue, started in 1923, where the magnificent lime trees, nearly two hundred years old, were cut down. Private builders suffered badly during the Depression, though it is said that later in the 1930s they were 'shown how to make money' by an Australian speculator, Albert C Baker.

The result of all this activity was that, like many towns, Witham underwent one of the greatest transformations of its long history. In 1920 there were about 900 houses, all privately owned. During the following twenty years about 800 were built. Meanwhile nearly 200 had been demolished, most by public action, leaving a balance of 1,500. And now for the first time about a quarter of the total was owned by the Council. There had been an exodus from the town centre, which contained nearly half the residences in 1920, but only one in six of them by 1939.

Not everyone appreciated the change. In 1939 the Chamber of Commerce bemoaned the dispersal of its customers, and in the same year the MP for Norwich mentioned in a speech that Witham's new houses were 'disgusting, debased, loathsome things'. This might have passed unnoticed but it was quoted in the new magazine *Picture Post,* which had a circulation of over 1¼ million. The councillors wrote to the offending MP, who told them he was referring to houses on the main road. This could not mean Council houses, so they were reassured.

Sociable Witham between the Wars

One of Witham's claims to fame in the world at large is that the novelist, playwright and theologian Dorothy L Sayers lived here (her statue is shown on colour page 14). She arrived in the early 1930s with her husband Major Atherton Fleming. It was he who mixed most with the townsfolk, being a regular at the Red Lion. She was mainly known for her eccentrically mannish appearance as she bought fish for her cats at a nearby shop. No doubt her main interest in Witham was its accessibility to her publishers and associates in London. But she later made a contribution to the local War effort.

During the 1920s and 1930s the town's growth brought new facilities and events of which the residents were suitably proud. In 1920 the 'the Nurses'

The Nurses' Bungalow (46 Collingwood Road, now a house). It was opened in 1920 as a War memorial. There were two maternity beds and accommodation for two district nurses; this shows Sister Agnes Hynd and Nurse Irene Buckley. The place was fondly remembered by many mothers. Taken in about 1933.

Bungalow' opened. The initial subscription was started by Dr Charles Knight as a 'practical' War memorial (he had demanded a hospital but others felt that it would be too costly). There were often financial difficulties – local perception was that the bungalow was funded by the ladies of the committee, but in fact nearly all the money had to come from the public purse. The nearest Witham has come to a hospital was at Black Notley, five miles north, where a sanatorium was opened in 1930 and later acquired other functions (it closed in 1998).

In 1932 a 'magnificent' new concrete water tower (the town's third) was built in Cross Road, supplied from Bradwell Springs near Silver End. At the opening ceremony the 'more venturesome' councillors climbed down into the tank. It was said to be a 'great day' and someone forecast that the tower would last sixty years (it was demolished in 1975). At the same time a recreation ground was laid out in Rickstones Road near the new houses. Grants did not materialise for the planned tennis courts, toilets, quoits, football stand and caretaker's cottage, but the play area and football pitches were very welcome. Part of the field was dedicated as a cemetery in 1933. This facility had been under consideration since 1914 but other proposed sites had been found to be unsuitable.

Farming was still important. In 1929 Witham again hosted the peripatetic Essex Agricultural Show – Mr Crittall lent a field for the purpose. More than one in seven of the town's male workers were still in agriculture in 1931. Another reminder of the countryside came in 1935 when two hundred of Mr Horner's sheep strayed onto allotments in Maldon Road from an adjoining meadow, and feasted on the vegetables.

But the times were characterised by urban delights, including a new cinema. Earlier schemes included a 'cinematograph show' in a portable building near Mill Lane in 1916, and film showings at the Public Hall around 1920. But the luxurious Whitehall, opened in 1928, was a proper cinema (shown on colour page 14). At the first night the large gathering was treated to a spectacular display of 'glowing electric lights of rainbow colours', using the town's brand new electricity supply. The 'talkies' arrived in 1930 with a showing of 'Sunnyside Up' at August bank holiday.

Another new facility was the free library. By 1926 the old one had been disposed of because of lack of space in the tiny Council office. After some of the books had been given to schoolchildren, the rest were sold to a

The outdoor swimming pool behind the Swan in the 1930s. It was so popular that during its first Whitsun holiday, emergency sheeting had to be bought to make more changing cubicles. There were 'tea gardens' alongside. At the back are the 'Waterworks cottages'.

Chelmsford second hand dealer for £4 (his Witham counterpart, Sammy Page, didn't want them). Requests from the Women's Institute and other residents eventually earned Witham a branch of the new County Library service. It opened in October 1932 under the supervision of Edith Wakelin, a farmer's widow. To start with, it had about 450 books, but after the second day of opening there were nearly 500 readers and the shelves were almost empty – it was hoped to obtain another 50 volumes.

In 1933 a new open air swimming pool came into use. In earlier years the only formal swimming place had been in the river Blackwater behind the sewage farm. The Council had provided a diving board there, and someone to keep the younger swimmers in order, but it was closed in 1929 because of pollution. As early as 1913 it had been suggested that two disused water tanks behind the Swan should be converted for swimming, but like many projects this one was delayed by the First World War. The pool was finally opened by Sir Valentine Crittall in 1933, and one of the councillors pointed out that without Crittall's factory there would not be enough people to justify it. It was a great success, though sometimes there were doubts about the water quality. It closed at the beginning of the Second World War.

After he failed to obtain a Hospital, Dr Knight re-directed his energies to another of his post-war projects, a 'Workers' Club'. When his supporters voted in 1919 to ban alcohol, he parted company with them. His projects were very successful for a while, especially the dances, where local 'young ladies' gave instruction. They were an exciting change from pre-war public entertainment which had been characterised by rather earnest concerts. But concerts continued too, some still organised by the indefatigable Mr Afford, who brought the famous pianist Myra Hess to the Public Hall in 1931, attracting 260 people from all over the county.

The Hall was taken over by the Council in 1934 and refurbished. Many thriving clubs and societies used it, often with late buses and trains laid on. They also met in the cinema, Rowley's Hall, Crittall's new social club (1937) and several smaller venues. As well as dances there were plays, 'vigorous' political meetings, shows by the Witham Amateur Operatic Society (founded in 1921), and a Pigeon Society. In addition, three different evangelical churches built new premises during the 1930s. The ever-increasing part played by women was symbolised by two 'firsts' reported in 1932. In September, when Ellen Bright married Hugh Derrett, she omitted the promise to 'obey' him, and in October six women sang in the choir at the parish church as an experiment (though they remained out of sight).

An annual Carnival was started in 1929, raising money for Essex hospitals. This procession is at the bottom of Newland Street in 1936. On the float, left to right, are June Osborne, Rosemary East (later Mrs Brown, half hidden), Marie Pinkham, Doreen East (Carnival Queen), Peggy Butcher (later Mrs Blake). There were also fairground amusements to replace the ones banned in 1891.

The Co-op's annual treat continued to flourish. Meanwhile its Newland Street business grew to become a combined department store and food shop incorporating a modern butcher's and bakery, with an extensive milk business. Its new dairy in Highfields Road served a wide area including London. The arrival of new facilities in the town continued in 1937 with the building of a fine police station in Newland Street, and the first Secondary school, Bramston School, in Spinks Lane. In 1939 there came a new post office in Newland Street, and a separate telephone exchange in Collingwood Road.

Town Planning

In 1930 the Council began to prepare a planning scheme under new legislation. Their experience of the Depression alerted councillors to the importance of jobs, and in December 1931 they asked the Board of Trade to direct new industry to Witham's 'good factory sites'. Their speeches extolled the virtues of the town as a place for expansion, with its road and rail facilities, and desirable housing. There was little immediate response from new employers but the tone was set for the town's future ambitions. When councillors in Halstead Rural District suggested in 1933 that planning was 'unnecessary in this part of Essex', their Witham colleagues disagreed.

In 1936 a regional report was received, including suggestions for 'aerodromes at Bishops Stortford, Braintree and Bocking and possibly near Saffron Walden'. A young local consultant, Tom Henderson, prepared a scheme which entailed a four-fold increase in population for Witham town from about 5,000 to 20,000 (he stayed here himself till 2003). There was a Public Inquiry in 1938, but the War intervened before its findings could appear. However, in 1937 Essex Fruit Packers built a large centre on Colchester Road at the proposed new industrial estate, paving the way for the future.

War approaches

Many agreed with a Witham councillor who had fought in the First World War and suggested in March 1935 that 'the country's money could be better spent on houses than on Arms'. But during the next few years, anti-gas training and Air Raid Precautions were established. Those initials, ARP,

This newspaper advert appeared in May 1934. Before the Second World War the Fascist Party of 'Blackshirts' attracted several young Witham men, mostly from the business community. At one time it was rumoured that a local member had been 'put away' by the police. They wore the uniform, went to rallies, and greeted each other with salutes. In 1935 they travelled to London to hear Oswald Mosley, and a passer-by put his fist through the window of their coach. A self-styled 'Witham Fascist' wrote angry letters to the paper about the Jews. Others, including a 'Witham anti-Fascist', responded. In 1936 the message 'Mosley right, Eden wrong' was chalked in huge white letters on the pavement outside Crittall's factory.

BLACKSHIRT MEETING
GROVE HALL, WITHAM
WEDNESDAY, JUNE 20th
8.0—10.0 p.m.
This is the First Big Meeting of the Witham Branch of the B.U.F.
Come and Ask Questions!
Lt. Col. H. E. CROCKER
C.M.C., D.S.O.,
EXPLAINS BLACKSHIRT POLICY
There is a limited number of Reserved Seats at 1/- and 6d. Obtainable from any Blackshirt or write—North Corner Av. Rd., Witham

were to become familiar. With Germany's invasion of Austria in March 1938, local Councils were given many new duties, such as organising gas masks, training, and an Auxiliary Fire Service. The old Police Station in Guithavon Street was earmarked as a Control Centre. Crittall's started producing gas-proof doors and windows. Young men of 20 and 21 were conscripted for military training. During the 'National Emergency' of late September 1938, deep trenches were dug to create public shelters at both of the Recreation Grounds and at the top of Church Street. The immediate crisis passed with the Munich agreement of 29 September, but a state of readiness continued to prevail during the following year.

The Second World War, 1939-1945

On Friday 1st September, a special train puffed into Witham station. Several hundred small evacuee children from Edmonton in north London alighted with their teachers and some mothers – all clutching gas masks. The planning paid off. Coaches took them to Bramston school where they each received a tin of corned beef and other 'iron rations', and then they went on to their new homes in Witham, Silver End and the surrounding villages. That evening was windy and rainy, and for the first time the black-out darkened the streets.

Two days later, on Sunday morning, the vicar's daughter stayed at home to listen to the wireless. During the first hymn she came into the parish church and gave her father a message. He announced that England was at War. Soon after the service the siren sounded. It was a false alarm, but that night the first of many mysterious aeroplanes was heard.

Councillors and their staff were deluged with new instructions from higher authority, and devoted themselves to endless extra duties. Their versatile clerk, Harry Crook, must have worked nearly 24 hours a day. Soldiers took over empty buildings, and vehicles with new labels rushed about. The police tried to enforce a black-out. Gas masks were carried everywhere and Cissie West's shop advertised coloured satchels for them, some with white spots.

The young evacuees were instructed by their teachers in the crowded schools, and sweet shops benefited from a 'minor boom'. There were tales about the poor state of the children's clothes and shoes, and their chasing sheep and catching rabbits. At Christmas special parties were arranged. Disillusionment set in as nothing much happened. By January, more than

ARP wardens and First Aid workers during the Second World War. Norman Dickson, the head warden, stands in the middle in a light jacket; his family bred sweet peas for Cullen's and named one new variety 'Air Warden'. Well known faces include Fred Gaymer (back row, third from right), and Dr Tom Benjamin and Dr Jim Denholm (second row from the front, left and right ends).

5. 1901-1945

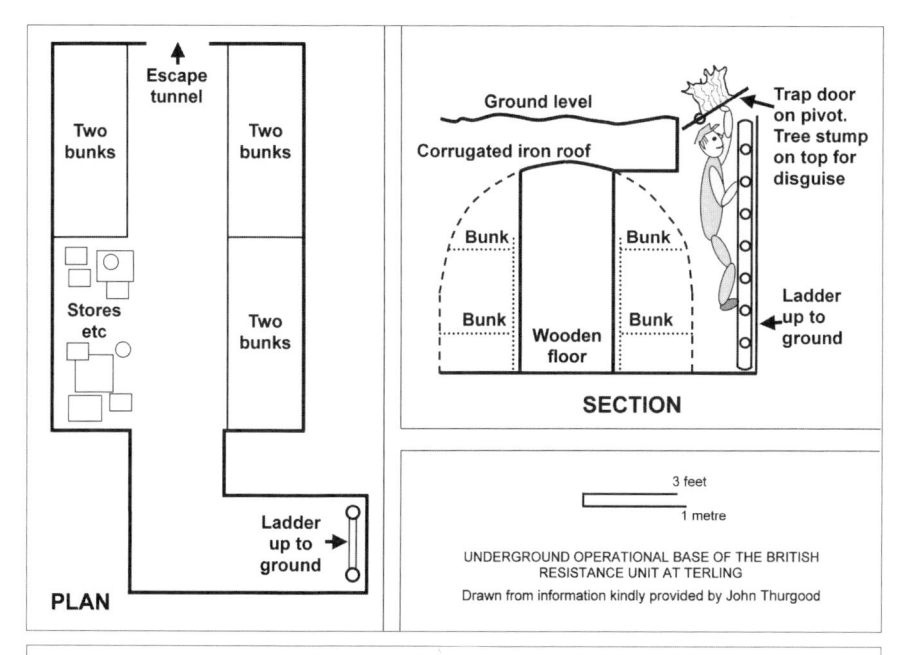

PLAN / **SECTION**

UNDERGROUND OPERATIONAL BASE OF THE BRITISH RESISTANCE UNIT AT TERLING
Drawn from information kindly provided by John Thurgood

> A sketch of the British Resistance Organisation's 'operational base' at Terling. The six men of the Witham and Wickham Bishops unit had a similar one near Langford Grove. In secret they were issued with commando daggers and revolvers, and spent weekends learning guerrilla tactics. If the Germans had invaded, they would have retreated underground and tried to cause trouble. My drawing is derived from a description by John Thurgood, a member of the Terling unit. He thinks now that they would not have survived very long.

half of the Urban District's 1,156 evacuees had gone home to London. Rationing and other restrictions caused many complaints. The ARP centre closed temporarily for lack of volunteers. A fright came at 5 am one February morning in 1940. Two wardens misheard a phone message and sounded the siren on Crittall's factory roof, causing alarmed townspeople to leap out of bed and seek shelter.

The spirit of dedication returned at the end of May 1940 with the evacuation of Dunkirk and the fear of invasion. Road blocks were guarded by the new Local Defence Volunteers – they were soon renamed the Home Guard and eventually over a hundred Witham men joined, in three platoons. One of their leaders, watchmaker Harry Barham, put his hobby to good use and became pigeon officer. Six men were secretly hand-picked for a unit of the British Resistance Organisation, given an underground base at Langford Grove, and rigorously trained to harass the Germans if they invaded.

134   A HISTORY OF WITHAM

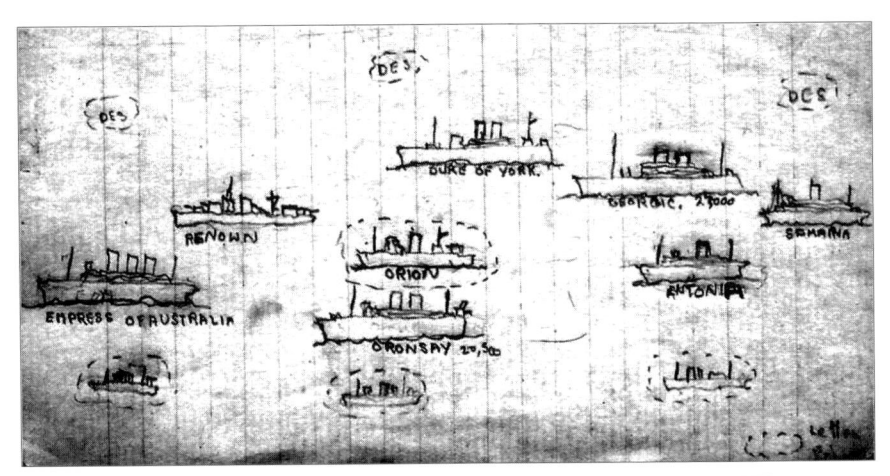

Halifax
Nova Scotia
Canada.
Monday August 19th

Dear Mum & Dad
(Canada calling) (Canada calling)
We left England on Sunday Aug 11th at 4AM. I was slightly seasick but recovered. The ship was HMT NOT ALLOWED TO SAY we were in convoy with seven other liners and a battleship also 8 destroyers I had a good journey. The sea was not too bad all across. We saw Destry Rides Again Marie Antoinette Over the Moon on respective days. I received

> In 1940 schoolboy Fred Richardson was evacuated to Canada on the *Oronsay* and drew this picture (top) of the convoy – the *Antonia* and the *Duke of York* were also carrying evacuees, whilst the three ships on each side were destroyers. The rest were liners (one of them, *Empress of Australia* had been in Yokahama in Japan at the time of the 1923 earthquake and saved 3,000 lives). The dotted lines show vessels that left the convoy on 16 August. When Fred arrived he sent this cheerful letter to his parents (below). On another page he wrote 'I do not want you to worry as I am happy as a sand boy'.

In mid 1940, the government set up a scheme to send children to safety in the Dominions. The thirteen-year old Witham schoolboy Fred Richardson of Church Street was keen to go, though his parents were less enthusiastic. He was selected, and in August crossed the Atlantic from Liverpool to Canada on the ship *Oronsay* with hundreds of others (one of his drawings and a letter are on the facing page). In September another evacuees' ship, the *Benares*, was sunk by a torpedo. Nearly all the children, escorts and crew on board were drowned, and no more were sent. But Fred stayed in Canada after the War and became a successful headteacher.

At home, protection from air raids became a priority again in July with the Battle of Britain, and the ARP Control centre re-opened. Shelters began to be built (rather slowly) at the schools. Rather more quickly builders were engaged to make private underground rooms in some of the gardens in Collingwood Road and elsewhere. Tenants of the bright new Council estate in Church Street felt conspicuous and asked (unsuccessfully) for camouflage. The first air-raid warnings sounded on 13th August, and schoolchildren became very familiar with their damp, cold and dark shelters. On the 19th, three people were killed by a bomb nine miles away in Chelmsford, and on the 24th someone was injured in Homefield Road by a bullet from a German plane.

This was next to Crittall's factory, which after a slowish start with war contracts, was now very busy. Products included Bailey Bridges, mesh landing mats, and parts for six-inch shells. The most unusual was a rocket-fired 'parachute and cable', intended to intercept low-flying enemy bombers approaching airfields. Workers included many newly recruited women, some from as far away as Norwich. Meanwhile the adjoining British Oxygen plant produced vital supplies for airmen.

On the night of Saturday 7th October 1940, 430 Londoners were killed as the Blitz began. Witham's experience was small but shocking. It was thought that 'no-one was ever going to bomb Witham'. But on the same night three bombs fell in Cressing Road. One did not explode till next morning, when it tragically killed roadsweeper Arthur Burmby and two soldiers. Lesser incidents continued. One day a 'small boy' found an unexploded incendiary near Elm Hall and took it home. Luckily his mother noticed – the police took it away and put it in a pail of water. Nevertheless, Witham was still a 'reception' area, and the 200 remaining evacuees in the Urban District were soon joined by over 600 more, some of them made homeless by the Blitz.

The remains of the power house at Crittall's after the second bombing raid on the factory, at 2 pm on 5 January 1941. The heroes of the day were the roof spotters. Although there had been no public warning, they saw the plane in time to send the workers to the shelters and thus saved their lives.

On 4 December 1940 town centre property was damaged by night-time bombing, and five people at the Control centre were injured. Then there were two raids on Crittall's window factory. The second and more serious one, in January 1941, demolished the power house. Next day a bomb fell near Pinkham's glove factory. Soon afterwards, an attack in the Highfields Road area affected about thirty houses and the Co-op creamery, and injured four people. Mr and Mrs Hodges' house next to the railway was ruined. He was a taxidermist and the children who rushed to look next morning found a stuffed owl much the worse for wear.

In February 1941, three people died in an air raid in Braintree, and in May seventeen workers at Marconi's in Chelmsford were killed, including a young man from Witham, Alfred Griggs. But then the bombing died down as the fighting moved to distant countries. Most of Rickstones recreation ground was ploughed in the 'Dig for Victory' campaign, and sheep and cows grazed in Maldon Road Park. Soldiers stationed in Witham included the No 2 Mobile Bath Unit at Medina Villas, who travelled all over Essex and beyond. In August 1941 they 'bathed' over 30,000 soldiers.

In July 1941 the Council opened a British Restaurant (at 67 Newland Street), and it was soon crowded with workers, schoolchildren and others, in spite of unpopular experiments with ling (a type of cod). 11,000 dinners were served during the first four months, and a weekly supply of pies was sent to Hatfield Peverel under the 'Rural Pie Scheme'. There was another such restaurant in Church Street for a time. Helpers were sought for innumerable other projects, and also busied themselves with economies and salvage. Blacksmith George Shelley was sent out to list useful iron railings, though none were taken down (as explained on page 15 of the colour section).

Meanwhile, bombs returned to Britain in spring 1942. Witham builders combined to send men for 'rescue and demolition' in London and elsewhere. In May, Anderson and Morrison shelters were taken round by Council lorry. In July Crittall's was bombed again, at 7.30 one morning, causing much alarm but few injuries. Afterwards, Walter Crittall refused to let in an inspector from the Ministry of Home Security because of the factory's secret work – the relevant civil servants were very annoyed. This was the last major attack on Witham, though vigilance continued. Anti-aircraft guns were installed on Crittall's roof. The Home Guard were issued with the new spigot mortar guns (see colour page 15), and members were sent on training courses which included leadership, field craft, grenades, and street fighting. Nearby towns were still to suffer grievously from bombing.

In June 1942 the Public Hall was vacated by soldiers, so dances could return, and the Home Guard could practise there in winter (provided they did not wear their studded army boots). In October, building started on a new airfield at Rivenhall, four miles to the north (one of several in north Essex). The contractors engaged Irish navvies and went up to Holyhead to meet them. Eventually there were 1,000 workmen on the site and heavy lorries pounded through Witham. The manageress of the British Restaurant, Mrs Haste, happily provided an all-day canteen. But the Irishmen proved very troublesome and by March 1943 the Council had given up the contract.

In January 1943, councillors decided after considerable discussion to appoint a Conscientious Objector, a Quaker, as Rating Officer. They also recruited Dorothy L Sayers to help with paper salvage by picking out the books worth saving for libraries. A compulsory fire watching scheme was laboriously launched – 800 people were trained, deployed round the clock, and gradually equipped with helmets and whistles (one each for reasons of hygiene). Mrs Mildred Hadfield was made organiser and had a thankless task. One exercise had to be cancelled when the firewatchers from Pinkham's factory refused to join in 'on account of the rain'.

Some American soldiers came to Witham during 1943, livening up dances, and damaging roads with their vehicles. Their airmen started arriving at the new Rivenhall airfield in January 1944; one of them wrote home about the 'terrible tasting water' and the malfunctioning toilets. The Americans were replaced by the RAF in October. Four Witham men, including a sailor, were killed in France soon after the D-Day landings of 6 June 1944. Then the first flying bombs fell on London and 100 new evacuees arrived, mostly mothers and small children, causing a multitude of problems for the splendid organiser, Mrs Irene Royffe. In October the Whitehall cinema and 44 houses suffered slight damage when a doodlebug fell in fields a mile away. But conditions at home were rapidly improving. Six specially screened street lights were switched on, and others had followed by the time the conflict in Europe ended in May 1945.

About 35 Witham men had been killed. A third of them were in the Air Force and several in the Navy. Some were brought to England for burial, but others lie in France, Belgium, Norway, Canada, Egypt, Libya, Italy, Japan, Burma and Singapore.

One of the VE day parties celebrating the end of the War in Europe. This one is in Millbridge Road. Mr and Mrs Hodges' ruined house in Highfields Road, bombed in 1941, is visible in the background.

VE day, celebrating the end of the War in Europe in May 1945, was marked by the customary huge bonfire in Newland Street, and by street parties around the town. The airmen at Rivenhall continued their celebrations into June, when they heard a talk by Dorothy L Sayers about 'The Playwright and the Theatre'. The sandbags and blast walls were removed from the Police Station, and in the General Election in July Witham acquired a new Labour MP, Tom Driberg (he had initially been elected as an Independent at a by-election in 1942). In July there were still over 100 evacuees; some had problems finding anywhere to go. At VJ Day in August the beer ran out.

Crittall's started turning back to making windows instead of Bailey Bridges, and invited demobbed men to join them. There were 71 applications for the job of Sanitary Inspector with the Council. Economy and salvage continued and the new Witham Pig Club was glad to take the waste food. In October the British Restaurant in Newland Street was closed, despite a petition to keep it. In January 1946 the Rivenhall air base closed, and RAF officers planted six commemorative oak trees in Witham Park. In due course the airfield housed former Polish prisoners of War.

Witham recovers

Houses were now desperately scarce. Several homeless families were allowed to live in the disused searchlight station near Blue Mills hill. As happened after the First World War, only the Council was permitted to build new houses at first. By early 1946, twenty-eight 'temporary' pre-fabs had been put up in Bramston Green (they stayed until 1982), and then the pre-war programme was resumed in the Church Street area.

By 1943 councillors had started going to conferences about the importance of post-war town planning. They had reviewed their own proposals, which fitted well with the principles of Patrick Abercrombie's Greater London Plan of 1944. He wished to restrict the growth of London, and house the resulting 'overspill' population and industry in areas like Witham, beyond the Green Belt. The long and tortuous process by which this actually happened would justify another book. Suffice it to say that during the coming decades many new residents were to move to Witham from London and elsewhere, helping to create a vibrant and active community which it is a pleasure and a privilege to live in.

WALK 1
ROUND THE ANCIENT EARTHWORKS

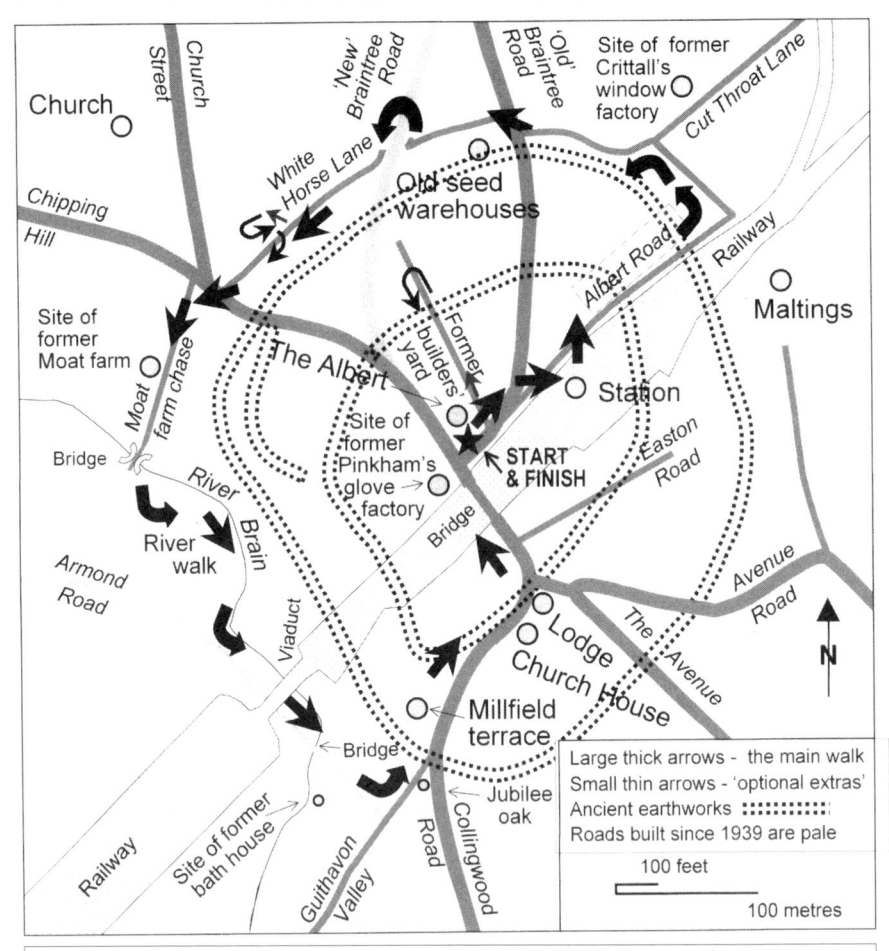

The route of walk 1. The circular earthworks enclose about 25 acres (10 hectares). There were two rings, the inner one higher, so today there is a 'dome' effect. This originated as an Iron Age 'hill fort' probably strengthened by the Saxons in 913 AD. For centuries afterwards the main Witham manor had its headquarters here. The walk starts in the centre, goes down to the edge, and then round about two thirds of the outside anti-clockwise (looking out for the old embankment), and back to the centre again. Other interesting features include the late Victorian and Edwardian buildings of the 'Temples Estate' of over 100 houses, started 1882.

WALK 1. THE EARTHWORKS

The distance is rather less than a mile ($1\frac{1}{3}$ km). Street numbers are given in brackets in the text (but not marked on the map). Landmarks may of course change or even disappear as time goes by. Pages 16 to 20 of the colour section show examples of bricks, railings, street furniture etc.

Start on the pavement at the edge of the Albert car park, opposite the railway.

The **Albert** and the **Grange** (hidden behind) – on site where Knights Templars and Hospitallers had chapel and farm buildings till 1500s. Albert a pub since 1842 – once had ship's figurehead of African chief outside (1880-1990s), brought from London by innkeeper George Best (some thought it insulted Prince Albert).

Right of Albert car park, unexplained **rise** up to adjoining taxi parking place. **Long yard** visible – workshops and warehouses. Belonged to Joseph Smith and Son, prolific builders 1882-1914 (see pages 86-88). They were 'builders, contractors, and brick manufacturers' with a 'steam joinery works & sawing & planing mills'. Had 40-foot brick chimney (12 metres) Old sawing shed now the carpet warehouse on far left (optional trip there and back). **Tiny building** on road side (1A) – taxis – built 1911 as haulage office. Then Employment Exchange in 1920s (manager Frank Cundy also taught typing). Then George Thompson, 'coal and coke merchant, cartage contractor, firewood, logs, buyer and seller of old Tudor tiles and bricks'.

Cross both Braintree Road and Albert Road to reach railings by railway, i.e. passing snack bar, formerly a bus shelter, on your left.

Deep **cutting** dug by hand through earthworks for railway in 1843 (see pages 62-65). **Station** built 1906 after old one crushed by fatal crash of Cromer express (1905). Before, main entrance was on far side, and smaller one here. New 1906 station well built – lengthy specifications, e.g. 'bull nosed' bricks, brass fittings etc. Ironwork made by Crittall's at Braintree (they had to build a new plant specially) – firm's name visible under middle of three windows (and elsewhere in station) See colour pages 16 and 17.

Car park across rails was coal yard. Various industries came to that area 1880s onwards, including Cooper Taber (seeds) – from 1956 to about 1990 they had a prize-winning glass building by Chamberlin, Powell and Bon,

The Temperance Hotel (9 Albert Road) in the 1890s. Its builder and first owner was Robert Moore (from the same family that founded a well-known local carriers' business in 1815 – it continued as a 20th century bus company). He was a member of Witham's 'Temperance Ark', founded in 1875 to campaign for total abstinence from alcohol. To start with, he also had an undertakers' business here. The boy on the horse is his son Robert Gladstone Moore. Note the decorated wooden gable end, and the moulded bricks between the upper and lower windows.

later the architects of the Barbican in London. Only industry remaining now is the **maltings** – taken over by Scottish company Hugh Baird, 1920s, much rebuilt since 1961.

Continue on down the hill, crossing to the left hand side sometime before the pavement runs out.

Opposite the station – in 1848 were stables, forges, workshops etc for building Maldon and Braintree railways. **House** (4) where William and Rebecca Pinkham first made gloves c 1904-05 (see colour page 12). **Fern Cottages** (5-8), built 1887 as part of new 'Temples estate', in which displays of dates, names and moulded bricks and chimneys were popular. Former **Temperance Hotel** (9) with large balcony, built 1883. **Pair of tall semi-detached houses** (13-14), the Pinkhams' second glove-making place (1905-12) – family lived in far one, about ten girls worked in other – connected by internal door.

Keep left at bottom – **edge of earthworks** is on your left – shown by raised houses – note level of front doors above road. Look at (but don't follow) **Cut Throat Lane** on right – once a main road to Rivenhall. Disappointingly for some, it's a corruption of 'Cut Athwart Lane' – lane cut across a field – there are others elsewhere in Essex. Has yellow **brick wall** – only surviving relic of vast **Crittall's** metal window factory – transformed Witham 1920 – war work in Second World War – several bombings (see pages 110-112, 136, and colour page 13). Demolished 1992, now site of supermarket (designed to look rather like Crittall's – long horizontal windows). In **Albert Road**, houses high up on old earthworks – bank dug into for car parking.

WALK 1. THE EARTHWORKS

Your view as you approach the end of Albert Road. In the house at the far end of the row on the left (23), Edgar Sainty's 'wireless doctor' business started in the 1920s. This row of houses and the big hedge are well above the level of the road. This is because they are on top of the old earthworks, which were started in the Iron Age and enlarged in 913 AD. The white building behind the right-hand end of the hedge is mostly along the bottom of the embankment. It used to be one of Cullens' seed warehouses.

Staggered cross-roads. Narrow **Braintree Road** to your left – interesting 1880s houses – incredibly this road carried all traffic to and from Braintree until 1970. Going across into **White Horse Lane** (formerly called Hill Lane because of earthwork), you go to the right of an attractive tall **weatherboarded building** – former seed warehouse. Built 1890s for Thomas Cullen – brick extension added 1908. Now home of popular Witham Technology Centre. The drive-in at far end of it is up steep slope because of old earthworks. Archaeological excavation here in 1970 (when 'new' Braintree Road was built) rather inconclusive.

At the dead end, take path sloping up to right and cross the busy road carefully.

From the road, see the pleasantly **'wild' area**. This and car park on land formerly bought by parish officers in 1600s, with money left by Dame Katherine Barnardiston. Rent paid for bread for the poor every Sunday till early 1900s. Once a gravel pit for road mending. Had playground with swings in 1900. Now known as **Bell field** (though name originally further east). Probably not for making bells – Witham's church bells all made in other towns. Considered for Council houses in 1919 – Government commissioner said 'too far beyond the town and shopping centres'.

To left of the field, take path between metal railings, leading down into the rest of White Horse Lane.

Immediately on right, **concrete base in corner** was site of Hurrell and Beardwell's motor engineering and omnibus business's first site (1920). **New houses** (2004) on right – replaced offices, earlier busy builders' yard (1914-74), first John Dean's, then Adams and Mortimer's, whose stock, auctioned in 1974 (391 lots), included '100 squints and splays', 'complete contents of paint shop', '2 planks of African pear', and sacks and sacks of nails. On **left** side of road, **earthworks** again, this time in back gardens of bungalows. All formerly the Cullens' garden, between their seed warehouse and their house.

Just past new cul-de-sac called 'Bellfield Close', a red brick **house**, 1928, inscribed **'Stefre'** between the top windows. Previously site of butcher's slaughterhouses, with pig styes, 'sticking pound', bullock pound, stables, hay loft, bone shed and chicken house. Built by Frederick Fuller (named after Stella and Fred) with Council subsidy. Electricity just arriving then – specifications asked for either nine gas points or sixteen electric points. It is said that wooden panelling inside the house was damaged by machine-gun fire from plane during Second World War.

Black weatherboarded **office building** – optional trip round it anti-clockwise, past its door into long car park – has stone on its left wall with the initials of John Coote, 19th century resident of 4 Church Street whose back door you can see.

Back in White Horse Lane, continue to the White Horse, then cross over the main Chipping Hill road and down Moat Farm Chase, nearly opposite you (walk 2 crosses here).

House at bottom on left uses name **Moat farm** – in fact was outbuildings – farmhouse was on right (built 1500s, demolished 1950s). Medieval house here sometimes called 'the Moot' – perhaps place for Saxon 'moot' or meeting – these held in a banked square – perhaps where there was a square pond near the river in the 1800s?

Brick **bridge** (built 1700s) once had a ford alongside on left – both used for carts and animals crossing to meadows – brick barrier narrowing the bridge is quite new.

WALK 1. THE EARTHWORKS   145

At the other side of the bridge, turn left along the path or by the river towards the viaduct (after which you'll turn left up the road).

The **River Walk** follows the river Brain nearly two miles through the town – established by Witham Urban District Council early 1970s. **Meadow** between path and river – previously, since Domesday (1086) and before, belonged to Powershall, over a mile away – people came from there to grow hay and graze animals. Given to Council 1937 as memorial to Philip Hutley, farmer at Powershall – known at first as 'Hutley Memorial Recreation Ground'. The **earthworks** on left now on other side of river in gardens, partly natural. Through **railway viaduct** 30 or 40 feet (10 metres) high – built 1843, blocking view between Chipping Hill and rest of the town.

Going over river and up Armond Road, looking to right, area of **grass and bushes** about 30 yards away was place used for working and washing skins and cloth in medieval times, with house called 'the Watering' in early 1500s. Then at end of 1700s was a small bath house and cold water pool – special path from the mansion at the Grove. More recently, several cottages by river, picturesque but damp and crowded, demolished 1930s in Council slum clearance programme (see page 124-25).

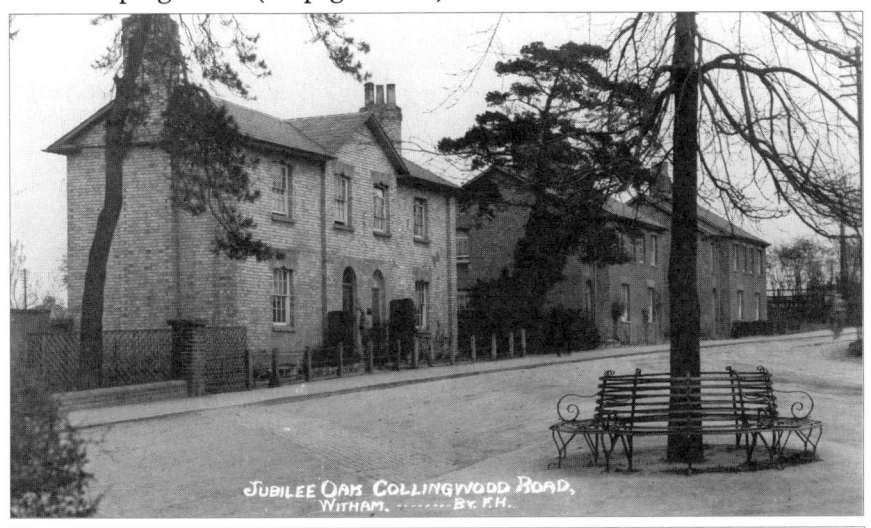

The Jubilee Oak in the early 1900s, and part of Millfield Terrace, built 1827-1858 by the Crump family of Freebournes farm. At first there were no roads here – the houses stood on their own. A 'sweet briar hedge' grew along the front and the field produced 'very fine crops of corn'. They were quite good dwellings – the stationmaster lived in one – but too early to have drains or running water.

At T-junction turn left up the hill; you are now in Guithavon Valley.

Now climbing outer **earthworks**. **Jubilee Oak** – on traffic island on right – 'moss cupped oak' planted 1887 – Queen Victoria's Golden Jubilee. Suffered unauthorised 'mutilation' by electricity workers in 1935 – looked like lamp post for a time. Small plaque on ground by it for Queen Elizabeth's Golden Jubilee, 2002. Continue uphill into main **Collingwood Road**, built 1869, was fields till early 1900s, then large houses came. 'The most fashionable road in the place' in 1919 according to postcard sent by a soldier to his mother.

On left, up the hill, **Millfield Terrace** (2-8, 57-67) – white brick – some dated, e.g. 57-59, the earliest two, with ogee arches (S shaped) over the windows, have 'I C 1827' for Iohannes (John) Crump. At 59 from 1880s to 1930s was dressmaker Elizabeth Smith with 'Miss Smith, Robes' on brass plate. Two newer houses inserted 1990s.

As you go on, look at buildings across Collingwood road, right to left. Red brick **bungalow** (46) with wooden fence – built 1920 as 'Nurse's bungalow' (see page 126) – innumerable Witham babies born here – intended as War memorial, but sadly plaque by door recording this now hidden by bushes. To its left, **Warwick House** (48), tall, original cast iron railings (see colour page 19). Built 1910 for William Heddle, bishop of the Peculiar People. His son had shop here for credit drapery business till 1970s – men known as 'johnny fortnights' collected payments at your door. Two **newer houses** (48A-50) on site of former **YMCA hut**, built 1915 as social centre for soldiers billeted in Witham for training. **Church House**, built 1909 as a meeting hall – funded by anonymous donation (now known to be from Hester Holt) – designed by well-known Chelmsford architects Chancellor and Son. All these buildings have steep banks behind them from the earthworks.

Still looking to the other side of the road, **junction** with long straight **Avenue** marks edge of inner earthwork – gradient at this end formerly one in two – reduced in 1960 to one in twenty – old slope survives in pavements. **Lodge**, one **gatepost**, and small piece of **railing** between them, survive from when Avenue was in grounds of mansion at the Grove – people could walk here if they behaved. Burton family lived in lodge early 1900s – six red-headed children – bedrooms in attic reached by fold-down ladder in living room. House-building started 1920s and magnificent lime trees cut down. One of earliest houses was **'North Corner'** (45) – white – down between the two roads – said to be first Witham house with Crittall's metal windows.

WALK 1. THE EARTHWORKS

The top of the Avenue. The top picture is from the 1890s; the porch of the Grove is at the far end, and Avenue Road on the left. The other pictures show (bottom left) part of the same view in about 1903, with the lodge, gateposts and ornate iron gates which were added in 1898 (the architect, George Sherrin, was designer of Spitalfields market in London), and (bottom right) one of the gates in 2004, now at Great Ruffins, Great Totham – (moved there in the early 1920s when houses started to be built in the Avenue).

Still looking over to the other side, **Avenue Road** – branching off to left of the Avenue – for centuries the only road between Newland Street and Chipping Hill. Edwardian wall **letter-box**. **Pair of houses (62-64)** at top on left dating from 1884 (then part of new 'Temples estate' like others in Avenue Road, some very imposing). Earlier the site of first (tiny) Church School, built 1813. **Black brick wall** further left – former site of parish pound for stray animals (till 1880s). Left again, past Easton Road, **Slythe's** monumental masons – one of oldest Witham businesses still working. James Slythe came to town about 1840 – his son moved to this site early 1860, had the two white houses built 1862. Last of the family died in c 2000. **Railway station** entrance originally on this side. After it moved to the other side in 1906, the third James Slythe was too impatient to go across by road – used to scramble down the bank and across the rails – also complained about the soot from the steam trains.

The cattle market in 1931, with the Christmas prize bull from Tolleshunt Darcy. He weighed more than half a ton (nearly 600 kg),. and butcher Frederick Fuller of Church Street paid £60 for him (over £3,000 at today's values). Church House is behind. In spite of the railings, there were occasional exciting escapes into the road by bullocks. Now the site of the Labour Hall.

WALK 1. THE EARTHWORKS 149

Cissie West at her shop, the Cabin, which formerly stood by the railway bridge. Before she came it was part of the office for the cattle market, and was used as a temporary mortuary after the Cromer express rail disaster of 1905. Probably taken in the 1930s; a celebration seems to be in progress, to judge from the flags.

Back on your own side of the road, **Labour Hall**, opened 1962, seriously damaged by fire June 2005. The site was formerly the cattle market. Just past it was the market office, of which part became a shop ('The Cabin') in 1930s, replaced 1990 by **red brick office building**. Graffiti on fence beyond (illustrated). Continuing across **railway bridge** (widened 1960), on left, **Templemead flats** (1990s) – on the site of old **glove factory** which was built for William Pinkham in 1912 (replacing the Albert Road house seen earlier), extended 1948, closed 1961 (see page 98). Then, for a time, Guys Mechanical Engineers – one of first companies to move from London in 1960s. The walk ends here, back at the **Albert**.

Historic graffiti from the 1990 campaign against the community charge or 'poll tax'. It is on the wooden fence behind the red brick office building (between that building and the railway bridge). Similar inscriptions can be seen in the car park behind the Newlands precinct. The original 'Peasants' Revolt' against the poll tax was in 1381.

WALK 2
THE VILLAGE OF CHIPPING HILL

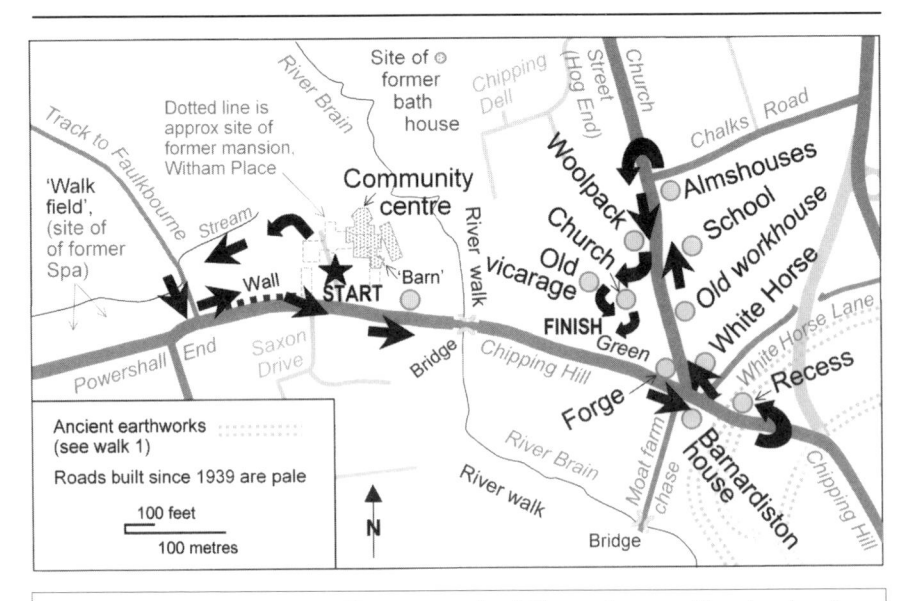

The route of walk 2. Chipping Hill was once a flourishing settlement, with a church and a market. It became less important after Newland Street was set up in about 1200. But many of its fine medieval houses still survive, some built in the 1300s, and there is a 'village' atmosphere. Note that my ideas about the details of Witham Place have changed since I wrote 'Witham 1500-1700: Making a Living' (and are still unproven).

The distance is about two thirds of a mile (1 km) (or ¾ of a mile (1¼ km) if you return all the way to the starting point). Street numbers are given in brackets in the text (but not marked on the map). Landmarks may of course change or even disappear as time goes by. Pages 16 to 20 of the colour section show examples of bricks, railings, street furniture etc.

Start in the car park at Spring Lodge Community Centre, Powershall End (sometimes known in the past as Post Hall End).

Community Centre – foundation stone just inside, laid by Council chairman Ted Smith in 1973 – first used 1975, formally opened 1976, much used and enjoyed ever since. **Witham Place** once stood here (see the map)

WALK 2. CHIPPING HILL

'The Barn', now a meeting room at the Community Centre, as it was in 1914 when it was 'in danger of falling to pieces'. Originally part of the mansion at Witham Place, built in the 1500s. The rest was demolished c 1850; materials auctioned then included panelling, wrought iron, and exotic trees. There have been several reports of a ghost. © Crown Copyright NMR.

- a large mansion (built just before 1556), 90 yards across (82 metres), round a courtyard. In 1745 it was 'a very ancient and excessive pile of building'. A small part survives in the Community Centre as 'the Barn'.

Walk straight along the drive through the car park, away from the road, for about 75 yards (70 metres). Then turn 90 degrees left into the narrow grassy area to go lengthways along it.

Walking on grass or path or tarmac (or some of each), keep fence on left and houses on right. **Overgrown ground** with willow trees on right was Witham Place's lake. After about 150 yards (140 metres) (at lamp-post 36), **track** crosses at end of path (leads to village of Faulkbourne). Facing you on the other side of it is **Walk field** (formerly a long 'walk' or avenue of trees). At its far end was Witham Spa (c 1735-54) with a pump and several buildings (see pages 37-38). Considered for cemetery in 1930 but found to be too wet.

Turn left along the track, then left again along the road (Powershall End).

On your right side are **white cottages** (26-30) – 26 was used for worship by local Catholics 1800 to 1851, and named after Lord Stourton, Catholic resident of Witham Place in late 1700s. On left side, **long red brick wall** (probably late 1500s) of Witham Place, 80 yards survive (75 metres). Faded diamond-shaped pattern in darker brick. On right, **housing estate and Saxon Drive** built 1970, had been site of Church allotments since 1841. On left just past entrance to Community Centre, **Spring Lodge** (3), grey brick house built c 1840 for farmer Robert Bretnall. Also **Mill House** (1) – 1857 to house the miller, extended 2001 by weather-boarded facsimile of former water mill which burnt down 1882 (as had an earlier one in 1776). Mill pond – in 1929 'nothing but an open cesspool' (no sewers in Powershall End then). On right **two red brick houses** (6-8, one now called Spring Cottage) – c 1870. Springett family lived here and at earlier house c 1820-1970s – caught eels in the river.

Cross the road where you can, and continue over the bridge using the wooden footway; afterwards continue on the right side of the road up the hill.

Brick bridge over river Brain built 1770 to replace a wooden one – took only three weeks (see page 46). Substantial repairs 1815, footway added 1973. Approaching far end, carving on top of near parapet, virtually invisible now, made in 1915 by soldiers from Royal Warwickshire regiment, billeted in Witham for training. **River Walk** crosses here.

Up the hill, **Bridge House** (55A), built 1980s – named after the card game. A barn here earlier, probably the tithe barn. The **next three houses** built in the 1400s. First (**55**), wrongly called 'manor house' – Chipping Hill didn't have one. Old stonework found under the road in front in 1983. Milk sold from basement early 1900s. Shoemakers' shop c 1850-1970s – at first the Abbott family, of whom Walter left 1860s and later had chain of big London shops – they were sold 1937, some to Clarks, others to K Shoes (Witham folklore reverses this to say wrongly that Abbott's started K Shoes). Second (**53**) – wall paintings inside, date 1606. Third (**51**) – base of brick chimney stack (restored 1966) – would have been inserted in older building, perhaps in 1600s. **Telephone pole** – markings show it was put up by the GPO in 1957, 36 feet long and medium girth (it is pictured on colour page 20). **'Chauntry Villas'** (47-49) with name and date – 1897, on site of four earlier tiny cottages – no known association with a chantry.

WALK 2. CHIPPING HILL

Chipping Hill green and the parish church in about 1916, with three Scots soldiers on the left-hand pavement. The cottages left of centre (32-34) were demolished as unfit in 1932. Owner Charles Richards wanted to build a new house in their place, but the Council bought the land instead because the green was 'considered by a great number of people to be a beauty spot'. Local residents contributed to the purchase money

Pause to look across the road at **the green**, market place till late 1300s. Travelling fairs closed 1891 (said to attract 'the worst characters of the neighbourhood'). Since 1978, site of Church's annual Medieval Fayre. **Oak tree** first planted 1937 to commemorate George VI's Coronation died. This replacement presented by Harry Ashby 1944 – has original 1937 plaque. **House** to left of churchyard entrance (28, formerly 26-30) once known as 'Druggles and Struggles', built c 1350. Resident Edmund Taylor imprisoned in Tilbury fort 1685 for preaching in favour of uprising against James II. **Large houses** to their right (26 (Mole End) and 24 (formerly 22)), partly from 1400s – together were home of Lollard family of Roydens in early 1500s, and of nonconformist George Lisle in 1660s, imprisoned in Colchester for preaching to 70 or 80 people here. In 1672 both Taylor's and Lisle's houses licensed for nonconformist worship. **Brick fronted house** further right (20-22) built early 1700s, became New White Horse then Kings Head (till 1863). One of several places said to have a tunnel to the church – none have yet been found.

Back on your own side of road, **house with shop window** (45), built 1400s and 1500s, formerly Post Office – a 'shrill whistle' was sounded at 7 p.m. to warn of the last post. A pump nearby was a meeting place. Once was a mile post here, but black dome left of window probably newer. **'Old House'** (43), same age, home in 1934 to 'Madam Elicia of London, a clairvoyant, palmist and crystal reader'. **House set back** (41), perhaps mid 1700s. Wide **newer house** (39) on site of old shops. **Tall house** (37, Oaklands) with date 1880 – early one of Joseph Smith's, moulded bricks from James Brown's catalogue, and cast iron railings (shown on pages 15 and 17 of the colour section). **Telephone pole** much newer than previous one – see markings – put up by BT in 1991, 9 metres long, light in girth. Code '2 I' tells BT where the pine tree was grown and by whom.

Crossing Moat Farm Chase, you also cross over Walk 1. **Barnardiston House** (35), partly from 1500s, many additions including imposing brick front. Wrought iron railings with cast tops. Named after Dame Katherine Barnardiston of Witham Place – owner, not resident – in 1630 she gave the rent to charity for preaching or schooling. Refreshments for Spa customers served here 1740s. 'Young gentlemen's boarding school' 1858 to 1894. Francis Crittall, future philanthropic industrialist, a pupil 1870s – found it like 'the sunwashed fragrance of a spring day', compared to 'fear-wracked' schooldays in Braintree. **Brookcote** (29), built 1897 as a 'small cottage', 'arts and crafts' style – builder hoped for five more next door, but drains inadequate. Designer George Sherrin – notable architect, work includes Spitalfields Market in London. In Second World War, hostel for evacuee children, then day nursery.

A few paces further, cross Chipping Hill, ready to return

'**Recess**' (14), elegant white brick, built early 1840s (shown on colour page 19) cast iron railings and gate. Once called 'Beatenberg' (changed after First World War by new occupants, the Dean family – they had been criticised for having a German relative). '**Bramstons**' (16), home (1840s to 1880s) of prosperous Miss Mary Ann Bramston (elder sister of the vicar) – was looked after by coachman, cook and housemaid in 1881. **Forge and house** (18), the most photographed place in Witham – house partly built c 1375 (roof structure is shown on colour page 2), wooden additions and shutters late 1600s, renovated by Braintree District Council and County Council 1970s.

Go up left side of White Horse into Church Street (once called Hog End – it was the main road to Braintree until the railway cut across the top of it in 1848).

The blacksmith's forge at Chipping Hill during the first year of the First World War. The soldiers and horses are from the Army Service Corps Territorials. Blacksmiths started up here before 1600, and horses continued to come till 1992. The business now receives commissions for special ironwork from all over the country (see also page 28).

The **White Horse** (2), built 1600s, public house since 1680 or before. **Two houses** (4-6), formerly one, built late 1500s. Previous house was home of Raven family of Lollards early 1500s. John Coote here c 1820-81 – prosperous furniture maker, upholsterer and auctioneer. Divided 1880s – at far end was home and office 1880s-1890s of George Mason Ball, important Agricultural Union organiser – many farmworkers lived in Church Street. Across the road, square **door** in wall – possibly for emptying former privy.

Shopping precinct (8-16), built 1955 (local architect Stanley Bragg included features like gables and 'panelled Essex plaster', attempting to echo medieval styles nearby). Previously, old shops included butcher's with own slaughterhouse behind. **Red brick house** against pavement (22, near end has mark from roof of previous neighbour). Used for Church of England Infants' school 1866-1900 – winding stairs, up to 100 pupils, some as young as two. British Restaurant 1941-43. Row of **plastered cottages,** formerly parish workhouse (24-40). Main part purpose-built 1714, one of earliest small-town workhouses in England. Plaque with date and initials of parish officers (probably Thomas Woodgate, Samuel Newton, Francis Raven,

William Skinner). Temporary Union workhouse 1834-1839, then became cottages (see pages 48-50, 59, 99). Still known as 'Charity Row'. Combined attic from former workroom. Two original black and white door numbers (26 and 30) provided by the Council in 1922 (one shown on colour page 20).

Set back, 'new' **Infants School**, built 1902 by non-denominational Witham Board. Temporary cookery and woodwork centre 1930s. Many extensions in last thirty years. Former site of one of the parish gravel pits. No evidence for a wool market as sometimes suggested. **Red brick house** (42) - ornate 1930s oak porch from cut-down gable ends, replacing older iron porch. **Three white cottages** (44-48), built c 1700 by Matthew Lurkin – paid 'one good fatt Turkey' annually for the site. Furthest one (44), grocer's and baker's shop c 1840-1989, shop front removed 1992. Formerly haunted by cat sitting on the stairs. On the corner, **Greene's almshouses** (50-52) founded before 1493 – rent of land in Springfield provided the residents with twopence a week and wood and candles. Rebuilt 1860.

Stop on corner of **Chalks Road,** look up Church Street. Behind little houses on the corner was Richards builders' yard c 1860s-1970s, with deep saw pit. Just past, was a road block in Second World War. Further up, both sides, **small terraced houses**, occupants very poor till mid 20th century, many farmworkers (see page 89 and colour page 19). Others called it 'Little Hell'.

Cross Church Street to walk back.

Tall brick house (11), 'Totscott', built 1732. Typical early 1700s – blue-black panels surrounded by red in front, chequered brick at back. Fine cast iron railings. Disused **Quaker burial ground**, behind wall and gate with yew trees, founded 1667 when Quakerism illegal. Headstones not used at first, but some from 1800s. **Bungalow** (9), sub-Post Office and shop till 1970s. **Woolpack** (7) built 1600s.

In corner of **churchyard** till mid 1800s was a small cottage for parish clerk (James Dace 1816-64 – his son founded the well-known local music shops). Flint boundary **wall** of churchyard probably late 1800s. Iron **arch** over gateway in memory of Wadley family, shopkeepers nearby. From the gateway see the **parish church** mostly from c 1330s, probably replacing an earlier one on a bigger site. Originally called St Nicholas, spelling changed to Nicolas 1930s. Looking at this **east end** – on left side the south **chapel**

WALK 2. CHIPPING HILL 157

The Woolpack in about 1881. It was never connected with the local wool industry, which had virtually disappeared when these two houses first became an inn in about 1800. Landlord Thomas Hook is standing outside with his wife Betsey and some of his children. The photo belongs to his great-great grandson, who lives in Canada. There used to be a bakery and a brewery in the yard (now flats).

(built c 1444) for a chantry (bequests by rich residents for prayers) – on right a **vestry** (late 1300s) of 'rag' stone, formerly two storeys. All the end except the vestry refaced in flint in 1850s.

Turning into the churchyard take the right hand path so that you go round the church anti-clockwise.

Past the vestry, the wide window of another small chantry chapel. After this, north side of original church – walls of flint and stone with medieval bricks (see colour page 17) (and a very few Roman ones). Out to your right, tall extravagant **monument** with draped urn – for prosperous vicar Andrew

Canon Francis Galpin, vicar of Witham 1915-21 and rector of Faulkbourne 1921-33. He was a world famous authority on ancient musical instruments, with over 600 in his collection (most now at the Museum of Fine Arts in Boston, U.S.A.). Here he is demonstrating a horn. He was also an eminent student of archaeology and botany.

Downes, died 1820 (name now invisible). In front of you, large **old red brick Vicarage**, now private house. Mostly mid-1700s for Reverend George Sayer – also had gardens landscaped (see pages 33-34 and page 6 of the colour section). Several alterations since. Francis Galpin, vicar 1915-21, had a world-famous collection of 600 historic musical instruments, but sold many of them in about 1917. Old extension on left demolished 1939 – probably because too big – another suggestion is that it was haunted. Sold 1960s – smaller house purchased nearby for vicar (known as rector since 1994).

Church tower – started life shorter with a wooden turret. Latter replaced by higher red brick top 1743, in turn replaced with present tower 1877 after much argument. Eight bells, early 1600s to 1932, one of latter to celebrate a century of ringing by the Chalk family. **West door** has Ordnance Survey benchmark from 1870s carved to right of it (rather battered). Round to the **south side** of church – walls refaced in flint in 1850s. In front of **porch**, by the path, the oldest surviving **tombstone** – Matthew Nicholls, 1700, former Quaker, became a churchwarden (see page 27). Carved skull on stone is a style of the time (nothing to do with plague). Flowering **trees** planted by Harry Richards 1945 to celebrate 60 years in church choir.

Church interior (if accessible) – somewhat denuded by past restorations, particularly in 1877. South **entrance arch**, re-used from a building of date c 1200. **Church chest** from 1300s (north aisle). Carved **chancel screen**, lower part from 1400s in oak. Three **helmets** or 'armets' in the south chapel. (there used to be four – see the illustration on the facing page). **Boards** on walls under the tower recording charities. **Monuments: 1500s** – recumbent judge John Southcott and wife Elizabeth (opposite south door, formerly in north chapel); magistrate Francis Harvey and wife Mary (chancel). **1600s** – funeral hatchment of Richard Kenwelmarsh (north wall); Robert Barwell the younger (chancel, florid memorial); George Lisle (south wall – omits his nonconformist activities). **Later, in chancel** – Pattissons, especially William and Sarah, drowned 1832 on honeymoon; Easts, from Berkshire, used to have some of Witham tithes paid to them, was said of Sir Gilbert East's funeral procession (1828) that 'as respects ostentation and grandeur, it has never perhaps been exceeded in this county, excepting in the instance of her late Majesty'. **West window** donated 1849 by famous architect Sir George Gilbert Scott in memory of his employee, Witham carpenter Henry Green Mortimer (who died in a fall from scaffolding during rebuilding of St Nicholas church at Hamburg in Germany; some said he was pushed).

Leaving the church by the main door, go forward through the churchyard onto the green. If you want to return to the start, turn right down the hill.

Four helmets from the parish church, dated c 1580-1750, displayed on a tombstone. When this photo was taken in 1914 they were kept in the vestry and the choirboys used to play with them. Three are still the church. The fourth, 'one of the most handsome examples of its type remaining in the country', was stolen in 1966. It's now in Royal Armories at the Tower of London (via a Bermondsey street market). © Crown Copyright NMR.

WALK 3
THE TOWN CENTRE

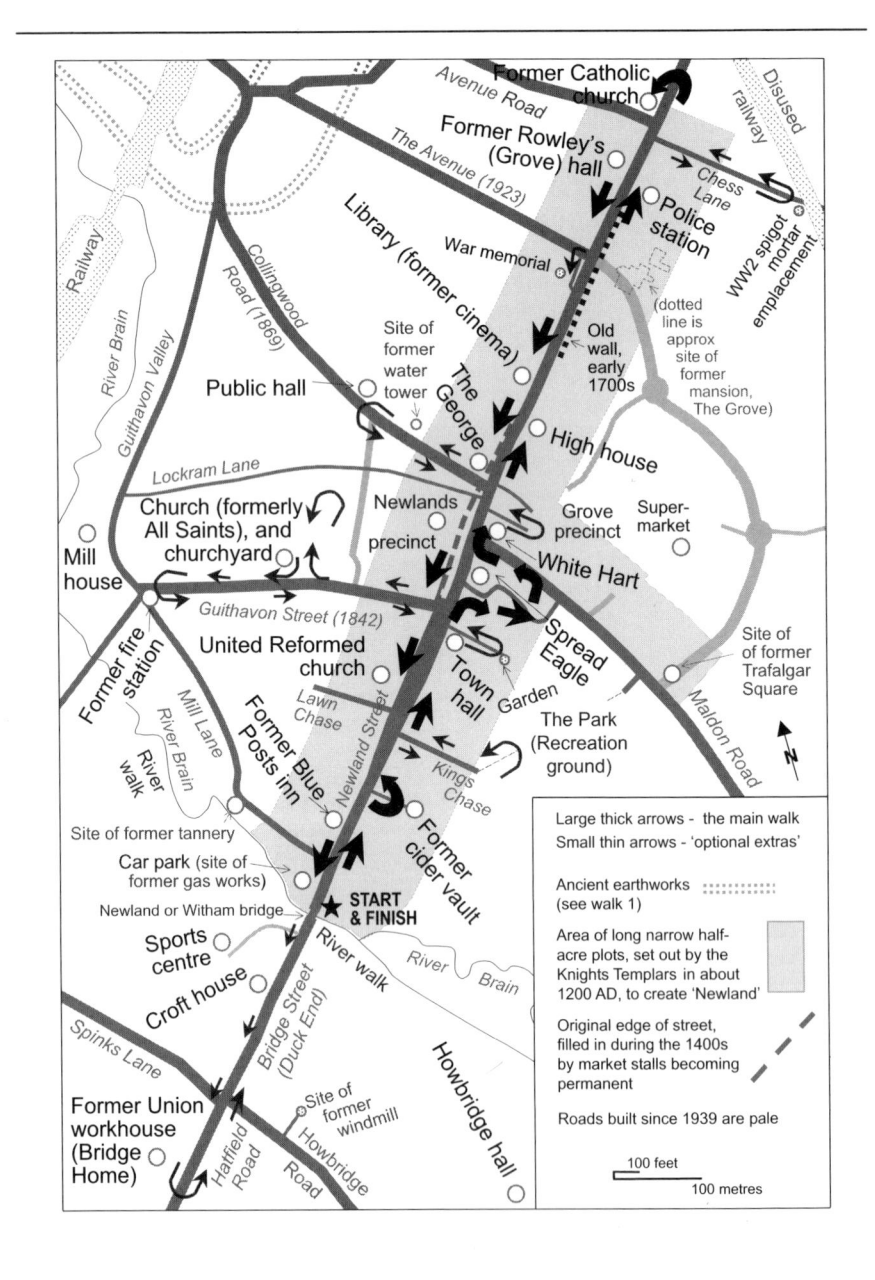

WALK 3. THE TOWN CENTRE

> On the facing page is the route of walk 3. The long main street is Newland Street (also known as High Street). The Knights Templars set up their new town here in about 1200, with narrow half-acre plots. The oldest surviving buildings are medieval (i.e. before about 1500), but the highlight is the varied brickwork from more recent times – much of it known as 'Georgian' because it dates from the time of the four King Georges (1714-1830).

A little over a mile (1¾ km) just to see Newland Street. Optional extras would add about another mile. Street numbers are given in brackets in the text (but not marked on the map). Landmarks may of course change or even disappear as time goes by. Pages 16 to 20 of the colour section show examples of bricks, railings, street furniture etc.

The walk goes up Newland Street from the bottom, on the right hand side. Start on the river bridge, opposite Mill Lane car park.

River Brain, probably site of a small Saxon settlement called 'Wulversford'. Later – industrial and hard-working end of street. River Walk now crosses town alongside it. **Bridge** built 1900 – nearly twice as wide as previous one – just in time for motor vehicles. **Tall building** (155-157), mostly built 1911 – decorated columns on top. Architect, Harry W Mann of Witham, killed First

> View up Newland Street in about 1905. The buildings to the right of the telegraph pole are now the site of Barnfield Place (143-47). At one of the old cottages, cows were kept in the back yard in 1850 – they had to walk through the building to get out. Another was home to the talented Poulter family in the early 1900s. An 'Electric Theatre' (i.e. a cinema) was proposed here in 1913, but never built.

World War. Initially Glovers' motor works. Later Ginetta made cult sports cars here (1962-88). The **Swan** (153), built about 1790. Right side has faint remains of words 'Home brewed beer' in black, just above the three iron crosses. Had Second World War pill box in front, guarding the bridge.
Telephone pole – successor of one into which Admiral Sir William Luard had his fatal fall in 1910. Old iron **water hydrant. Behind the Swan** was Witham's first waterworks (1869-1904) – its tanks were popular swimming pool in 1930s (see page 128). Afterwards Witham's third fire station (1940s to 1966). All now replaced by flats.

Long building (149-151), built 1600s. Iron fittings of old shop awning, probably mid 20th century, inscribed 'J Dean, Maker, Putney' (see colour page 16). He had a Chelmsford agent.. Old slots for boarding up windows during rowdy events. **New houses** (143-147, Barnfield Place). **Dental surgery** (141), built 1913, replacing Carpenters Arms, previously the Fleece, a lodging house – visitors in mid-1800s included soldiers (one was a 'Polish officer'), two ordnance surveyors, travellers (some Irish), a grinder, an American 'printer compositor', drovers, hawkers (one of them Canadian), and a Suffolk 'hydrophonist'.

Two small shops – the second (137) formerly Ardleys' bakery (c 1820 to 1939), with ovens behind. Then the former **Ardley's yard** – inside to right, past the plastered building, a building from the early 1700s, with red and black 'chequered' brickwork (ruined at the time of writing). **Doctors' surgery** (129, probably built 1700s) – nice iron foot scrapers (see

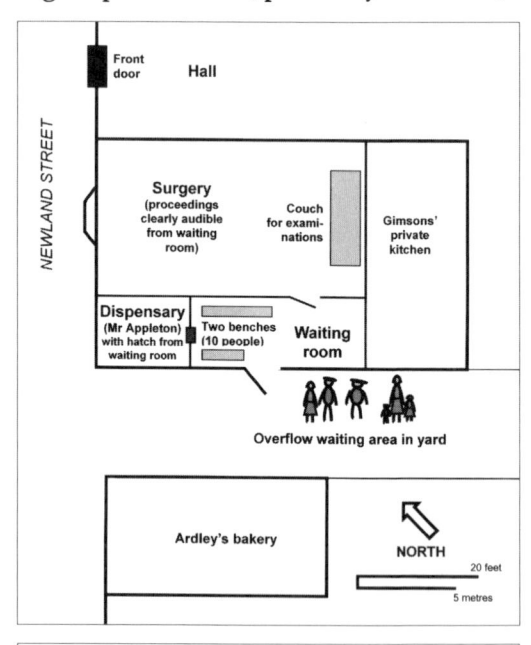

A plan of the of the doctors' surgery (129) in the 1920s, from a sketch by Walter Peirce. Grander patients than the ones shown, would ring the bell at the front door and be ushered in by a maid 'in a black dress and white apron and cap'. You took your own bottle for your medicine if you had one.

colour page 16). The practice is over 300 years old, either here or nearby (see page 44). Dates of alterations on side wall (some probably estimates). **'The Gables'**, aptly named (125-127) – incorporated into surgery 1990s. Victorian porch, wooden 'barley sugar' columns. Horizontal timbers just visible above windows, where upper floor once projected. When first built (1600s) housed Richard True, prosperous cloth-maker – he died 1665 in the Plague.

Next, **'Gimson's yard'** – small cottage (123) over old **cider vault** built 1700s – steps down to it in front, top of arch visible near ground on left side (see page 43). On way back to main street, notice **backs** of the buildings. On corner (**121**) – gabled back from 1600s, brick front from 1800s. Next up the street, **tall pair** of buildings (117-119) (previously (1600s) site of tenterfield for stretching new-made cloth). Built c 1730s – brickwork at front and back is best and second-best styles of the time respectively. Cellars projecting in front – most of Newland Street has cellars, important for cool storage. The further building (119) was visited in 1816 by 15-year old artist Edwin Landseer (best known today for the bronze lions in Trafalgar Square in London). His host Dr Dixon found him to be an 'incessant talker', and no good at shooting. He sketched the doctor's gun dog for a future painting.

Next four buildings (103-115), either side of Kings Chase, all formerly part of Witham Co-op, who took the nearest one in 1896 (rebuilt 1930 with 'WCS' on parapet). Second one is Pelican House, incorporated 1914 (built 1840, has pelican on parapet, emblem of Pattissons, then owners). Buildings past Kings Chase built 1930s – making the Co-op into a large department and food store. **Kings Chase** named after three generations of King family, grocers and drapers (here 1830s to 1904). At back made tallow candles – a smelly process using animal fats. 1920s manhole cover by Ham Baker, of Westminster, London, made at Langley near Birmingham (shown on colour page 16). Down the chase, **the Park** (or Recreation ground, see illustration on next page), made 1900 from earlier garden, worth a visit – some 200-year old trees. In early 1700s, the nearest end was a noisy cattle market.

Earlier **building** at 101 was Constitutional Club briefly (c 1899-1908). **Bank** (99), purpose-built 1910 by Joseph Smith for Capital and Counties Bank, classical style. Manager and family lived above. Became Lloyd's about 1920. **Yard** to its left (97 – buildings demolished 2004) – in early 1900s was Arthur Ralph Brown's (first 'carriage builder', then motor works promising 'aeroplanes and flying ships' to order) (see page 95), then after 1908, Cullen and Nichols' 'motor carriage & engineering works'. **Newer bank** (95), built

Peace Celebrations, Witham, 19.7.19.

> The Park (also known in the past as the Recreation ground), is accessible from both Kings Chase, off Newland Street, and Maldon Road. It was opened to the public in 1900 when many families lived nearby in the town centre, so children played there often. In addition it has always been a place for special events like the national 'Peace Day' in 1919, following the signing of the Treaty of Versailles, which concluded the negotiations after the First World War. This appears to be the 'Blindfold Race' for discharged soldiers, which according to the newspaper was won by 'R Griffiths and Miss B Cutmore'.

1960s – predecessor a café, like others it served many motorists before the by-pass of 1964. **Small buildings** with plaster fronts (89-93), from 1700s.

Two **red brick buildings** (85-87). First (**87**), built 1760s by bricklayer Samuel Humphreys – distinctive style – mansard roofs with windows in – similar ones by him across the road (64 and 66). Original black and white house number over the door, fixed by Council 1922 (not many left, but see 83, 55 and 5). Bright's solicitors came about 1930 from Collingwood Road. Railings not threatened in Second World War – needed for safety. **85** refronted about 1750, Witham's second Post Office 1853-1887 – in 1865 novelist Anthony Trollope, Post Office surveyor, visited – recommended increased salaries, and left his umbrella behind. From 1887-96, was the first shop of the new Witham Co-operative Society (see pages 90-91).

Shop with archway (83), birthplace in 1786 of Daniel Whittle Harvey, lawyer, politician and journalist (founded *Sunday Times* newspaper (1822), first Commissioner of new City of London Police (1839)). Afterwards was the Richard Wrights' clockmakers' business (1790s-1830s, see colour page 6 for one of his clocks). Later baker's shop 1900-89, ovens behind – closing of Gilbert's left sorrowful customers. **Grey-brick building** (67) **and yard**

WALK 3. THE TOWN CENTRE

(through archway) – site of Red Lion c 15th cent to 1700. Thomasin's brush shop and works in 1800s (see pages 66-67). Brush yard sometimes called Newland Place – in 1850 had '15 or 16 cottages … manufactories of mops and brushes … drainage and ventilation are exceedingly defective, and every inch of space is encumbered with the rubbish belonging to the trades'. Works closed 1871, most of cottages demolished 1930s as uninhabitable. Part of front was war-time British Restaurant 1941-45. Completely rebuilt 1960s and reduced from three storeys to two.

Grey-brick house (65), built 1855, Bawtrees' solicitors for several decades. **Shops** (63 and 63A) – building of mixed age – nearest part (63A, low) is oldest, with roof timbers from the 1400s. Never an inn as sometimes suggested. Main shop (63) was a chemist's 1830s-1904 – his home-made wooden drawers with steel bases still survive. After him, Ortlewell's hardware business moved from across the road with manager Albert Mondy.

Albert Mondy at his house and hardware shop (63) in the 1930s. He was 'not impressed' with Witham when he first arrived, but in the end he bought the business and stayed for over fifty years. He sold it in 1951 aged 83 – his odd-job man Ted Chaplin was 91. The shop still attracts customers from faraway places for essential but mysterious objects.

The Bank (right, now Town Hall, 61). Taken before 1910. In that year the town clock was installed here (it or its predecessor was formerly on the old Constitutional Club which burnt down). Note the iron foot scrapers (still there) and the false windows at the top, where the medieval roof goes down behind the newer parapet. In the middle is no.59 (replaced 1939); on the left Witham House (57, formerly the Pattissons' family home).

Town Hall (61). Part of the George 1400s to c 1807 – largest and busiest Witham inn. In 1700s had 'dining parlours of all sizes', 'elegant bed-chambers', stables for 50-60 horses, inn sign with 'elegant and much admired representation of St George slaying the dragon'. In 1807 became Witham's first commercial bank, with new brick front – 'false pointing' to make the bricks look regular (see colour page 17). Restored 1994 as Town Hall for Witham Town Council, with Heritage Centre (look inside). Seat dedicated to Albert Poulter, 'gentleman' (1907-2002), local historian who often sat here. Behind Town Hall, 'medieval garden', founded 1996. Example of Knights Templars' medieval ½ acre plots (here and no.59 together). When leaving garden, stone on wall on right reads 'This wall belongs to Mills Bawtree and Co.' (bankers 1826-1891, between two financial collapses).

'New' bank (59), built 1939. Before 1807, site part of the George. Briefly an iron foundry in 1870. Later called Horwood House. Montessori school 1917 onwards for eight small poor children from London. A helper wrote a book, *The Unrelated Family* (c 1920) – called it 'an old-fashioned house in an old-fashioned town'. **Witham House** (57) built c 1750 for first Jacob Pattisson. Family home till 1859 – saw many dramas and tragedies. On right, gateposts to carriage yard, and disturbed brickwork behind first-floor window where formerly was an enclosed footbridge to next door. Solid cast iron railings. **Two red-brick buildings** (53-55) built late 1700s to let by second Jacob Pattisson. **Spread Eagle** (47-51), mostly from 1500s – an inn ever since (see page 77 for photo). Early gables, later decorative barge-boards. Date '1300' on front is invented. One of Witham's five coaching inns in early 1800s.

Turn right under the Spread Eagle arch, go through the yard till you reach Maldon Road, to turn left up it. Note the following en route.

Yard – in 1820s the Royal Mail coach came daily – half-past midnight to Norwich, 2 a.m. to London. Foreign mail to Harwich twice a week. Also three other coaches a day each way. Stables for over seventy horses. Also in 1839 for few years, small silk factory. On right as you reach Maldon Road, **Freeland House** (20), designed 1862 by Frederic Chancellor, renowned Chelmsford architect and civic figure (started career with Witham's James Beadel). Coming out into the road and looking down (right) and across, a large Holm oak and a grey brick gatepost – marking former garden of **the Retreat**, a private 'lunatic asylum' (1812-c 1914), founded by Dr Thomas Tomkin (now bungalows). Walking left up Maldon Road, former **Baptist chapel** (1828-1975), now a care centre (see page 71). **Former house** (2), with '1889' on front (this style has the 9 in the middle), built for William Ward, 'noted for his cart horses'. Shop **with two gables** (2b), built as public toilets (1929-1960s) – a boon to motorists travelling the old A12. Visible across Maldon Road, brick house with blue-black panels from early 1700s, behind White Hart.

'Central Buildings 1927' (39-41) on corner. On site of the Angel (since c 1720, earlier the Greyhound) – in which market held indoors mid 1800s, after street market closed. The three first tenants after 1927 were London Central Meat Company (note initials in tiles in front of doorway, also decorative ironwork above shop window, and two original Crittall metal doors),

The new shop at 41 Newland Street about to open in January 1928. The rest of the new 'Central Buildings' was still empty.

East Anglian Electric Supply Company (just arrived in town), and the Tax office (in 1931 the assistant tax inspector, Arthur R Thompson, wrote a fascinating book, *Nature by Night*).

Cross Maldon Road at traffic lights to continue along Newland Street.

Maldon Road has old blue and white name plate – probably from 1914 when Council first fixed them – few survive. **White Hart** (thought to be haunted) – oldest parts from 1500s but much altered. Rebecca Cook, innkeeper in the 1840s, mistakenly claimed explorer Captain Cook as an ancestor. In 1902, petrol sold here – in 1908 served Royal Automobile Club members 'by appointment' – also had billiards. Entrance to **Grove shopping centre** (completed 1988, now home of fortnightly 'farmers' market'). Optional trip into it to see converted **maltings** on left, built about 1700 (12, Superdrug in 2004) – chequered' brickwork – at first, upper floors were nonconformist meeting-house. Back on the street, **Woolworth's** (35), built 1934 – no upper floor, just bricks and false windows there – the company's standard design for its 'fifth grade' shops. **Three small shops** (29-33) restored 1989 – medieval timbers visible inside.

Collins Lane – Edmund Collins built 'little court' of cottages here before 1700. At times also called Hubbards Lane, Alma Place or Cutts Yard. Next to smelly maltings mentioned above. In 1850, 'state of terrible dilapidation' – privies and rubbish overflowing – inhabitants 'the picture of wretchedness'. **Three shops** (9-13), built 1600s – 'timbers' added to front 1920s. **Red Lion** (7), nearest part built late 1300s, rest 1600s. Called Black Boy in 1700s, with cock fights. Became Red Lion c 1790 (third place with this name).

Pair of shops (5A and 5B) inscribed '1934', by local tax officer and part-time architect William John Redhead – he also 'designed' the church for Dorothy L Sayers' novel 'the Nine Tailors'. At the imposing **High House** (5) (see facing page), when Dr Payne moved out in 1924, his 'surplus furniture' included a sideboard and six chairs made by Chippendale. Three storeys till 1934, when top one removed. **Former Post Office** (1939, Witham's fourth), with 'GR' for King George VI. Attractive narrow bricks like many 1930s Essex POs. 1980s extension on right. Closed 1990s (except sorting office). At earlier building here, William Perry made an experimental mail coach in 1770. **Statue** (1994), novelist, theologian and Witham resident Dorothy L Sayers (see colour page 14), by local sculptor John Doubleday.

The drawing from which High House (5 Newland Street) was built. It was published in a book in 1757 by Abraham Swan, a London architect. He said that he hoped to appeal to 'gentlemen of moderate fortunes'. The first owner was probably Thomas Crispe, who also had a share in a plantation, slaves in the West Indies, and several ships. His brother Nicholas was a well-known London porcelain maker (British Library, shelf-mark 61 h5). Page 7 of the colour section. shows the house in an engraving of 1832.

Freebournes (3), timbered, 1600s, restored 1989 – named after John Freeborne – Quaker clothmaker – died here 1675 (see page 26). After that a farmhouse with 300 acres (1675-1960s). Never dressed up in brick. 'Witham fires' started here in haystacks – 5 November 1828. Was said in 1869 that its 'farm yard and cattle open to the street ... amidst some of the best houses'.

Large **Office building** (1974, since extended), part of town expansion scheme – a major employer. **Brick wall** (mostly early 1700s) of former mansion **the Grove** (see pages 30 and 40). Originally 430 feet long (135 metres) – two-thirds remains. Full height visible from behind it. Nearest section best preserved – special curved bricks near top (shown on colour page 17). Land sold in plots 1920s onwards. Winston Churchill considered buying the mansion. Fixtures auctioned 1932 – e.g. marble fireplaces, chandeliers, electric motor. Remains demolished soon afterwards. Former stable block became a house – taken down 1966 after fire. **Victorian letter box**, small 'C' type, six inch aperture, c 1890s. Wall breached by **Grove road** (1970s) and **Police station** (1937), latter once 'quite the most ornate building in Witham'. **Seat** given by German town of Waldbrohl to celebrate twinning with Witham and Juterbog. Inward-sloping surfaces symbolise friendship. Two old cedar trees, relics of the Grove's gardens.

Important junction – Avenue Road (opposite), was formerly the only road to Chipping Hill, whilst Chess Lane on your side led to thirty-acre Broad Mead since Domesday Book of 1086 and before (name perhaps from 'chase' (lane), not chestnuts). **Optional trip** down the lane and back, leads across Armiger Way, then at end is concrete **spigot mortar emplacement** from World War Two (shown on page 15 of the colour section) – on right near fence, just after wooden level-crossing gateposts for old railway to Maldon (closed 1960s, now the Blackwater trail).

Returning up Chess Lane to the main road, five **Grove cottages** – originally 'furthest house on the south side of Newland Street'. Made 1830s into to seven cottages, later on two pairs were combined. **Striped post** – remnant of cast iron signpost (about 1920), inscription of Maldon Ironworks.

Cross Newland Street at the junction to turn back.

Former **Catholic church** (1851), now a house. Earlier was site of Witham's first fire station (of four), built 1807 (15 feet by 14 feet, 4½ by 4¼ metres). Earlier still, a small field called Gallowscroft – site of medieval gallows. **Garage** – art deco vase and gatepost on corner – others similar have gone (see colour page 16). **Former Rowley's hall** next door now sells car parts. **Royal British Legion Hall** (1957) also accommodates Baptist services. **Garage**, 1930s stepped fascia – Glover's, founded at far end of street over a hundred years ago. A mansion once stood where **The Avenue** joins

The former Rowley's Hall or Rooms (late 1920s), afterwards the Grove Hall (1932 onwards). There were weekly dances with a band (and late night buses home), also dinners and whist drives. For the 1935 Jubilee, 800 children had tea in two sessions. The front verandah where teas and coffees were served is now the shop window. Taken in 2003.

Newland Street, replaced mid-1700s by avenue of eighty magnificent lime trees, part of the Grove estate. Fields used by First World War soldiers. House building began 1923 – trees felled. Gardens with **War memorial** – includes many ordinary Witham families not often commemorated.

In 1762, this area was called 'an open, airy, part of the town' – fashionable. Red brick **Newbury House** (2) – Frederick Shelley moved here in 1936 and set up a bookmaker's business – named the house after the racecourse. Previously Congregational church's manse (1875-1936) – in 1916, Reverend David Picton and Scots soldier accidentally killed here by hand grenade. Cast iron railings, integral foot scrapers, here and at larger **Avenue House** (4), (see pages 30-31, and page 7 of the colour section) whose history is complex – some medieval inside, chequered bricks from early 1700s on left wall, and 1757 red brick frontage (necessitating rainwater outlet – left side – high up – date and initials of gentleman William Wright and his wife Mary – see pages 30-31). In mid 1800s occupants the Misses Du Cane had five servants.

The **next fourteen buildings** fronting the street – early to mid 1800s – all white or grey brick frontages, so distinctive. Include **6-12** (Grove Terrace, c 1840, replacing cottages). Not for servants as sometimes suggested (they had humbler existences) – but retired tradesmen and widows, most with their own servant. **14, set back**, the odd one out, built 1891 for the groom at Avenue House. Large **Roslyn House** (16) (see colour pages 17 and 18) – four stages visible. First, near side (and back), timber frame with 'carpenters' marks' (Roman numerals scratched on wood). Second, far side, 'chequered' brick (c 1715 when 'great workhouses' were built, perhaps for weaving). Third, white brick everywhere else, from conversion to 'capital mansion house' in 1813. Note many diagonal pressure marks on white bricks (more commonly used in the 1700s). Fourth, Victorian conservatory in front, and cast iron railings. **Whitehall** (18, library since 1981). Mostly built early 1830s, home of Blood family – prosperous solicitors – had six servants in 1851 – claimed relationship to both Captain Blood (tried to steal Crown jewels 1671), and General Sir Bindon Blood (Boer War) – (connection in both cases either mythical or very distant). Later was the cinema (1928-64, see colour page 14). Inside, poster for first performance, and original notice board – also, visible through left-hand doors, a board painted 'TO CYCLE HOUSE'. Upstairs windows give views of surprising backs of neighbouring buildings.

Tiptree Villa (20), built 1876, initials of Edward Harvey and wife Amelia Charlotte (of Tiptree). Inherited the site from Edward's distant relative Miss Charlotte King (of 24) – heiress who 'lived a long life in extreme penury, scarcely allowing herself common necessaries'. She also left him the **next three houses** (22-26) and he put up fine cast iron railings and gates in front of all four, inscribed 'Davey, Paxman and Co, Colchester' (two Davey brothers from Witham helped James Paxman start famous engineering works at Colchester in 1865, one of them left in 1871 - see also pages 176 and 182, and page 16 of the colour section) . The three houses are medieval inside – each has a different frontage from the 1800s – all 'stock' bricks – with bits in, rather cheap, perhaps chosen by Miss King ? Known colloquially as 'Dorothy Sayers' Cottages' after the novelist – she lived at 22-24 c 1930 to 1957. They fell into disrepair for a time – were restored in 1975 thanks to Essex County Council. Row of **four shops** (28-34), formerly houses, built in 1800s – 34 was once Witham's main photographic studio (c 1891-1939). The **George** public house (36) (so called since early 1800s after previous George (61) was closed). Public library started in the back room here in 1932.

For an optional extra, go part-way into Collingwood Road, up the right hand side, back on the other.

Collingwood Road (built 1869) – now the main road north. Named after Admiral Lord Collingwood (battle of Trafalgar, 1805). Accommodated new red-brick water tower, 80 feet (24 metres) high – on right – (see pages 84-85) demolished carefully 1935 – contractors wanted to 'throw' it instead (i.e.

push it over). Mostly high hedges for several decades – in 1890, sheep were damaging the path. Gradually built up from early 1900s.

Behind the George, **Ben Sainty Court** – named after one of three signalmen who prevented worse carnage at the rail disaster of 1905 (see page 94 and colour page 11). **Large block** for various health organisations. Former **office** of Witham Urban District Council with initials (1934, when it was enlarged to include Rivenhall and Silver End). **Public Hall** (1894), classical, home to multitude of events. Late Victorian **letter box**, medium 'B' size, larger than Witham's others. **Constitutional Club** (1910), replacing the one burnt down in Newland Street. Next **house** (16) built for the Miss Pattissons 1904 (see page 122). Returning on the other side – tiny **telephone exchange** (1939 inscribed on bricks), newer one behind (1975). Newland Drive goes to car park, where **wall** backing onto churchyard has anti-'poll-tax' graffiti (1990) and stone with 'E C SMITH' (1880s). He was first occupant of imposing red brick **Collingwood House** (c. 1880) (15, now Noel Pelly House), good moulded bricks. Next, site of Saturday **market** (since c 1970).

Back in Newland Street, compare position of **38** (Wimpy, on former site of Glover's) between Lockram Lane and Collingwood Road, on original building line of c 1200 AD, with that of projecting **40** (Lisa Marie since the 1960s), further forward because built on site of medieval market stalls.

The centre of Newland Street in 1961. The brick upper part of 'Modes' (36, far right) is on the original road line of c 1200, as is Glovers (38, now Wimpy), behind the George's hanging sign. But Bibbys (40, now Lisa Marie) and the buildings behind it project about 30 feet (9 metres) forward (i.e. leftwards). Their sites were once medieval market stalls, made more permanent from the 1400s onwards. The shops beyond Bibbys were redeveloped in 1967, and the new buildings (some of which front the Newlands precinct) were set back.

Lockram Lane – here centuries before Collingwood Road – started early 1400s as gateway from house into field behind. 'Lockram' was once a type of cloth but in 19th century meant 'rubbish' – lane then temporarily renamed Queen Street – government inspector wrote in 1850 'Why so dignified it would be impossible to discover, as nothing can well be imagined more filthy and disgusting …'. Blue street name plate from 1914 (see colour page 20).

Newer shops (42-54) (built 1967) – nearest one replaced Spurge's drapery shop, once one of the wonders of Witham. Entrance to **Newlands precinct** – c.1967– rather outdated now – but has always had some splendid shops – and who knows, concrete might be fashionable again one day! After another new shop, **older building** on pavement line (56) was in the shoe trade from the 1850s till 2004 – refronted 1886, date in moulded bricks. Two **two-storey shops painted white** above (58 and 58a) – together a butcher c 1820-1970 – earliest ones, Barwells, enjoyed being confused with rich Barwell family of the Grove. Early timbers and fireplace inside 58a. Two **three-storey red brick** buildings (60-62) built mid 1700s for the Pattissons to rent out. **Last one** of row (64), painted above, formerly 'Corner House', built 1760s, housed chemist's 1840s-1960s – formerly steps to corner door. One chemist, Robert Poynter Green, was also a dentist, serving 'Nobility, Clergy, Gentry' and others. His son Hubert, returning 1916 from twenty years of world travel, 'found Witham very much changed'.

Wide area is **former market place** and fair ground – original street width of 1200 AD again – was centre for most outdoor gatherings till precincts were built. **Coach House Way** – along old medieval line of street (name quite new). Across it, **imposing red brick** building, five windows wide (66), built 1780s by Samuel Humphreys in his own style (mansard roof etc., like his 87 opposite, and his 64 that you've just passed) – Drake's wine shop for over a century (1850s to 1970s). Adjoining **smaller brick building** on corner of Guithavon Street (68) – is copy (dated 2000) of its predecessor, built 1700s for Jacob Pattisson – second of three Red Lion

A flagon from Drake's wine shop. Francis Drake moved to 66 Newland Street (from 74-76) in the early 1900s. He blended whisky and sold it in London – one variety was called 'Cardiac'. The business continued here till the 1930s under the supervision of four of his children, Edward, Ethel, Winifred and Ada.

WALK 3. THE TOWN CENTRE

inns till c 1800 – also dealt with the post. Then c 1800-53 became Witham's first separate Post office. Had a clock and known as 'Clock House' – notice of local meetings gave their times as 'by the Town Clock'.

For another optional extra, turn into Guithavon Street, go up the right hand side, back on the other.

'Guithavon' is pronounced 'Guthayvun' – worthies who built and named it (1841) wrongly thought it was ancient form of 'Witham'. Once a quiet and genteel street. **Tall white building** (2-4) – probably built as cloth warehouse by Armond family – 1500s or 1600s. In 1700s was 'spacious and elegant assembly room' of Red Lion. **Seat** with two old plaques moved here for safe keeping – one from wall in Lockram Lane belonging to tanner James Matthews (1817), other from 46 Newland Street (1881). **Car park** (1960s), former site of National Schools (see page 61 and 74). **All Saints church**, completed 1842 for Anglicans, restored 1989 for Catholics (see pages 73-75).

Guithavon Street in the early 1900s, with gas lamp and telephone pole. The two houses have the National Schools beyond, with a flagpole. There was a slaughterhouse behind them. All now replaced by the car park. The church remains – formerly All Saints (C of E), it is now Holy Family and All Saints (Catholic).

1950s Ordnance Survey bench mark right of door. Explore peaceful interesting churchyard (nightingales used to sing here) – old cedar tree – original cast iron railings at front, and some others at back (along Lockram Lane) inscribed 'Davey, Paxman and Davey' from churchyard extension in 1867 (the older version of the firm's name, see pages 172 and 182 and colour page 16 – they cost nearly £90, equivalent of £4,000 today).

'Parsonage' (14) built 1849 for curate – interesting latch on iron gate.
'Woodhams' (16) built 1850s, called 'a charming country retreat'. First named 'Woodbine Villa', changed about 1900 after Woodbines became the 'poor man's cigarettes'. Sheltered housing at Rex Mott Court (built 1975) and Podsbrook (1973). Stop at **crossroads**, look over to **chapel** opened 1932 for the Peculiars (now Evangelicals). Previously site of steam and gas flour mills (1879-1925) – miller's brick house to right in the trees (water mill behind demolished 1948). **Green space** left of the chapel – Second World War Home Guard practised here. Further left was Territorial Army headquarters.

Crossing Guithavon Street to return – Witham's second **fire station** on corner (1850s to 1940s), 1950s Ordnance Survey bench mark lower right. Victorian **letter-box** – smallest size, fixed 1894 by builder Charles Richards (work cost 16s 6d (82½ p)) (see colour page 16). **Grassed triangle** in front – formerly Second World War air raid shelter for firemen. New telephone pole (2004 – colour page 20 shows it being put up). **Crown**, built 1860 – publican 1897-99 was Joseph A Kuner, Witham's first electrical engineer. **Mill Vale Lodge**, built 1986 – previous building was police station (1849-1937), report centre Second World War, afterwards clinic (toilets in old cells). Attractive brick **church hall** – originally was Methodist church, opened 1864 (see page 71) – architect Charles Pertwee of Chelmsford. School room added behind 1934, along whose right wall are foundation stones and names of benefactors (including Yorkshire flour miller Joseph Rank – helped Methodists worldwide, father of J Arthur Rank the film mogul – rare to find his name displayed like this, he was usually too modest to allow it).

'New' **Methodist church**, built 1961 – on site of 'Paradise Row', nonconformist almshouses. **Red brick terrace** (21-37) completed 1861. By 37, unusual fibre glass telephone pole (experiment of 1970s and 1980s – there's another further on). **Gate** and hidden path between 19 and 21 – short cut to Lawn Chase. **Colne House** (19), built 1850 as Savings Bank (founded 1818 in Newland Street, primarily for the poor). Church's role shown by cross in wall. Called a 'very pretty building' in 1869. Gothic style unusual for bank buildings then – more usually classical. **Terrace** (3-15) built 1843 for the Pattissons to rent out. Red bricks unusual then – perhaps chosen to match their 'Witham House' in Newland Street, proudly visible ahead of you (deceived compiler of 1970 official historic buildings list, who thought they were from 1700s). Original railings and coal-hole covers (see colour page 16).

When you reach Newland Street again, turn right into it.

1920s Ordnance Survey **bench mark** on corner behind the left leg of the road name (pictured on colour page 20). **Corner building** (70) – occupied c 1860-2001 by stationer and Richard Sutton Cheek (see the illustration below). **Three** attractive **red brick buildings** (72-78) from 1700s. The first (**72**) is earliest (c 1726) – typical blue-black brick panels – alleged spy lodged here 1756. Later (1782-1843), Norton family of coopers (barrel makers) had large timber yard. In 1802 Thomas Norton wanted son John to build over the left-hand gateway – he didn't – finally done 1980s (72a). **74-76** (about 1770) (now the post office), arched first-floor window – in early 1900s it was Mr Spurge's (less 'classy' than no. 42), called 'London House' At **78** (also 1770s), now with bow windows, some of Mr Spurge's shop girls lodged, with

A 19th century engraving of the wide part of Newland Street, published by Richard Sutton Cheek. His own 'printing office', and bookseller's and stationer's premises can be seen left of centre (now 70 Newland Street). He produced a scurrilous local newspaper here called *The Tomtit* from March 1869 to May 1870. Then it had to be closed after a libel action.

The town sign, designed by Roy Belsham to commemorate the Golden Jubilee of the Queen and the 50th anniversary of Witham Rotary Club. It was unveiled in February 2003 by Alan Hurst, MP, and dedicated by the rector, the Reverend John Suddards. The photo was taken soon after the unveiling, hence the flags (see also the front cover)

a housekeeper. Town sign, designed by Roy Belsham, and unveiled in 2003 by Alan Hurst MP to commemorate the Golden Jubilee of the Queen, and the 50th anniversary of Witham Rotary Club

Set well back, three tall **Medina Villas** (80 84, see the facing page) – with name and date (1883). Bricks from earlier Georgian building, Medina House, visible in right hand end wall. The Villas were too novel and imposing for Witham – only 80 succeeded just as a house, others needed single-storey **shops in front**. The first from about 1950s, others 1880s. The furthest (84) was new Post Office built 1887, when called 'more useful than ornamental'. First telephone exchange here in 1905 – twelve subscribers. In 1906, telegram about election results stuck in chute – found eleven years later. Post Office moved away 1939. Cooper's versatile drapery and haberdashery shop here 1963-99. **Telephone pole** – from markings and fittings, is over 40 years old – larger predecessor served the Post Office. Good place to view the **panorama** of lovely old buildings on the other side of the road.

Nice iron gate. **Shop** (86) – two storeys – Sammy Page's c.1910-1940s – wealth of second-hand goods. **Shop** (88) – three storeys with white edges – ironmonger's c.1830-1930s – in 1861 Carrington Wilson employed '7 men, viz. 1 coppersmith, 1 tinman, 1 bellhanger, 1 whitesmith, 1 shopman, 1 porter, 1 carman' (a carter). Now Holts' quality butchers, run by the family, here since 1952 (after a few years at 143).

United Reformed Church, formerly Congregational, built 1840 – architect

Set back are the three Medina Villas (80-84 Newland Street). When built in 1883 they were twice as tall as any other Witham houses of the time, with moulded cornices and chandeliers inside. Each had two indoor WCs and also the first plumbed-in baths in Witham. The town was not ready for such luxury and builder Joseph Smith had no offers at the first auction in 1884. Taken in 1990.

probably James Fenton (built many similar in Essex) (see page 71). Earlier small timber church built 1714 – by 1800s it was 'dear old patched up Meeting house'. Memorial right side, shown on colour page 20 – Jacob (the first) and Elizabeth Pattisson (died 1754 and 1750). Base of obelisk near front steps – Thomasin family, brushmakers. **Space** in front – formerly Witham Literary Institution building, changed briefly to Constitutional Club c 1908 – had town clock which was previously in Guithavon Street – all burnt down 1910. Two **tall red brick buildings** now joined (90-92), Original features from 1500s inside; some accidentally revealed by burst pipe in 1979. Frontages from late 1700s. Now Byfords – quality furnishing and gifts – (92 since 1955, 90 incorporated 1966) – third generation of the family.

Lawn Cottage (94), just before the chase – pointed gable, cheerful Gothic style, built 1865 for James Wright (shows date and initials) – indoor WC was served with rainwater from lean-to glass roofs (Witham had no mains till

1869). **Lawn Chase** was drive to **Lawn House** (c 1830-1970). Was imposing white brick building – whilst occupants (Luard family) away in July 1868, gardens opened to the public – nearly a thousand came. Almshouses in drive moved to Guithavon Street to 'improve' surroundings. **'Christmas House'** (96-98), 1960s, replaced older building of same name. **Batsfords** (100) – vast early red brick frontage, possibly pre-1700, judging from 'rolled' brick edges to windows (see page 45 and colour page 17). In early 1920s gifted broadcaster Peter Eckersley lived here – director, announcer and engineer of 2MT, Britain's first regular radio station. Known in Witham for cheerful life-style and parties. Building became hotel c 1980, restaurant and bar 2003. **Flats and shops** (102-116) built 1987 on site of Parion's caravan sales park. Earlier, small, crowded houses here, including Notts yard, named after Joseph Nott – sold clothes and groceries c 1820-1850.

Small plastered **shop** (118), part of structure is from late 1300s, one of oldest in Newland Street. Lead-glazed windows installed by builder Fred Gaymer 1930s. Highway Bookshop since 1988. **Tall gabled building** (124) – part is rest of medieval house – behind brick front from 1880s with moulded bricks. Mann's private boarding school for boys, with attic bedrooms and outside toilets, 1840s-1907.

Two attractive **red brick buildings** (126-128), **Blue Posts inn** c 1700-1845 (see pages 41-42). Innkeeper William Harlee in c 1700 'new fronted with brick' the medieval building on right (128), and also built new one on left (126). Busy coaching inn later – stabling for forty-five horses, pig stye, and skittle yard. After the railway, Smyths' seed-drill factory (1840s-1894), with blacksmiths, wheelwrights etc. from Suffolk. Later Coates' electrical shop (c 1930-1994), starting as 'wireless and cycle engineer'. **Public house** (130), founded c 1840, called **'the Crotchet'** from c 1890-2000, so named by publican (who was a music teacher). Single storey part on left was formerly blacksmith's forge. **Shop, corner of Mill Lane,** formerly **Globe** (c 1845-1917). Parish 'cage' was in yard, probably for centuries, for petty offenders – became store 1849, demolished 1920s. **Takeaway** originally built 1921 as Lawrence's fried fish shop, demolished 2005, replaced by new building. Look up **Mill Lane** - past row of houses on left was a large tannery till the 1960s.

Cross Mill Lane to the car park. For an optional extra, continue straight on up the right hand side of Bridge Street (formerly known as Duck End), back on the other – only selected places are mentioned.

WALK 3. THE TOWN CENTRE

Car park – site formerly gas works (1834-1960s) – had manager's house on corner (see pages 66, 115-16 and colour page 14). **Bramston Sports Centre** and swimming pools (named after former vicar, opened 1974, part of town expansion scheme). **Croft House** (10), Newmans' dairy 1899-1945. **Elmy House**, site of former Elmy's yard (or 'Buffalo Row', after escaped buffalo was cornered there). **Bridge House** (28), built 1700 – refuge for unmarried mothers 1888-93. **Bridge Street Motorcycles** (30) – here since 1959, founded 1953. **Grass** on corner, former site of almshouses (1712-1967). Cross **Spinks Lane**, to **Hatfield Road**. Vet and horse-dealer William Spink lived at red brick **Poplar Hall** on corner in mid-1800s. One-time house name – Cambridge Villa (c 1874-1906) sometimes visible on end wall. 'Cottage home' for poor children from workhouse c 1908-1915. Former **Union workhouse**, forbidding, built 1837-39 (see pages 58-61). Architects Scott and Moffatt (Sir George Gilbert Scott later famous – designed St Pancras Station). Closed 1880. Since known as 'the Bridge' – various uses for housing disadvantaged people. Closed 2003, converted into flats (a purpose considered, but rejected, in 1922). Many new houses on its land behind – potentially a very valuable archaeological site, on Roman road and not far from Roman Temple at Ivy Chimneys – not sure whether anyone looked.

Approaching Bridge Street from Hatfield Road (c 1910). All the features in the foreground have now gone. On the left, the hedge in front of Poplar Hall and the Bridge Street almshouses (brick). On the right, the corner of Howbridge Road, where the RAFA club now stands. Standing there is Robert Fleuty, the fourth Fleuty to be a master wheelwright in Witham; his yard was off the edge of the photo to the right.

Faragon Terrace (59-67 Bridge Street). Shown below are enhanced photos of the inscription, which is in darker brick on the upper part of the building. 'GMT' stands for George and Mary Thomasin, original owners, and 1869 is the date. Below the main picture is the inscription on the front railings, 'Davey, Paxman and Davey, Colchester'. The two Daveys were Witham men and helped to start the firm in 1865. One of them left in 1871 so this is the oldest version of the firm's name. Contrast the post-1871 version shown on colour page 16, and also see pages 172 and 176.

Crossing over Hatfield Road to return, over **Howbridge Road,** along which once stood a windmill (mid 1830s-1850, now site of Tudor Close). **RAFA club** (opened 1959). **Faragon Terrace** (59-67), illustrated above. The name (origin unknown) and 'GMT 1869' are picked out in black brick on the upper part of the building. GMT were George and Mary Thomasin, owners of the brushworks (see pages 66-67), for whom the terrace was built. In front are rare original cast iron railings inscribed 'Davey, Paxman and Davey, Colchester'. Offices in **former George and Dragon** (29), rebuilt 1889 after fire, date on back. **Three half-timbered houses** (23-27), built 1500s, sculpted timbers on 27 (see page 22). Narrow **bottleneck** here on main road to London (A12) before 1964 by-pass. Former **Morning Star** (13), now a house, set back – built as pub 1950s to replace one of same name on roadside. **Alfred Cottages** (3-9), with name and date (1891, see colour page 20), built by Edward Sayer, named after his Baptist father Alfred, bootmaker at no 1 for over fifty years. Over the bridge you are now back at the start.

OTHER PLACES TO SEE

The manor houses and their surroundings (see page 4 of the colour section)

Powershall, Terling Road, 15th and 17th century barns in front. **Blunts Hall**, Blunts Hall Drive, 18th and 19th century house, medieval earthworks to west. Nearby, **Cuppers farmhouse**, 19 Blunts Hall Road, small medieval farmhouse; had large traction engine business 1870-1910. **Howbridge Hall**, Howbridge Road (see colour page 4). 16th century, adventurous restoration of interior by Basil Ionides in 1920s with mixture of fittings from other ages and other countries. Opposite, **house formerly smallholding** (63), one of six in Witham by Essex County Council in 1913 to encourage farming. **Benton Hall**, on road to Wickham Bishops. Nearby, over brick **bridge** built 1730s, the attractive **Blue Mills**, formerly Machins mill, and further on, **Chantry Wood** up the hill, once a hundred acres, a vital part of Witham's economy since Domesday.

North Witham

In **Rickstones Road. Rickstones school and college** (opened 1977). **Evangelical church** (next to 24). **Houses** at **6-8** (1926), and all of **Manor Road** nearby (1924) were built for Crittall's new factory workers, designed by C H B Quennell of London (1872-1935), associated with 'arts and crafts' movement, more usually planned grand houses, e.g. for Hampstead Garden Suburb in London. With his wife Marjorie also wrote many popular children's history books, e.g. the 'Every Day Life' series.

In **Cressing Road**. Witham's pioneering **Council houses** (the earliest are 17-27, completed 1923, shown on page 14 of the colour section). **Templars estate**, more pioneering houses, completed 1966, traffic-free layout, for first residents coming with jobs from London under Town Expansion scheme. In front,

The evangelical church in Rickstones Road, designed by Terence Wynn of Maldon and opened in 1996. There has been a church here since 1932, when the original one was established by Mrs Marion Blyth and her daughter, of the Mill House in Guithavon Valley.

opposite 143, is where roadman Arthur Burmby and two soldiers were killed by an unexploded bomb in 1940 (see page 135).

South Witham

In **Maldon Road. Parkside Youth Centre,** built 1837 as British School, became Board School 1895 (latter date on building). Masonic Hall, former **Quaker meeting house** (29), re-built 1801-02, late revival of 'chequered' brick work. **Sauls bridge**, best seen from field on the left going from Witham). Further away on that side was once a wooden viaduct carrying the railway line to Maldon (demolished 1960s; a similar one survives at Wickham Bishops).

In **Maltings Lane** (formerly Made Lane). **Denholm Court**; weatherboarded part was a 16th century tannery, became maltings 18th century when brick section and kiln added (see page 47). Lead glazing factory for Crittall's in 1920s. **Victoria Cottages** (1890s), on site of seven others said in 1850 to be one of the healthiest places in the parish. The Pavelin family lived here 1841

Sauls bridge in Maldon Road, built 1814. Predecessor named after 15th century John Salle. Now the oldest iron bridge in Essex, the second ever built in the county, designed for Ransomes of Ipswich by 29-year old William Cubitt. He was later Sir William, knighted in 1851 after the Great Exhibition, when he chaired the building committee which included Brunel, Robert Stephenson and Charles Barry. Taken in 1988.

These people worked at Crittall's lead glazing works in the old maltings, Maltings Lane (see pages 47 and 111). It was only open during the 1920s. The girls soldered the lead. As a precaution against poisoning they had to gargle before going home, and drink barley water. When I published a similar photo in the local newspaper it was thought the girls worked at Pinkham's – many thanks to the people who produced more information and pictures.

to c.1980. Previously, in early 19th century, the 'pest house' was here, for people with infectious diseases. In **Hatfield Road**. **Old Ivy Chimneys**, various ages, earliest part probably 16th century. Home of the three Miss Luards c.1880-1947, daughters of the Admiral – they went about the town doing good works. Nearby the site of an important **Roman Temple**.

East Witham

Colchester Road. Milestone, showing 38 miles to London, opposite Crittall Road (see page 39). 18th century stone behind early 19th century cast iron plate (latter probably by Ransome's of Ipswich). 1870s Ordnance Survey bench mark on the stone.

Witham associations in the countryside

E.g. **Cressing Temple** and its medieval barns (see page 14). **Terling** village (17th century Puritans, see pages 24-25). **Silver End**, garden village, started 1926 by Crittall's. 'Modern movement' houses, now regarded as a historic site (see page 112).

SOURCES OF INFORMATION

Following is a list of some of the publications that I have used. However, much of my information came from original documents which are housed in various places, especially the Essex Record Office. In due course I shall try and put details of these sources, and other additional information, in the Essex Record Office and Witham Library. I know a lot of people promise this and don't manage it, so I apologise in advance if I become one of them.

Witham books and articles
Henrietta Barnewall, *A Hundred Years ago: or, a narrative of events leading to the marriage and conversion to the Catholic Faith of Mr and Mrs M Sidney* (1877).
Rev. John Bramston, *Witham in Olden Times: Two lectures delivered at Witham Literary Institution* (1855).
R H Britnell, 'The Making of Witham', in *History Studies,* volume 1, no. 1, May 1968.
A F J Brown (ed.) *Witham in the 18th Century* (Workers' Educational Association, 1963).
Edward Cresy, *Report to the General Board of Health on a Preliminary Inquiry into the Sewerage, Drainage and Supply of Water, and the Sanitary Condition of the Inhabitants of the parish of Witham* (HMSO, 1850).
Rev Henry Du Cane, *A few Hints to the Inhabitants of Witham on the occasion of Dr Wiseman's recent exercise of his assumed Spiritual jurisdiction in the Town* (1851).
Essex County Council Archaeology Section; *Origins of Witham* (Essex County Council, 2001).
R C Fowler, *The Church of St Nicholas, Witham* (Wiles, 1911).
Janet Gyford
    Memories of Witham: Shops (Janet Gyford, 1983).
    Domesday Witham (Janet Gyford, 1985).
    Men of Bad Character: the Witham Fires of the 1820s (Essex Record Office, 1991).
    Witham 1500-1700: Making a Living (Janet Gyford, 1996).
    Public Spirit: Dissent in Witham and Essex 1500-1700 (Janet Gyford, 1999).
    Images of England: Witham (Tempus, 1999).
    Witham Park: 100 Years Old (Witham Town Council, 2000).
    'The Witham hoard of 17th-century tokens and George Robinson the issuer' (with R H Thompson), in *Essex Archaeology and History*, 3rd series, volume 20, 1989.
    'Mike Wadhams and 'Cocksmiths' (22-26 Newland Street, Witham), in *Essex Archaeology and History News*, April 1991.

'Cornelius Walford, junior and senior, versatile Victorians', in *Essex Family Historian*, December 2004. Some of my books are out of print, but see the web sites mentioned below.

T A Henderson, *The Parish Church of Saint Nicolas, Witham, Essex* (Witham Parochial Church Council, 1986).

W Pinkham and Son Ltd
The Story of a Lamp (c.1948).
Sixty Years of Progress (1959).

Albert Poulter (booklets, all published by Albert Poulter)
In the Yards, Up and Down the Steps (1996).
Albert's Witham (1997).
Landgirls links with Essex (1998).

B W Quintrell, 'Gentry Factions and the Witham Affray, 1628', in *Essex Archaeology and History*, 3rd series, volume 10, 1978.

Warwick Rodwell, *The Origins and Early Development of Witham, Essex: a study in settlement and fortification, prehistoric and medieval* (Oxbow, 1993).

Maurice L Smith (booklets, all published by Maurice Smith)
A brief History of Witham Congregational Church (1965).
1. *Early History of Witham* (1970).
2. *Markets, Manors and Manorial Rolls* (1970).
3. *St Nicolas Church* (1970).
4. *Postal History of Witham* (1971).
5. *Witham Schools* (1971).
6. *Witham River Bridges* (1972).
7. *Witham Roads* (1972).
8. *Fires in Witham* (1975).

Speciality Publishing Co., *The Pictorial Record: special local edition for Witham and District* (c.1900) (also a reprint by Essex Libraries, 1982).

James Taverner, *An Essay upon the Witham Spa. Or, a brief Enquiry into the Nature, Virtues and Uses of a Mineral Chalybeate Water at Witham in Essex* (1737).

David Trump, 'Blunts Hall, Witham', in *Transactions of the Essex Archaeological Society*, 3rd series, volume 1, part 1, 1961.

M C Wadhams, 'The Development of Buildings in Witham from 1500 to circa 1800', in *Post-Medieval Archaeology*, volume 6, 1972.

A Vera G Wright, *The Unrelated Family: being an account of a woman's experiment in Child Education* (Jarrolds, c.1920).

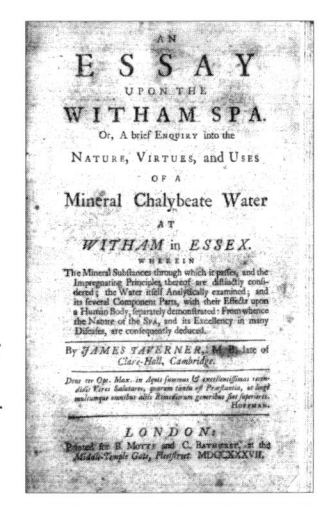

The title page of James Taverner's book promoting Witham's 18th-century spa. It was published in 1737 (see pages 37-38).

Other books with particular Witham content or relevance

D D Andrews (ed.), *Cressing Temple: a Templar and Hospitaller manor in Essex* (Essex County Council, 1993).

Clyde Binfield, *So Down to Prayers: Studies in English Nonconformity 1780-1920* (Dent, 1977).

David J Blake, *Window Vision: Crittall 1849-1989* (Crittall Windows, 1989).

A F J Brown (all published by Essex Record Office)
English History from Essex Sources 1750-1900 (1952).
Essex at Work (1969).
Chartism in Essex and Suffolk (1982).
Meagre Harvest, the Essex Farm Workers' Struggle Against Poverty 1750-1914 (1990).
Prosperity and Poverty, Rural Essex 1700-1815 (1996).

Miller Christie, *A History of the Mineral Waters and Springs of Essex* (1911).

Penelope J Corfield and Chris Evans (eds.), *Youth and Revolution in the 1790s: letters of William Pattisson, Thomas Amyot and Henry Crabb Robinson* (Alan Sutton, 1996).

Ronald and Ann Cowell, *Essex Spas and Mineral Waters* (Ian Henry, 2001).

Mr and Mrs F H Crittall, *Fifty Years of Work and Play* (Constable, 1934).

Samuel T Davies, *Odd Fellowship; its history, constitution, principles and finances'*(Richard Sutton Cheek, 1858).

Leonore Davidoff and Catherine Hall, *Family Fortunes: Men and women of the English middle class, 1780-1850* (Hutchinson, 1987).

Michael Gervers (ed.), *The Cartulary of the Knights of Jerusalem in England. Secunda Camera. Essex* (British Academy, 1982).

Anthony Langley, *Hicks Bros., Ltd., An Essex Bus Company* (privately published, 1991).

Beatrice A Lees (ed.) *Records of the Templars in England in the Twelfth Century* (British Academy, 1935).

Philip Morant, *The History and Antiquities of the County of Essex,* volume ii, (1763-8).

J Morris (ed.) *The Troubles of our Catholic forefathers related by Themselves* (Burns and Oates, 1872).

Andrew Phillips, *Steam and the Road to Glory: the Paxman Story* (Harvey Benham Charitable Trust, 2002).

Elinor M C Roper, *Seedtime: the History of Essex Seeds* (Phillimore, 1989).

Bob Walklett, *31 Years of a British Specialist Car Manufacturer Ginetta: the Inside Story* (Bookmarque, 1994).

Unpublished works

Penelope J Corfield (with Mary Clayton and Janet Gyford), 'Reputation and Loss in a Victorian Family: the Pattissons of Witham in 1859', 1997 (ERO T/B 587/9).

Department of the Environment, 'List of Buildings of Special Architectural or Historic Interest: Witham', 1971.

Dorothy L Sayers Historical and Literary Society, 'Talking of Dorothy L Sayers ...' (typescript, 1979).

Janet Gyford
    'Shop People and their Customers: Witham, Essex, 1900-1939' (MA oral history project, 1981).
    'Men of Bad Character: the Witham Fires of the 1820s' (MA dissertation, 1982).
    'Survey of dated buildings and structures in Witham' (1992 – ERO Acc A8888).
    'Witham before 1500' (1996 – ERO T/P 655).

Helen Irons, 'The Idle, the Ignorant and the Positively Hostile: a Study of Outdoor Poor Relief in Witham, Essex, 1820-34' (dissertation, 1995).

Maurice L Smith, typescripts on many subjects (ERO T/P 506).

Shirley Watson, 'Nineteenth Century Witham: the Role of Local Government' (BA dissertation, 1978).

Web sites

Essex Record Office catalogue, http://seax.essexcc.gov.uk

Janet Gyford, http://www.gyford.com/janet includes information about my books including lists of surnames mentioned in them. Also the full text of *Memories of Witham: Shops*, and *Men of Bad Character*, which are out of print.

Phil Gyford, http://www.gyford.com/domesday is an improved version of my *Domesday Witham*, which is out of print.

Ian Hunter, http://www.essexpub.net/Witham/witham.htm has pictures and histories of Witham pubs.

John V Nicholls, http://www.milestonesonline.co.uk specialises in Essex milestones, sign posts and boundary markers.

The National Archives catalogue (formerly Public Record Office) http://www.catalogue.nationalarchives.gov.uk

Many other web sites too numerous to mention were a constant source of information, and also led me to some very inspiring, knowledgeable and helpful people who advised me about obscure but fascinating subjects.

INDEX

Italics indicate people and places from outside Witham.
Bold type indicates that there is a relevant illustration on the page in question.

Abbott family (shoemakers), 152
Abercorn family and Lord Paisley (peers), 30, 40; colour page **7**
Abercrombie, Patrick (town planner), 139
aborigines (Australian), 79–80, **80**
Abrey, Shafto (retired sea-captain), 100, 104
Adams and Mortimer (builders), 144
Adcock, John (blacksmith), **28**
Adnams family (brushworks proprietors and brewers), 66–67, 90
adultery, 23, 25, 73
aeroplanes, airfields and airmen, 63, **95**, 104, **107**, 121, 130, 132, 135, 137, 138, 139, 144, 163. *See also* bombing
Afford, Bernard (stationer and music promoter), 108, 129
Africa, colour page **10**. *See also South Africa*
AFS. *See* Auxiliary Fire Service
Ager children (paupers), 60
Agricultural Customs, Select Committee on, 68
Agricultural Shows. *See* Essex Agricultural Show
Agricultural Society. *See* Witham Agricultural Society
agriculture. *See* farms and farming
airfields and airmen. *See* aeroplanes
Air Raid Precautions (ARP), 131, **132**, 133, 135
air raids. *See* bombing
air raid shelters, 131, 135, **136**, 137, 176
Albert, the (2 Chipping Hill), 15, 140–41, 149
Albert (prince), 141
Albert Memorial, the (London), **59**
Albert Road, 115, 141–43, **143**; colour page **12**. *See also* Fern Cottages (nos.5-8); railway station; Temperance Hotel (no.9)
Aldgate (London), **39**
Aldous, Mary (pauper), 60
Alfred Cottages (3-9 Bridge Street), 182;
colour page **20**
Algore, John (fuller), 21
Allectus Way, 9
Allen, George (police superintendent), 92
Allen, Thomas (schoolmaster), **31**
allotments, 125, 127, 152
All Saints church (now Holy Family and All Saints), 73–75, **74**, 102, **108**, **116**, **175**
Alma Place (Newland Street). *See* Collins Lane
almshouses, 156, 176, 180, **181**
ambulances, 117, 118
America, 25, 42, 77, 79, 83, 138, **158**, 162
Amiens, Peace of (1802), 52
Angel inn (formerly the Greyhound) (39-41 Newland Street), 38, **77**, 167
Anglo-Saxon Chronicle, 10–12, **11**
Anglo-Saxons, 9–14, **11**, 16, **140**, 144, 161; colour page **2**
Angria (pirate), 32
Antonia (ship), **134**
apothecaries, 43
apprentices, 33, 46, 55
Arch, Joseph (farmworkers' union leader), 88, 90
archaeology, 8, 9, 10, 143, **158**, 181
archbishops. See *Canterbury; Westminster*
architects, **59**, 71, 73–74, 83, 104, **112**, 142, 146, **147**, 154, 155, 159, 161, 167, 168, **169**, 176, 178–79, 181, 183
Ardley family (bakers and taxi proprietors), 106, **162**
Ardley's yard (Newland Street), 162
Armiger Way, 170
Armond family (gentry and clothiers), 175
Armond Road, **8**, 145
Army Service Corps Territorials, **155**
ARP. *See* Air Raid Precautions
Arras (France), 108
arson. *See* fires
artists. *See* paintings and painters (art)

Ashby, Harry, 153
assemblies. *See* dancing
astronomy, 79
Asuni, Ghillini Di (musician), 38
asylums, 57, 84, 167
Athaneum club (London), 81
Attlee, Clement (civil servant, politician and Prime Minister), 100
Australia, 56, 58, 79–80, **80**, 81, 88, 125; colour page **9**. *See also Empress of Australia (ship)*
Austria, 131
Auxiliary Fire Service (AFS), 131
Avenue, The, 30, 31, 103, 125, 146, **147**, 170; colour page **7**
Avenue House (4 Newland Street), **31**, 37, 102, 171; colour page **7**
Avenue Lodge (Collingwood Road), 146, **147**
Avenue Road, 86, 88, **147**, 147–48, 170; colour page **16**. *See also* North Corner (no.45); Taber family

Bacon, Denise (landowner), 17
Baddow, Great, 94
Bailey Bridges, 135, 139
Baird, Hugh (maltsters), 142
Baker, Albert C (building developer), 125
bakers, 14, 16, 19, **117**, 130, 156, **157**, 162, 164
Balaam, Florence, nee Saward (trade union organiser and magistrate), 110, 114
Balfour, Betty (suffragist), **101**
Balfour, Mrs (lecturer), 79
Ball, George Mason (farmworkers' union leader), 89, 155
balls. *See* dancing
bands, 66, 102, **103**, 104, **108**, 109, 112, **171**
bankruptcy. *See* debt
banks and banking, 163–64, **166**, 176–77
Bannister, Thomas (signalman), colour page **11**
Baptists, 70, **71**, 77, 90, 167, 170, 182
Barbican, the (London), 142
Barham, Harry (watchmaker and Home Guard officer), 133
Barnardiston, Katherine (Dame), 21, 24, 76, 143, 154; colour page **5**
Barnardiston House (35 Chipping Hill), 37, **54**, 154
Barnfield Place (Newland Street), **161**, 162

barns, **14**, 15, **21**, 27, 55, 70, **151**, 152, 183, 185; colour page **4**
Barry, Charles (architect), **184**
Bartlett, William Henry (artist), colour page **1**
Barwell family (butchers), 84, 174
Barwell family (clothiers and gentry), **26**, 30, 158, 174
basketmaker, 99
Basset, John (woolmonger), 18
Bath (Somerset), 42
Bath field, colour page **6**
baths. *See also* swimming
   for soldiers, 136
   indoor, 34, 102, 123, 179
   outdoor, 30, 35, 145; colour page **6**
Batsfords (100 Newland Street), 45, 115, 180; colour page **17**
Battle of Britain, 135
Bawtree family (bankers and solicitors), 165, 166
Bayles, Thomas (lawyer), 25
Bayonne (France), battle of, 53
Beadel family (farmers and builders), **51**, 88, 167
Beardwell (motor engineer). *See* Hurrell and Beardwell
Beatenberg (14 Chipping Hill), 154
beer, 24, 38, 48, 60, 68, 139, 162
Belgium, 138. *See also Frezenberg; Passchendaele; Waterloo; Ypres*
Bell Field, 102, 143
Bellfield Close, 144
bells, 63, 143, 158, 178
Belsham, Roy, inside front **cover**, **178**
Benares (ship), 135
benchmarks (Ordnance Survey), **39**, 158, 176, 177, 185; colour page **20**
Bengal (India), 100
Benington, Thomas (landowner), 17
Benjamin, Tom (doctor), **132**
Benton Hall farm and manor, 12, 17, 183
Berkeway, William, 17
Berkshire, 67, 159
Best, George (innkeeper), 141
Bethlem asylum (London), 57
Bevington, L F (Captain), 113
Bibles, 20, **24**
Bickmore, John (labourer), 52
bicycles, 65, 96, 100, 118, 172, 180
Billericay, 17

billiards, 168
Bird, William (railway policeman), 62
Birmingham, 53, 58, 100, 163
bishops
 Irish, 35
 of London, 16, 73, 74, 75
 of the Peculiar People, 146
Bishops Stortford, 130
Black Boy. *See* Red Lion (3rd)
Black Death (1348), 17
Blacker Bombard (guns). *See* spigot mortar emplacements and guns
Blackshirts. *See* Fascists
blacksmiths, 14, **28**, 68, 104, 137, **155**, 180
Blackwater, the (river), 8, 128. *See also* Blue Mills
Blitz, the, 135
Blood family (solicitors), **67**, 172
Bloomfield, Amy (Co-op committee member and tanner's wife), 99
Blue Mills (formerly Machins), and Blue Mills Hill, 68, 139, 183
Blue Posts inn (126-28 Newland Street), **41**, 42, 52, 54, 67, 180
Blunts Hall Drive. *See* Blunts Hall farm and manor
Blunts Hall farm and manor (Blunts Hall Drive), 12, 16, 17, 84, 97, **105**, 183
Blunts Hall Road, **69**. *See also* Cuppers (no.19)
Blyth family (millers), 96, **183**
Board of Health. *See* Witham Local Board of Health
Board Schools. *See* Chipping Hill (Board) School (Church Street)(opened 1902); Maldon Road School (1837-1966)
boars. *See* pigs
Bocking, 100, 130
Boer War, 65, 172
Bolivian, 120
Bombay (India), 32
bombing and air raids, 132, 133, 135–36, **136**, 137, **138**, 142, 144, 184
Bond Street (London), 99
bonfires and Guy Fawkes night, **72**, 75, 108, 139
bookmaker, 171
books, **24**, 34, 35, 37, 68, 79, 80, 127, 137, 166, 168, 183. *See also* libraries
bootmakers. *See* shoemakers
Boreham, 37

Boulogne (France), Count Eustace of, 14
bowls, 96
Boy Scouts, 122
Bragg, Stanley (architect), 155
Brain, the (river), **8**, 16, 18, 21, 30, 34, 65, 84, 85, 144–45, 152, 161; colour page **1**. *See also* Chipping bridge; Chipping Mill; Moat Farm bridge; Newland bridge; Newland Mill; Sauls bridge
Braintree, 110, 130, 136, 141, 154
 railway to, 63, 65, 142; colour page 11
 road to, 154
 Union and workhouse, 61, 100, 114
Braintree District Council, 154` farm; Crittall family; Employment Exchange
Bramston, Clarissa (vicar's wife), **73**, 75
Bramston, John (vicar), **73**, 73–75, 76, 154
Bramston, Mary Ann, 154
Bramston Green, 139; colour page **6**
Bramstons (16 Chipping Hill), 154
Bramston Secondary School (Spinks Lane) (opened 1937), 130, 131
Bramston Sports Centre (Bridge Street), 121, 181
Branwhite, Bloss (pauper), 57–58
Braxted, Great and Little
 Braxted Lodge, 29
 Braxted Park, 96
Brazil, 110
bread, 19, 26, 50, 51, 68, 76, 143. *See also* bakers
Brentwood, **54**, 62, 123
Bretnall family (millers and gentlemen), 50, 58, 64, 81, 152
breweries and brewing, 28, 67, **157**
Brewster, Gladys (baker's driver), 106
bricklayers, **46**, 164, 174
brickmakers and brick kilns, 46, 74, 85, 87, 141, 154, 181
bricks, **21**, 27, 30, **31**, 35, 44–46, **45**, **46**, 60, 85, 86, 141, 144, 152, 156, 157, 167, 168, 170, 171–72, 174–75, 177–78; colour pages **17**, **18**, **19**
 moulded, 87, 142, 154, 173, 174, 180; colour page 17
Brictmar, 13
Bridge, Frank (musician and composer), 93
Bridge Home / Hospital (Hatfield Road), **39**, 58–60, **59**, 61, 106, 181. *See also* workhouse (Witham Union)

INDEX

Bridge House (28 Bridge Street), 181
Bridge House (55A Chipping Hill), 152
bridges, 62, 63, 120, 135, 152, 161, 167, 183, 184. *See also* Catholic bridge; Chipping Hill bridge; Moat Farm bridge; Newland bridge; Sauls bridge
Bridge Street (formerly Duck End), 16, **22**, 96, 180–81, **181**, 182. *See also* Alfred Cottages; (nos.3-9); Bramston Sports Centre; Bridge House (no.28); Croft House (no.10); Elmy's yard; Faragon Terrace (nos.59-67); George and Dragon (no.29); Morning Star (no.13); RAFA Club
Bright, Ellen (later Mrs Derrett), 129
Bright family (solicitors), 114, 164
British Broadcasting Corporation (BBC), 115
British Gas Company, 97
British Legion, 113, 170
British Oxygen Company, 111, 135
British Resistance Organisation, **133**
British Restaurants (67 Newland Street and 22 Church Street), 136–37, 139, 155, 165
British School. *See* Maldon Road School (1837-1967)
Britten, Benjamin (composer), 93
Broad Mead, 170
broccoli, 30
Brockes family (blacksmiths), 104
Brookcote (29 Chipping Hill), 154
Broomfield, 121
Brotherhood, the, 96, 113
Brown, Arthur Ralph (coachmaker and motor engineer), **95**, 96, 163
Brown, James (brickmaker, of Moulsham), 87, 154; colour page **17**
Brown, Jeremiah (innkeeper), 42
Brown, John (architect, of Norwich), 74, 75
Brown, John (houseowner), 17
Brunel, Isambard Kingdom (engineer), 81, **184**
brushmakers and brushmaking, 77, 78, 164–65. *See also* Thomasin family
brush yard (also known as Newland Place, Newland Street), 66, 164–65
Buckingham, Duke of, 34
Buckinghamshire, 34
Buckley, Irene (nurse), **126**
buffalo. *See* cattle
Buffalo Row. *See* Elmy's yard
building and builders, 16, 17, **21**, **22**, 27, 44–46, **45**, 73–75, 85–88, **87**, 110–12, **112**, 121–25, 137, 138–39, 141, 144, 156
Building Society. *See* Witham Building Society
bulls. *See* cattle
Bunny, Robert (innkeeper), 23
Burchard, Elizabeth, 32
burh. *See* earthworks
burials, tombstones and memorials, 26, **27**, 33, 48, 50, 73, 75, 84, 145, 156, 157–59, 179; colour pages **5, 20**. *See also* funerals
Burma, 138
Burmby, Arthur (roadsweeper and bombing victim), 135, 184
Burnett, Reverend and Mrs (nonconformist minister and teacher), 36
Burton family, 146
Bury St Edmunds (Suffolk), 33
buses and charabancs, 62, 64, 109, 112, 117, 118, 120, 129, 131, 144, **171**
Busshegge family (common scolds and eavesdroppers), 19
Butcher, Peggy (photographer), **129**
butchers, **15**, 18, 19, 28, 50, 84, 130, 144, **148**, 155, 167, 174, 178
Butler, Lilly (vicar), 34
Butler, Thomas (grocer and draper), **72**, 78
butter, 68
Byfords (furniture and gifts), 179
by-pass, **119**, 120, 121, 164, 182

Cabin, the (Collingwood Road), **149**
cabinet maker, 42
cafés and restaurants, 37, 40, 112, 121, **128**, 136–37, 139, 155, 164, 165, **171**, 180
cage, the, 180
Calcraft, Sarah, 60
Calcraft, William (public executioner), 60
Caldow, John (teacher and clergyman), 36
Cambridge Villa (also known as Poplar Hall, Hatfield Road), 181
Campion, George B (artist), colour page **7**
Canada and Canadians, 35, 79, **82**, 83, **134**, 134–35, 138, **157**, 162
candles, 35, 48, 116, 156, 163
Canterbury (Kent), Archbishops of, 25, 33; colour page **6**
Cape of Good Hope (South Africa), 32
Capital and Counties Bank, 163
Capon, Arthur (coal carter), **115**
'Captain Swing', 56

carding. *See* wool carding
carnivals, **129**
Carpenter's Arms (previously the Fleece, 141 Newland Street), 162
carpenters, 19, 46, 171. *See also* cabinet and chairmaker
carriers and carts, 17, **18**, 39, 50, 52, 59, 62, 65, 97, 100, 103, 106, 115, 118, 141, **142**, 144, 178
cars. *See* motor vehicles
Carter, Martin (gentleman and lawyer), 37
Case, Charles (nonconformist minister and teacher), 35
Castle, John, 59
Catholic bridge, **120**
Catholics and Catholicism, 20, 21, 23, 24, 25, 27, 30, 37, 51, 75–76, 152, 170, 175; colour page **5**
cattle, 25, 39, 96, 106, 136, 144, 145, **148**, **161**, 169, 181
cattle market (1st, Kings Chase), 39, 163
cattle market (2nd, Collingwood Road), **148**, **149**
celery, **67**
cellars, 163
cemetery, 127, 151
censuses, 60, **67**, 71, 73, 78, 98
Central Buildings (39-41 Newland Street), **167**
Chalk, John (property owner), **86**
Chalk family (bellringers), 158
Chalks Road, **86**, 94, 156
Chamberlin, Powell and Bon (architects), 141–42
Chamber of Commerce, 125
Chancellor family (architects), 146, 167
chantries, 13, 152, 157, 183
Chantry Wood, 13, 58, 183
Chaplin, Ted (shop assistant), **165**
Chaplin family (soldiers and hospital helper), 108, **109**
Chapman and Andre (mapmakers), 29
Chappelow, Grace (suffragette, of Hatfield Peverel), **101**
chariots. *See* coaches
charity and charities, 26, 33, 34, 35, 76, 100, 102, 154, 158
Charity Row (24-40 Church Street), 60, **99**, 156. *See also* workhouse (Witham parish)
charity shop, 100
Charles I (king), 25
Charles II (king), 25

Charlotte (queen), **40**
Chartists and Chartism, 70, 77–78, 83
charwomen. *See* washerwomen and washing
chauffeurs, 96, 117
Chauntry Villas (47-49 Chipping Hill), 152
Cheek, Richard Sutton (newspaper proprietor and printer), **177**
cheese, 68
Chelmsford, **41**, 46, 48, 55, **56**, 57, 64, **73**, 78, 87, 97, 110, 115, 128, 135, 136, 146, 162, 167, 176. *See also Moulsham*
chemists, 165, 174
chess, **19**
Chess Lane, 170; colour page **15**
Chignell children (paupers), 60
children, 23, 30, 35, 37, 40, 46, 48, 57, 60, **61**, 68, 75, 76, 81, 84, **89**, 98, 101, 102, **103**, 125, 131, 132, **134**, 135, 136, 137, 138, 154, **164**, 181. *See also* schools
China, 81, 110
Chippendale (furniture maker), 168
Chipperfield, Thomas (yeoman), colour page **4**
Chipping Dell, colour page **6**
Chipping Hill, front **cover** and **reverse** thereof, 10, 12, **13**, 14, 16, 18, 27, **28**, 43, 63, 66, 73, 84, 85, 92, 104, 148, **150**, 152–54, **153**, 170; colour pages **2**, **20**. *See also* the Albert (no.2); Barnardiston House (no.35); Beatenberg (no.14); Bramstons (no.16); Bridge House (no.55A); Brookcote (no.29); Chauntry Villas (nos.47-49); Druggles and Struggles (no.28); the forge (no.18); the Grange (no.4); Kings Head inn (nos.20-22); Oaklands (no.37); post office (no.45); Recess (no.14); Vicarage (Old)
Chipping Hill (Board) School (Church Street) (opened 1902), 104, 156
Chipping Hill bridge, **46**, 152; colour page **18**
Chipping Hill Terrace (100-134 Church Street), **86**
Chipping Mill (1 Powershall End), 18, 152
Choat, Des (cartoonist), **7**
cholera, 83
Christmas, 60, 64, 103, 113, 132, **148**
Christmas House (96-98 Newland Street), 180
Church, James (gas works manager and Methodist), 70
church, parish (St Nicholas/Nicolas), front **cover** and **reverse** thereof, **13**, 16, 17, 20,

23–25, **24**, **27**, 33, 40, 51, **73**, 74, 76, 84, 94, 100, 124, 129, 132, **153**, 156–59, **159**, 176; colour pages **1, 2, 5, 17**
churches and chapels, 13, 104, 141; colour page **1**. *See also* All Saints church; Baptists; bells; the Brotherhood; Catholics; church, parish; Congregational church; Evangelicals and Peculiars; manorial chapel, Methodists; minster church; Quakers
Church chest, 158
Church House (Collingwood Road), 114, 146, **148**
Church Schools. *See* National (Church) Schools
Church Street (formerly Hog End), 12, 20, 26, **54**, 68, 70, 71, 85, **89**, 99, 104, **107**, 124, 131, **134**, 135, 139, 154–56; colour pages **2, 19**. *See also* British Restaurants (no.22); Charity Row (nos.24-40); Chipping Hill (Board) School (opened 1902); Chipping Hill Terrace (nos.100-134); Greene's almshouses (nos.50-52); National (Church) School (Church Street) (1866-1900); post office (no.9); Totscott (no.11); White Horse (no.2); Woolpack inn (no.7); workhouse (Witham parish) (nos.24-40)
Churchill, Winston (politician and Prime Minister), 121, 170
churchwardens, 23, **24**, 25, **27**, 32, 34, 48, **49**, 158
cider vault (123 Newland Street), 42, **43**, 163
cinema, 127, 129, 138, **161**, 172
circuses, 61, 118. *See also* fairs; menagerie
civil servants, 98, 100, 123, 124, 137
Civil War, the, 25–27
clairvoyant, 154
Clark, Charles (publisher and poet), 63, **72**
Clarks Shoes, 152
Claudius (Roman emperor), 9
Cleland, John (sea captain) and Mary Amelia, 32
clock, town (1st, at 68 Newland Street), 175
clock, town (2nd, on the 2nd Constitutional Club between 88 and 90 Newland Street), 94, **166**, 179
clock, town (3rd, at 61 Newland Street), **166**
Clock House (68 Newland Street), 175
clockmakers, 42, 79, 164; colour page **6**
clothiers, 22, 23, **26**, 27, 30, 32, 45, 46–47, 169

cloth industry, 18, 21–23, **26**, 27, 46–47, 48, 50, 145, 156, **157**, 163, 172, 174, 175
clothing, 19, 28, 41, 43, 47, 48, 60, 64, 76, 132
Clothing Club, 76
clubs. *See* societies and clubs
coaches and coachmakers, 7, 31, 34, 39, 40, **41**, 42, 62, 63, **64**, 74, 80, **95**, 96, 163, 167, 168, 180; colour page **7**
Coach House Way, 174
coal and coke, 35, 47, 50, 60, 65, 76, **115**, 116, 117, 141, 177; colour page **16**
coal yard, 141
Coates (electrical shop), 180
cock fighting, 38, 168
Cocks farm (Braintree Road), 15
Coe, Sarah (laundress), 98
coffee, 37, 40, **171**
Coggeshall, 59
Coke-oven field, 47
Colchester, 9, 10, 21, 22, 25, 26, 33, **40**, 46, 62, 121, 153, 172, 182; colour page **16**
Colchester Road, **39**, 75, 130, 185
Coldstream Guards, 53
Collier, John (of Sussex), 46
Colling, James Kellaway, (illustrator), **74**
Collingwood, Admiral Lord, 172
Collingwood House (15 Collingwood Road), 173; colour page **17**
Collingwood Road, **85**, 99, **103**, 116, 130, 135, 145–49, **149**, 164, 172–73. *See also* Avenue Lodge; the Cabin; cattle market (2nd); Church House; Collingwood House (no.15); Constitutional Club (3rd); Jubilee Oak; Millfield Terrace (nos.57-67); National (Church) School (1813-1842); Nurses' Bungalow (no.46); Pelican Cottage (no.16); Public Hall; Warwick House (no.48); YMCA hut
Collins, Edmund (builder), 35, **49**, 168
Collins Lane (also known as Hubbards Lane, Alma Place or Cutts Yard), 27, 62, 77, 168
Colne House (19 Guithavon Street), 176
combing. *See* woolcombing
Commons, House of. See Parliament
Communist party, 114
Community Centre. *See* Spring Lodge
concerts, 38, 93, 104, 112, 129
Coney, William (blind man), 57
Congregational church (now United Reformed), 27, 32, 36, 47, 50, 59, 66, **71**,

71–72, **72, 73**, 76, 78, 88, 90, 100, 109, 171, 178–79; colour page **20**
Conservative Party, 97, 100, 101
Constable, John (painter), 80
Constitutional Club (1st) (101 Newland Street), 163
Constitutional Club (2nd) (between 88 and 90 Newland Street), 94, 173, 179
Constitutional Club (3rd) (Collingwood Road), 173
Cook, Captain James, 168
Cook, James (farmworker, hanged in 1829), 55, **56**; colour page **9**
Cook, Rebecca (innkeeper), 168
Cooper, Mrs, 73
Cooper, Selina (suffragist), 101
Co-operative Society. *See* Witham Co-operative Society
Cooper's (drapers and haberdashery), 178
coopers, 31, 177
Cooper Taber. *See* Taber family
Coote family (upholsterers, furniture makers and auctioneers), **54**, 144, 155
Copford, 74
coppersmith, 178
Corner House (64 Newland Street), 174
corsets, 117
Cottis, Charles (herbalist), 43
Council housing. *See under* houses
Council School. *See* Maldon Road School (1837-1966)
Councils. *See* Braintree District Council; Essex County Council; Witham Town Council; Witham Urban District Council
Country Life (magazine), colour page **4**
courts of law, 14, 15, 18, 42, 55–56
courtyards. *See* yards
cows. *See* cattle
Cressing and Cressing Temple, front **cover** and **reverse** thereof, 12, **14**, 17, 21, 185
Cressing Road, 94, 97, 114, 121–24, **123**, 135, 183–84; colour page **14**. *See also* Templars estate
Cresy, Edward (architect and public health investigator), 83–84
cricket, 38, 79–80, **80**
crime, 18–19, **19**, 23, 30, 35, 39, 41, 48, 50, 55–56, **56**, 57–58, **159**, 180
Crispe, Nicholas (porcelain maker), **169**
Crispe, Thomas (gentleman), **169**

Crittall family (window manufacturers), 7, 110–14, **111, 112,** 123, 127–29, **131**, 133, 135-37, **136,** 139, 141, 142, 146, 154, 167, 183–85, **185**; colour pages **13, 16**
Crittall Road, 185
Crocker, Lieut.Col. H E (Blackshirt speaker), **131**
crocodile, 67
Croft House (10 Bridge Street), 181
Cromer (Norfolk), 94, 141, **149**
Crompton's (electrical engineers of Chelmsford), 97
Cromwell, Oliver (Protector), 25
Crook, Harry (Clerk of Witham Urban District Council), 132
Cross Road, **123**, 123–24, 127
Crotchet inn (130 Newland Street), 180
Crouch, the (river), 68
Crown, the (Guithavon Street), 97, 176
Croxall family (gas manager etc.), **115, 119**
Crump family (farmers), 55, 81, **145**, 146
Crusaders, 14
Crystal Palace (London), 79
Cubitt, William (engineer), **184**
Cullen family (seedsmen and motor engineers), 88, 97, **132, 143,** 144, 163
Cundy, Frank (manager of Employment Exchange), 141
Cuppers farm (19 Blunts Hall Road), 70, 183
curates, 20, 33, 176
curriers. *See* tanning and leather-making
Cutmore, Miss B, **164**
Cut Throat Lane, **116**, 142
Cutts Yard (Newland Street). *See* Collins Lane
Cuxhaven (Germany), 40
cycles. *See* bicycles

Dace family (musicians), 52, **73**, 156
Danbury, 103
dancing and balls, 23, 36, 37, 38, 79, 104, 129, 137, 138, **171**
Daniel, James (lawyer and poet), **72**
Darby, John (elder and younger, clothiers), 46
Darby, Mary (milliner), 43
Davey and Paxman (ironfounders and engineers), 172, 176, **182**; colour page **16**
Davies, Samuel T (writer and photographer), 75, 76, 79
Dazley family, 104
D-Day (1944), 138
Dean, J (of Putney, maker of shop awnings and

blinds), 162; colour page **16**
Dean family (builders and diarist), 104, **107**, 144, 154
debt and bankruptcy, 19, 30, 34, 35, 80–81
Defoe, Daniel (writer), **29**, 30; colour page **7**
demonstrations. *See* meetings
Denholm, Jim (doctor), **132**
Denholm Court (Maltings Lane), 184
Denmark and the Danes, 10, **11**
dentists, 112, 174
Depression, Great (1930s), 113–14, 125, 130
Derrett, Hugh and Ellen, 129
Devon, 97
Dibben, William (hairdresser), 104
Dickens, Charles (writer), 73
Dickson, Norman (seedsman), **132**
dinners and lunches, 35, 38, 40, 62, 66, 70, 75, **80**, 137
disease. *See* health and disease
disorder. *See* riots
dissenters. *See* nonconformists
Dissolution of religious houses, 20–21
District Visitors, 76
Dixon, Henry (doctor), **44**, 60, 62, 65, 75, 80, 163
doctors, surgeons and physicians, 33, 35, 37, 43–44, 50, 84, 96, 106, 112, **162**, 162–63
dogs, 23, 41, **98**, 104, 163
Domesday survey (1086), 13–14, 145, 170, 183
donkey, **122**
Doole, Josiah (railway porter), 94
'Dorothy Sayers Cottages' (22-26 Newland Street), 172, colour page **16**
Doubleday, John (sculptor), 168
Douglas family (gentry and soldiers), 32
dovecotes, 15, 17
Downes, Andrew (vicar) and family, 35, **51**, 157–58
Dragoons, 32, 53
drains and sewers, **58**, 68, 83–85, **85**, 102, **145**, 152, 154, 165
Drake family (wine merchants), **174**
Draper, Mrs ('indifferent' singer), 38
drapers, 16, 28, 32, 78, 146, 163
dressmakers and milliners, 43, 99, 146
Driberg, Tom (MP), 139
drills and drillmaking. *See* seed drills
drinking and drunkenness, 23, 24, 25, 26, 54, 61, 129

Driver, Charlie (soldier and singer), 108
drovers, 162
Druggles and Struggles (28 Chipping Hill), 153
Drury Lane (London), 38
Du Cane family (clergymen and gentry), 75, 81, 171
Dudley, Hannah (pauper), 60
Duke of York (ship), **134**
Dunkirk (France), 133
Dunn, James (teacher), **36**
Durham, 33
dying and dyers, 16, 18

earthquake, **134**
earthworks and the burh, 8–10, **8**, **9**, 10, 12, 15, 17, 62, 86, **140**, 140–49, **143**, 183; colour page **1**
East Anglian Electric Supply Company, **116**, 168
Eastern Counties Railway Company, 62–64, **64**
East family (motor engineers etc.), **129**
East family (tithe owners), 159
East India Company, 32
Easton Road, 148
Ebenezer Close, 122; colour page **6**
Eckersley, Peter (radio engineer and broadcaster), 115, 180
Eden, Anthony (politician), **131**
Edinburgh (Scotland), 33
Edmonton, 131
Edward the Elder (king), 10, **11**, 12
Edward VII (king), **93**
Edwardian Witham, 92–102, **140**, 148
eels, 18, 152
Egar, John (soldier), 53
Egypt, 138
elderly, the, 35, 48, 53, 59, 60
elections and the franchise, 77, 78, 89, 97, 99, **101**, 113–14, 139, 178
electrical engineers, 97
electricity, 97, **116**, 116–17, 127, 144, 146, 168, 170, 176
elephant, 118
Elicia, Madam, 154
Elizabeth II (queen), inside front **cover**, 146, **178**
Elm Hall farm, 10, 135

Elmy family (brickmakers, plumbers etc.), 74, 85, 181
Elmy's yard, Bridge Street (also known as Buffalo Row), 181
emigration, 77, 81, 88
Emmens, Peter, 24
Employment Exchange (1A Braintree Road), 141
Empress of Australia (ship), **134**
engineers, 149, 172, **184**. *See also Brunel;* electrical engineers; motor engineers; radio engineers; water engineer
Essex Agricultural Show, 70, 94, 127
Essex County Council, 100, 121, 154, 172, 183
Essex Fruit Packers, 130
Essex Regiment, 102
Essex Yeomanry, 104, **107**
Eustace of Boulogne, Count, 14
evacuees, 131–35, **134**,138, 139, 154
Evangelicals and Peculiars, 71–72, 88, 106, 129, 146, 176, **183**
Exhibition, Great (1851), 79, **184**
exports, 21, 22, 23, 47, 68, 88

fairs, 16, 61, 79, 91–92, **92**, **129**, 153, 174. *See also* circuses; menagerie
Faragon Terrace (59-67 Bridge Street), **182**
farmers, 30, 47–48, 50, 52, 55, 56, 57, 68, 70, 78, 81, **87**, 88–89, 106, 116, 122, **145**, 152. *See also* yeomen
farms and farming, 17, **18**, 28, 34, 47–48, 60, **61**, 68–70, **69**, 86, 89, 94, 106, 116, 117, 127, 141, 144, 145, 169, 183
farmworkers, 50, 51, 55–57, **56**, 66, 68–71, **69**, 78, 88–89, **89**, 109, 113, 127, 155, 156; colour page **19**
Farrow, Thomas (brush worker), 66
Fascists, **131**
Faucelon, Alice (houseowner), 17
Faulkbourne, 13, 151, **158**
 Faulkbourne Hall, 29, 94
Fenton, James (architect), **71**, 178–79
Fern Cottages (nos.5-8 Albert Road), 142
fertilisers, 28, 48, 65, 68
fire engines and firemen, 55, 56, 94, 118, 131, 137–38, 176
fires, 32, 55–56, 94, 117, 152, 169, 170, 182; colour page **9**. *See also* bonfires

fire station (1st) (corner of Newland Street and Avenue Road), 170
fire station (2nd) (corner of Guithavon Street and Mill Lane), 176
fire station (3rd) (Newland Street behind the Swan), 162
firewood, 141, 156
Fish, Charles (shoemaker), 77
fish and fishing, 18, 39, 68, 126, 137. *See also* eels
Fisher family (farmworkers and servants), **99**
fishmongers and fish and chip shops, 18, 19, 180
Fleece, the. *See* Carpenter's Arms
Fleet prison, London, 25
Fleming family. *See* Sayers, Dorothy L
fletchers, 19
Fleuty family (wheelwrights), **181**
floods, 18
food, 48–52, 60, 61, **92**, 104, 106, 114, 121, 131. *See also* cafés and restaurants; coffee; dinners and lunches; tea
football, 112, 113, 127
foot scrapers, 162, **166**, 171; colour page **16**
ford, 144
Foreign Office (London), 98
forge (18 Chipping Hill), front **cover** and **reverse** thereof, 28, 154, **155**; colour page **2**
forge (130 Newland Street), 104, 180
forgery, **28**
Fox, George (Quaker), 26
France and the French, 13, 32, 36, 42, 53, 106, 138; colour page **10**. See also *Amiens; Arras; Boulogne; French Revolution; Loos; Napoleonic Wars; the Somme;* World War, the First; World War, the Second
franchise. *See* elections and the franchise
Franks, Richard (innkeeper), 42
Freeborne, John (clothier), **26**, 169
Freebournes farm (3 Newland Street), **26**, 55, 70, 116, 118, **145**, 168–69
Freeland House (20 Maldon Road), 167
French Revolution, 33, 51
Frer, John (poacher), **19**
Frezenberg (Belgium), **107**
Friendly Societies, 76–77, **77**
Friends, Society of. *See* Quakers
Fryatt, Abraham (trade union secretary), **89**
Fuller, Frederick (butcher) and Stella, 144, **148**
fulling and fullers, 18, 21

funerals, 25, 66, **87**, 102, **108**, 158, 159. *See also* burials
furniture, 15, 32, 34, 42, 80, 110, 117, 155, 168, colour page **4**
Fyzabad (India), 83; colour page **9**

Gables, the (125 Newland Street), **44**, 163
gadding to church, 24
Gallipoli (Italy), 106
gallows, 170
Gallowscroft, 170
Galpin, Canon Francis (vicar and collector of musical instruments), 110, **158**
games and sport, **19**, 23, 37, 38, **92**, 96, 104, 152, 168, 180. *See also* Bramston Sports Centre; cricket; football; swimming
'Gap', the (later Cross Road), **123**
garages. *See* motor engineers
gardens and gardening, 30, 33–35, **34**, 38, 94, 158, 163, 166, 170, 171, 180; colour page **6**
Garrard family (clothiers and yeomen), 22, 24
Garrett family (postmasters and postmistress), 65
gas and gasworks, 66, 70, 97, 99, 110, **115**, 115–17, **119**, 144, **175**, 176, 181; colour page **14**
gas masks and anti-gas training, 130, 131, 132
Gaymer family (farmers, carpenters etc.), **132**, 180
geese, **18**
gentry and ladies, 28–33, **29**, 35, **36**, 40, 42, 43, 48, 55, **67**, 76, 79, **80**, 100, 106
Geoffrey de Mandeville (baron), 13
George III (king), 40
George IV (king), **54**, 55. *See also Prince Regent*
George V (king), 81, 94
George VI (king), 153, 168
George and Dragon (29 Bridge Street), 182
George inn (1st, pre-1800, part now the Town Hall, 61 Newland Street), front **cover** and **reverse** thereof, 15, 23, 38, 41, 42, **166**, 172; colour page **17**
George inn (2nd, since c. 1800, 36 Newland Street), 172, **173**
Georgian Witham, 28–58, **161**
Georgic (ship), **134**
Germany and the Germans, 28, 40, 104, 106, 131, 154, 159, 170. See also World; War, the First; World War, the Second

Gernon, Robert *(baron)*, 13
ghosts, **151**, 156, 158, 168
Gilbert's (bakers), 164
Gimson family (doctors and nurses), **44**, 84, 106, 124, 163
Gimson's yard (Newland Street), 163
Ginetta (motor engineers), 162
Girling's (electrical engineers of Maldon), 97
Gladstone, W B, 96
glaziers. *See* windows
Glebe Crescent, 124, colour page **6**
Globe inn (132 Newland Street), 180
Glover family (motor engineers), 96, 117, 162, 170, **173**
gloves. *See* Pinkham family
Goldings, 17
Goodey, James (water engineer), 103–4
Gospel Standard Baptists. *See* Baptists
Grace, W G (cricketer), 80
graffiti, **149**, 173
granaries, 15
Grange, the (4 Chipping Hill), 141
Grant, Thomas (mathematician), 31
gravel, 8, 34, 39, 143, 156
Gray family (maltsters), 88
Great Eastern (ship), 81
Great field, colour page **6**
Great Torrington (Devon), 97
Green, William (farmer), 55
Green Belt, the, 139
Green family (chemists and dentist), 174
Greene, Jerome, 25
Greene, John (blacksmith), **28**
Greene's almshouses (50-52 Church Street), 156
greengrocers, 97
Greenwich, 81
Greyhound inn. *See* the Angel
Griffiths, R, **164**
Griggs, Alfred (bombing victim), 136
grocers, 32, 78, 156, 163
Grove, the (Newland Street), **26**, 29–30, **40**, 45, 98, 109, 145–47, **147**, 169–70, 171, 174; colour pages **7, 17**
Grove Cottages (Newland Street), 170
Grove Hall. *See* Rowley's Hall
Grove shopping centre, 168
Grove Terrace (6-12 Newland Street), 171
Guardians of the Poor, 59–61, 78, 100–101
Guithavon Road, 121

Guithavon Street, **74**, **175**, 175–77, 179, 180; colour pages **16**, **20**. *See also* All Saints church; Colne House (no.19); the Crown; fire station (2nd); Mill Vale Lodge; National (Church) Schools (1842-1967); Paradise Row; Podsbrook; police station (1st); Rex Mott Court; Woodhams (no.16)
Guithavon Valley, **124**, 146. *See also* Jubilee Oak; Millfield Terrace (nos.2-8); Newland Mill; the Watering
guns, 23, 26, 103, 110, 137, 144, 170; colour page **15**. *See also* shooting
Guys (mechanical engineers), 149
gypsies, 92

Hacker, John (preacher), 20
Hadfield, Mildred (fire watching organiser), 137–38
Haggard, Rider (writer), 68–69, **69**, 89
hairdressers, 79, 90, 104, 112
Hairpowder Tax, 30
Hales, Robert (King's treasurer), 17
Half Acres (also known as Newland), 16
Halstead, 130
Ham Baker (ironworks), 163; colour page **16**
Hamburg (Germany), 28, 40, 159
Hampstead (London), 81, 183
hanging, 55–56, **56**.. *See also* gallows
Hannar, Peter and Susan (drillyard manager and Methodists), 68, 70
hardware shops. *See* ironmongers
Harlee, William (innkeeper), 180
Harridge family (wine merchants), **36**
Harrington, Robert (clockmaker), 79
Harris, John, 26
harvest, 17, **18**, 34, 51, 60
Harvey, Daniel Whittle (politician and journalist), **45**, 164
Harvey, Edward and Amelia (property owners), 172
Harvey family (gentry), 158
Harwich, 39, 40, 42, 46, 61, 167
Haste, Mrs (manager of British Restaurants), 137
Hatfield Peverel, 57, 70, 72, **101**, 103, 137
  Hatfield Priory, 29, 31
Hatfield Road, 9, **39**, 98, 120, **181**, 181–82. *See also* Bridge Home; Cambridge Villa; Ivy Chimneys; Poplar Hall; Witham Lodge;

workhouse (Witham Union)
hats, 19, 24. *See also* dressmakers and milliners
hawkers, 43, 162
Hawkes, David (VC, soldier), **82**, **83**, 82-83; colour page **9**
Hawkes family (farmworkers), **82**, 82–83
Hayes, George (Crittall's worker), 113
health and disease, 17, 32, 35, 37, 50, 51, 53, 57, **58**, 60, 66, 76, 83–85, 90, 101–2, **124**, 124–25, 145, 163, 165, 168, 174, 185. *See also* doctors; hospitals; the Spa
Heatherley, John (surgeon), 43
Heddle family (drapers and Peculiars), 146; colour page **19**
helmets, 137, 158, **159**
Henderson, Tom (planning consultant), 130
Henry I (king), 10
Henry VI (king), 18
Henson, William (inventor of 'aerial carriage'), 63
herbalist, 43
Herde, John (butcher), **15**
Heritage Centre, 166
Hertford, Lord, 42
Hertfordshire, 14, 121
Hess, Myra (pianist), 129
Hetch, Peter (cider and winemaker), 42, **43**
Hicks (bus company), 118
Highfields Road, 130, 136, **138**
High House (5 Newland Street), 46, 168, **169**; colour page **7**
High Street. *See* Newland Street
Highway Bookshop (118 Newland Street), 180
highwaymen, 40
Hill Lane. *See* White Horse Lane
Hills, Joseph, 57
Hills, Thomas, tailor and preacher, 20
hippopotami, 96
Hodges, Mr and Mrs, 136, **138**
Hogben, John (hairdresser and councillor), 90
Hog End. *See* Church Street
Holt, Hester, 146
Holts (butchers), 178
Holy Family and All Saints church. *See* All Saints church
Holyhead (Anglesey), 137
Home and Colonial Stores, colour page **14**
Home field, colour page **6**
Homefield Road, 135
Home Guard (originally Local Defence

INDEX

Volunteers, 23, 133, 137, 176; colour page **15**
homeopathy, 66
Hook family (innkeepers), **157**
Horner, Mr, 127
horse mills, 47
horses, 7, 17, 27, 34, **41**, 41–42, 47, 50, 52, 53, 59, **64**, **67**, 80, 85, 94–96, **95**, 103, 104, 106, **115**, **117**, 118, 166, 167, 180; colour pages **4, 7, 14**
Horsnell, William (farmworker and leader of Peculiars), 71
Horwood House (59 Newland Street), 166
Hospitaller, Knights, 17, 21, 141
hospitals, 32, 100, 106, **109**, 122, 127, **129**. See also Bridge Home; Nurses' Bungalow
House of Correction, 48
houses, 10, 83–85, 84, 113, **124**, 130, **140**, 143, 145, 183. See also slums
 Council housing, 102, 114, 121–25, 123, 139, 143, 183; colour page 14
 new housing, 44–46, 85–88, 86, 102, 110, 112, 114, 121–25, 123, 138–39, 146, 171
Howbridge Hall farm and manor (Howbridge Road), 12, 13, 16, 88, 183, colour page **4**
Howbridge Road, **181**, 182. See also Howbridge Hall farm and manor
Hubbard family (farmworkers, carpenters etc.), 68, 90, **91**, 98, 99
Hubbards Lane (Newland Street). See Collins Lane
Hull (Yorkshire), 36
Humphreys, Samuel (builder and bricklayer), **46**, 164, 174
Hurrell and Beardwell (motor engineers), 144
Hurst, Alan (MP), inside front **cover**, **178**
Hutley family (farmers), 55, 57, 68, **69**, 78, 106, 145
Hutley Memorial Recreation Ground, 145
Hyde Park (London), 79
hydrophonist, 162
Hynd, Agnes (nurse), **126**
hypnotism. See mesmerism

imports, 66, 68, 113
Independents. See Congregational church
India, 32, 81–83, **82**, 100; colour page **9**
Indian Mutiny, 83; colour page **9**
industry, 7, 46–47, 65–68, 70, 88, 109–14, 116, 130, 139, 141–42, 161. See also brushes and brushmaking; cloth industry; Crittall family (window manufacturers); Pinkham family (glove manufacturers); seed drills; seed industry
influenza, 90
Ingatestone, 42
Ingles, David, Canon (vicar) and family, 101, 102
inns and innkeepers, 17, 19, 23, **27**, 27–28, 37, 38, 40, 41–42, 78, **92**, 165, 180. See also *names of inns*
inoculation, 50, 51
invasion, 52, 104, **105**, **131**, 133
Ionides, Basil, 183
Ipswich (Suffolk), 37, 40, 41, **184**, 185
Ireland and the Irish, 23, 30, 32, 34, 35, 51, 137, 162
Iron Age, **8**, 8–10, **140**, **143**; colour page **1**
ironmongers and hardware shops, 114, **165**, 178
ironwork, 66, 141, **147**, **151**,**155**, 156, 162, 167, 170, **184**, 185
 foundry, 166
 railings and gates, 137, 141, 146, 154, 156, 164, 167, 171, 172, 176, 177, 178, 182; colour pages 15, 16
Ishams farm and manor, 12, 13
Italy and the Italians, 99, 138. See also *Gallipoli*
Ivy Chimneys (Hatfield Road), 9, 181, 185; colour page **1**

Jackson, Charles, 73
Jackson, Thomas, **51**
Jackson family (clothiers), 32, 45, 48
James II (king), 153
Japan, 81, **134**, 138
Jews, **131**
John (king), 16
joiners, 86, 141. See also cabinet and chairmaker
Jordan, Police Constable, 121
Jubilee Oak (Collingwood Road and Guithavon Valley), **145**, 146
juries, 55–56
justices of the peace. See magistrates
Juterbog (Germany), 170
Kay-Shuttleworth, Edward (Captain), 97
Keatly, Charles (soldier), 52

Kedington (Suffolk), colour page **5**
Kelvedon, 38, 62, 79, 120; colour page **11**
Kent, 52, 56, 68, 70, 81. *See also* Canterbury
Kenwelmarsh family (gentry), 158
key, **9**
King, Miss Charlotte (heiress), 172
King family (grocers and drapers), 163
Kings Chase, 163, **164**; colour page **16**. *See also* cattle market (1st)
Kings Head inn (20-22 Chipping Hill, formerly New White Horse), 153
Kitchener, Lord, 102
Knight, Charles (doctor), 127, 129
K Shoes, 152
Kuner, Joseph (electrical engineer), 97, 176
Kynaston family (gentry), 30, **51**

Labourers Friend Society. *See* Witham Labourers Friend Society
Labour Party, 100, 110, 111, 121, 139
 Labour Hall (Collingwood Road), **148**, 149
lamplighter, 116
Lancashire, 101. See also *Liverpool; Manchester*
Lancaster, Thomas and Mary Ann (soldier and paupers), 53, 58
Landseer, Edwin (painter), 163
Langford, **133**
Langley (Birmingham), 163
Lapwood family (farmworkers), 68, **69**, 89
Laud, William (archbishop), 25
laundresses. *See* washerwomen and washing
Laurence, Percy (gentleman), 109
law. *See* courts of law
Lawn Chase, 176, 180
Lawn Cottage (94 Newland Street), 179
Lawn House (Lawn Chase), 180
Lawrence (fish and chip shop), 180
Lawrence, Thomas (painter), colour page **8**
Lawson, Cecil P (artist), colour page **9**
lawyers and solicitors, 25, 30, 33, 37, 39, **45**, 55, **72**, 80, 104, 114, 164, 165, 172
LDV (Local Defence Volunteers). *See* Home Guard
Leadenhall market (London), 22
leather. *See* tanning
Leighs, Great, 86
letter-boxes, 148, 170, 173, 176; colour page **16**
Liberal Party, 81, 87, 97–98, **98**, 100; colour

page **12**
libraries, 78, 94, 127–28, 137, 172
Libya, 138
lighting, 66, 97, 116–17, 138. *See also* candles
Lincolns Inn, London, 30
lion, **9**
Lisbon (Portugal), 52–53
Lisle, George (nonconformist minister), 27, 153, 159
Literary Institution. *See* Witham Literary Institution
Liverpool (Lancashire), 62, 135
Lloyd's Bank, 163
Lobb, Theophilus (doctor and nonconformist minister), 35
Local Board of Health. *See* Witham Local Board of Health
Local Defence Volunteers (LDV). *See* Home Guard
lockram, 174
Lockram Lane (also known as Queen Street), 173–74, 175, 176; colour page **20**
lodging houses, 57, 162
Lollards, 20, 153, 155
London, 17, 20, 22, 25, 29–31, 38–43 passim, **39**, 48, 57, **59**, 64, 68, 74, 77, 79, 81, 83, 88, 96, 98, 99, **101**, 102, 115, 126, 130, **131**, 135, 137–139, 142, **147**, 152, 154, 163, 164, 167, 174, 183. *See also under* bishops
 people from, 7, 20, 30, 31, 36, 39, 43, 59, 68, 100, 118, 131, 133, 141, 149, 154, 163, 166, 169, 183
 railway to, 62, 64, 86
 road to, 7, 9, 16, 39–42, 65, 77, 118–21, 119, 167, 182, 185
London House (74-76 Newland Street), 177
Long, widow (pauper), 48
Loos (France), **108**
Luard family (gentry, nurses, etc.), 76, 81, 84, **93**, 94, 98, 100, 106, 113, 162, 180, 185
Lucknow (India), siege of, 83; colour page **9**
lunches. *See* dinners
Lurkin, Matthew, 156
Lytton, Constance (suffragette), **101**

Macdonald, Ramsay (Prime Minister), 111–12
Machins mill. *See* Blue Mills
Mackmurdo, Arthur (architect), 104
Made Lane. *See* Maltings Lane

Mafeking, Relief of (South Africa), 65
magistrates, 25, 30–31, 33, 58, 72, 88, 92, 110, 114, 118–21,**120**
Mahomet Alli Khan (imaginery brigand), 103
mail. *See* post and postmen
Maldon, **11**, 32, 97, 170, **183**
  railway to, 63, 65, 142, 170, 183; colour page 15
Maldon Road, 31, 103, 104, 120, 127, **164**, 167–68, 184. *See also* Freeland House (no.20); Maldon Road School; Masonic Hall; Olivers farm; Park and Recreation ground; Parkside Youth Centre; Quaker meeting house; the Retreat; Sauls bridge; Trafalgar Square
Maldon Road School (also known as the British, Board or Council School) (1837-1967), 72, 90, 100, 184
malting and maltings, 28, 35, **47**, 88, 111, 142, 168, 184, **185**
Maltings Lane (formerly Made Lane), **9**, **47**, 74, 111, 184–85, **185**. *See also* Denholm Court; pest house; Victoria Cottages
Malyon, Charles, bricklayer, **46**
Manchester (Lancashire), 62
manhole covers, 163, colour page **16**
Mann, Harry W (architect), 161
Mann's (school), 180
Manor Road, 183
manorial chapel, 15
manors, 12–16, 17, 18, 21, 39, **140**, 152, 183
maps, **4**, **6**, **12**, **29**, 42, 102, **140**, **150**, **160–61**
Marconi's (radio engineers), 115, 136
markets, 10, 12, **15**, 16, 22, 64, 148–49, 153, 156, 167, 168, **173**, 174; colour pages **2**, **3**. *See also* cattle market
marriages, 32, 33, 40, 53, 66, 81, 129
Mary (Queen), 110
Masonic Hall, Maldon Road, 184
masons. *See* stonemasons
mathematics, 31, 36
Matilda (queen), 14
Matthews family (tanners and leather-makers), 43, 65, 175
Mawdsley family, 114
Mayhew family (surgeons), 43, **44**, 50
meals. *See* food
means test, 114
Mechi, Alderman (farmer), 68
medals. *See* Victoria Cross

medieval Witham, 12–19, **161**, 166; colour page 17
Medina House. *See* Medina Villas
Medina Villas (80-84 Newland Street), 87, 136, 178, **179**
meetings and demonstrations, 10, 52, 55, 62, 77–80 passim, 84, 85, 89, 90, 99, 100, **101**, 102, 109–14 passim, 129, **131**, 144, 175
memorials, 25. *See also* burials; War Memorial
menagerie, 61. *See also* circuses; fairs
Mens family (haulage contractors and librarian), 106
mesmerism, 79
Methodists and Methodism, 70–71, **71**, 176
midwives, 43
mileposts and milestones, **39**, 153, 185
militia, the, 52
milk and dairies, 48, 106, 118, 130, 136, 152, 181
Millbridge Road, 125, **138**
Millfield Terrace (Guithavon Valley and Collingwood Road), **145**, 146
milliners. *See* dressmakers and milliners
Mill Lane, 27, 46, **58**, 65, 85, 108, **119**, 127, 180; colour page **14**
Mill Vale Lodge (Guithavon Street), 176
Mills (bankers), 166
mills and millers, 13, 18, 19, 28, 47, 50, 96, 118, 152. *See also* Blue Mills; Chipping Mill; horse mills; Newland Mill; windmill
ministers (nonconformist), 27, 35, 36, 109, 153, 159, 171
minster church, 10, 12
Moat farm and Moat Farm Chase, 10, 22, 86, 144, 154
Moat Farm bridge, front **cover** and **reverse** thereof, 144
Moffatt, William (architect), **59**, 181
Mondy family (ironmongers), 114, **165**
Moore family (innkeepers, undertakers and carriers), **142**
Moot, the. *See* Moat farm and Moat Farm Chase
moots, 10
Morant, Philip (historian), 30, **34**, 46
Morning Star (13 Bridge Street), 182
Morses (silk factory owners), 57
Mortimer family (builders), 144, 159
Mosley, Oswald (Fascist politician), **131**
Motion family (farmers, gentry and poet), 94

motorcycles, 96, 97, **119**, 181
motor engineers, 88, **95**, 96, 97, 117, 129, 162, 163, 170; colour page **16**. *See also* the East family
motor vehicles, 7, **95**, 96–97, 103, 104, **111**, **117**, 117–21, **119**, **120**, 132, 137, 138, 144, 161, 164, 167; colour page **14**. *See also* buses; motorcycles
Moulsham, 87; colour page **17**
Mount, James (brushmaker), 77
Mountnessing, 62
Munich (Germany), 131
music, 35, 36, 40, 52, 54, 62, **73**, 80, 99, 104, 115, 116, 129, 156, **158**, 180. *See also* bands; concerts; organs; pianos

Napoleonic and French Wars, 47, **51**, 51–53, **53**, 93, 172
National Agricultural Labourers' Union (NALU), 88–89, **89**, 155
National (Church) School (Church Street) (1866-1900), 155
National (Church) School (Collingwood Road) (1813-1842), 148
National (Church) Schools (Guithavon Street) (1842-1967), 60, **61**, **74**, 74–75, 102, 108, 113, 114, 115, **175**
National Glove Company. *See* Pinkham family
National Insurance Act (1911), 100
naturalists, 79, 168
Neath (Wales), 66
Newbury House (2 Newland Street), 171
Newland bridge, 28, 161, 182
Newland Mill (Guithavon Valley), 19, 96, 176, **183**
Newland Place. *See* brush yard
Newlands shopping precinct, 174
Newland Street (also known as High Street), **15**, 15–16, 17–18, 27, 28, **45**, 45–46, 64, 75, 85, **92**, **95**, 96, 116–120 passim, **117**, **119**, **129**, 148, 159, 160–75, **160**, **161**, **173**, **177**, 177–81; colour pages **3**, **7**, **14**, **18**. *See also* the Angel (39-41); Ardley's yard; Avenue House (no.4); Batsfords (no.100); Blue Posts inn (nos.126-128); British Restaurants (no.67); Carpenter's Arms (no.141); Central Buildings (nos.39-41); Christmas House (nos.96-98); cider vault (no.123); Clock House (no.68); Collins Lane; Constitutional Club (1st, no.101, and 2nd, between nos. 88 and 90); Corner House (no.64); Crotchet inn (no.130); fire station (1st and 3rd); the forge (no.130); Freebournes farm (no.3); the Gables (no.125); George inn (no.61 then no.36); Gimson's yard; Globe inn (no.132); the Grove; Grove Cottages; Grove Terrace (nos.6-12); High House (no.5); Highway Bookshop (no.118); Horwood House (no.59); Lawn Cottage (no.94); London House (nos.74-76); Medina Villas (nos.80-84); Newbury House (no.2); Notts yard (nos.102-116); Pelican House (no.113); police station (2nd); post and postmen (nos.68, 85, 84, 5 then 74-76); Roslyn House (no.16); Rowley's Hall; Red Lion inn (no.67, then 68, then 7); Spread Eagle inn (nos.47-51); surgery (no.129); Swan inn (no.153); War memorial; Whitehall (no.18); White Hart inn; Witham Co-operative Society (no.85 then nos.103-115); Witham House (no.57)
New Lights. *See* Evangelicals and Peculiars
Newman, John (vicar), 56, 73
Newmans' (dairy), 181
Newport, Wales, 83
New South Wales (Australia), 56, 58; colour page **9**
newspapers and magazines, **7**, 35, 37, **38**, 41, 42, **45**, 50, 55, **56**, **63**, 75, **80**, 83, **85**, 88, **92**, 96, 101, **112**, 118, **120**, 121, 125, **131**, 164, 177; colour page **4**
Newton, Samuel, 155
New Zealand, 81
Nicholls, Matthew (innkeeper), **27**, 158
Nicholls family (labourers), 85
Nichols (motor engineer), 163
'Nine Tailors, the' (novel), 168
Nobel prize, 79
Noel Pelly House. *See* Collingwood House
nonconformists, 7, 26–27, 70–73, 75, 78, 153, 168, 176. *See also* Baptists; Congregational church; Evangelicals and Peculiars; Methodists; ministers; Quakers
Norfolk and Norwich, 39, 40, 74, 125, 135, 167. *See also Cromer*
Norfolk Island (Pacific), 58
Norman conquest, 13–14
Northamptonshire, 23

INDEX

North Corner (45 Avenue Road), **131**, 146
Norton family (coopers), 177
Norway, 138; colour page **20**
Notley, Black, 127
Nott, Joseph (shopkeeper), 180
Nottingham, 23
Notts yard, Newland Street, 180
Nova Scotia, Canada, 83
nurses and nursing, 84, 100, 106, **126**, 126–27, 146
Nurses' Bungalow (46 Collingwood Road), **126**, 126–27, 146

Oaklands (37 Chipping Hill), 154; colour pages **15, 17**
O'Connor, Fergus (Chartist), 77–78
Oddfellows, **61**, 76
Oliver, John, 24
Olivers farm (Maldon Road), 55, **56**
onions, 68
Ordnance Survey, 162. *See also* benchmarks
organs and organists, 52, **73**, 104, **116**
Orion (ship), **134**
Oronsay (ship), **134**, 135
Orsett, page **10**
Ortlewell's (hardware shop), 165
Osborne, John (tanner), 28
Osborne, June, **129**
overseers of the poor, 26, 27, 32, 48, **49**, 52, 55
Oxbrow, William (telegraph and postal worker), 65
Oxfordshire, 31, **105**

Page, John (landowner), 18
Page, Sammy (second-hand dealer), 128, 178
painting and painters (trade), 42, 68, 144
paintings and painters (art), 80, **86**, 99, 152, 163; colour pages **5, 8, 9, 11**
Paisley, Lord. *See* Abercorn family
Palmer, Edward (baker), **117**
Paradise Row (Guithavon Street), 176
Parion's (caravan sales), 180
Paris (France); colour page **10**
Park, Mr (judge), 56
Park and Recreation ground (Maldon Road), 39, 70, 79, 94, 112, 113, 115, 131, 136, 139, 163, **164**

Parkside Youth Centre (Maldon Road, formerly school), 72, 184
Parliament, 23, 25. *See also* elections and the franchise
Parliament, Members of, inside front **cover**, 97, 110, 111, 125, 139, **178**
Parnell, James (Quaker), 26
Parrish, Fred (signalman), colour page **11**
Partridge, R, **80**
Passchendaele (Belgium), 108
pattens and patten making, 47, 66
Pattisson family (grocers, solicitors etc.), 32–33, 37, 45–46, 47, 58, **72**, 72–73, 74, 80–81, 94, 106, **122**, 159, 163, **166**, 167, 173, 174, 177, 179; colour pages **8, 20**
Pavelin family (farmworkers etc.), 57, 60, 184
Paxman. *See* Davey
Payne, Dr, 168
peace, justices of. *See* magistrates
peas and pea-picking, 60–61, **61**, 88, 118
Peasants' Revolt (1381), 17, **149**
Peasenhall (Suffolk), 68; colour page **10**
Peculiars. *See* Evangelicals
Peirce, Walter, **162**
Pelican Cottage (16 Collingwood Road), **122**
Pelican House (113 Newland Street), 163
pence ladies, 76
Peninsular War, 53
pensions, 25, 52, 100
Perren, Robert (upholsterer), **54**
Perry, William (father and son, coachmakers), 42, 64, 168
Pertwee, Charles (architect), **71**, 176
peruke makers. *See* wigs and wigmakers
pest house (Maltings Lane), 50, 185
photographers, 172
pianos, 80, 99
Picton, David (Congregational minister), 109, 171
Picture Post (magazine), 125
pigeons, 129, 133
pigs, 66, 84, 85, 139, 144, 180
pillory, 18
Pinkham family (glove manufacturers), 97–99, **98**, 106, 109–10, 113, 114, 116, **129**, 138, 142, 149, **185**; colour page **12**
pirate, 32
Plague, the (1665), 158, 163
planning, town, 130, 139
playgrounds. *See* Recreation grounds

plays. *See* theatre
ploughing and ploughs, **18**, 70, 136; colour page **14**
Pluck family (shoemakers), 77
plumbers, 74, 85
poaching, **19**, 57
Podsbrook (Guithavon Street), 176
poets and poetry, **31**, 63, **72**, 94
Poland and the Polish, 139, 162
police and policemen, 40, 58, 62, 92, 96, 104, 118–21, 130, **131**, 132, 135, 139, 164, 170, 176
Police station (1st) (Guithavon Street), 131
Police station (2nd) (Newland Street), 139
Pollard, Lieutenant (trade union organiser), 110
poll tax, **149**, 173
poor, the, 25, 27, 35, 42, 46, 48–52, **51**, 54, 57–61, **58**, 65, 68, 70, 76, 78, 92, 96, 99, 100, 111, 117, 143, 156, 166, 176, 181. *See also* the workhouse
Pope, the, 17, 20
Poplar Hall (also known as Cambridge Villa, Hatfield Road), **181**
population figures, 16, 17, 23, 27, 42, 51, 57, 76, 79, 89, 103, 113, 125, 130, 139
porcelain maker, **169**
porters, 64, 94, 178
Portugal, 22, 75. *See also Lisbon*
post and postmen, 27–28, 39, 41–42, 65, 85, 90, 167, 168, 175. *See also* letter-boxes; post office (several)
Post Hall End. *See* Powershall End
post office, main (1st) (68 Newland Street), 175
post office, main (2nd) (85 Newland Street), 65, 66, 164
post office, main (3rd) (84 Newland Street), 65, 96, 115, 178
post office, main (4th) (part of 5 Newland Street), 130, 168
post office, main (5th) (74-76 Newland Street), 177
post office, sub (1st) (45 Chipping Hill), 153
post office, sub (2nd) (9 Church Street), 156
Potter, John (Archbishop of Canterbury), 33
Potto, Edmund (tailor and arsonist), 55–56; colour page **9**
Poulter family (nurserymen, shoemenders, politicians etc.), 114, **161**, 166
poultry, **18**, 38, 144. *See also* turkey

pound (parish, for animals), 148
Powershall End (sometimes known as Post Hall End), 10, 37, 50, 68, 70, **82**, 85, 125, 150–52. *See also* Chipping Hill bridge; Chipping Mill (no.1); the Spa; Spring Cottage (nos.6-8); Spring Lodge (no.3); Stourton (no.26); Witham Place
Powershall farm and manor (Terling Road), 12, 17, 55, 57, **69**, 106, 145, 183; colour page **4**
Prayer book, **24**
pre-fabs, 139
Presbyterians. *See* Congregational church
priests (Catholic), 30, 75
Prime Ministers, 96, 100, 111–12, 121
Prince Regent, 54. *See also George IV (king)*
printers, 162, 177
prisons, 25, 26, 39, 55, **56**, 57, 83, **120**, 153, 180
privies. *See* toilets
Proctor, Alexander (doctor), **44**
Public Hall (Collingwood Road), 93, 100, **101**, 102, 127, 129, 137, 173
public houses. *See* inns
Punch (magazine), **63**
Puritans, 21–25, **24**; colour page **5**
Putney, 162

Quakers and Quakerism, **26**, **27**, 70, **71**, 137, 156, 158, 169, 184
Queen Mary (ship), 115
Queensland (Australia), 88
Queen Street. *See* Lockram Lane
Quennell, C H B and Marjorie (architect and writer), 183

rabbits, 18, 114, 132
Rackham, Clara (suffragist), 100
radio, 104, 115, 132, **143**, 180
radio engineers, 115. *See also Marconi's*
RAFA Club, Bridge Street, **181**, 182
rail crashes, 64, 94, 141, **149**, 173; colour page **11**
railings. *See under* ironwork
railway goods yard, 65
railway navvies, 62
railways, 7, **8**, 61, 62–65, **63**, **64**, 66, **67**, 68, 86, 88, 94, 100, 106, 109, 111, 118, 129, 130,

INDEX

131, 141–42, 145, 149, 170, 173, 180, 184; colour pages **1, 11**
railway station, 62–64, **63**, 88, 141, 148; colour pages **11, 16, 17**
railway workers, **63**, 63–64, 86, **89**, 90, 94, 109, 113, 118, 121
rallies. *See* meetings
Randall family (hirers of agricultural machines), 70
Rank, J Arthur (film maker), 176
Rank, Joseph (flour miller and philanthropist), 176
Ransomes (agricultural engineers), **184**, 185
rates and ratepayers, 48, 51, 57, 75, 78, 83–84, **85**, 99, 106, 116, 137
rats, 113
Raven, Christopher and family (tailors and Lollards), 20, 155
Raven, Francis, 155
Rayleigh, Lord, and Strutt family, 29, 59, 74, 79, 84, 90, 97, 101, 106, 117
Rayners att Tye (later Elm Hall farm), 10
razor maker, 68
Read family (carriers), 39
Recess (14 Chipping Hill), 154; colour page **19**
Recreation grounds, parks and playgrounds, 143. *see also* Hutley memorial recreation ground; Park and Recreation ground (Maldon Road); Rickstones Road Recreation Ground; River Walk
rectors. *See* vicars
Red Cross hospital, 106, **109**, 122
Redhead, William John (tax officer and architect), 168
Red Lion inn (1st, 67 Newland Street), 164–65
Red Lion inn (2nd, 68 Newland Street), 38, 174–75
Red Lion inn (3rd, 7 Newland street, formerly the Black Boy), 38, 126, 168
Reformation, the, 20–21
refuse disposal, 113, 118, 123, 165, 168
Renown (ship), **134**
restaurants. *See* cafés and restaurants
Restoration, the (1660), 25–27
Retreat, the (Maldon Road), 84, 167
Rex Mott Court (Guithavon Street), 176
Rice, Barbara, **123**
Richard II (king), 16
Richards family (builders), **153**, 156, 158, 176
Richardson, Fred (evacuee and head teacher), **134**, 135
Rickstones Road, 97, 123–24, **183**
Rickstones Road Recreation Ground, 127, 131, 136
Rickstones Secondary School (Rickstones and Conrad Roads) (opened 1977), 183
Rifle Brigade, **82**, 83
riots and disorder, 23, 50, 55, 56, 92
Rivenhall, 13, 27, 88, 112, 137, 138, 139, 142, 173. *See also* Rivenhall Thicks; Tarecroft wood
Rivenhall Thicks, 13
rivers, 8, 10, 13, 28. *See also* the Blackwater; the Brain; *the Crouch*; the River Walk
River Walk, 34, 144–45, 152, 161; colour page **6**
roads, 9, **12**, 16, 17, 18, 20, 27, 39–42, 130, *See also* motor vehicles.
Robinson, Henry Crabb (writer), 33, 81
Robinson, John (suspected spy), 42
Robjent, George (postman), 85, 90
Rochdale Pioneers, 90
Rochford, Earl of, **41**
Roman Catholics. *See* Catholics
Romans, the, 8–9, **9**, 16, 157, 181, 185; colour page **1**
Root, Malcolm (painter), colour page **11**
Roslyn House (16 Newland Street), 36, 66, 171–72; colour pages **17, 18**
Rotary Club, inside front **cover**, **178**
Round family (gentry and soldiers), 102, **109**
Rowley's Hall or Rooms (also known as Grove Hall) (Newland Street), 129, **131**, 170, **171**
Royal Army Medical Corps, **103**
Royal Exchange (London), 74
Royal Naval College (Greenwich), 81
royalty, 10, 12, 13, 14, 16, 17, 18, 25, **40**, **54**, 61, 66, 75, **83**, 90, **93**, 94, 110, 141, 146, 153, **171, 178**
Royden, Christopher and family (gentry and Lollards), 20, 153
Royffe, Irene (evacuees' organiser), 138
Ruffins (Great Totham), 104, **147**
Rumsey, Charlie, 115
Russia, 66; colour page **10**
Ryan, Pat (researcher), colour pages **17, 18, 19**
Rydel, John (miller), 19
Rykedon, Robert (landowner), 17

Saffron Walden, 130
Saggart, John (carrier), 39
sailors, 32, 54, 81, 100, 104, 138
Saint George, 166
Saint John, Abbey of, Colchester, 21
Saint Nicholas and Saint Nicolas church. See church, parish
Saint Pancras station (London), 59, 181
Saint Patrick's Day, 23
Sainty family (signalman, wireless doctor etc), 115, **143**, 173; colour page **11**
Salle, John, **184**
Samaria (ship), **134**
Saracen's Head (Chelmsford), 78
Sauls bridge (Maldon Road), 15, 63, **184**
Savings Bank, 176–77
savings clubs, 76
Saward, Florence. See Balaam, Florence
Saxon Drive, 152
Saxons. See Anglo-Saxons
Sayer, Alfred (bootmaker), 90, 182
Sayer, Benjamin (pauper), 57
Sayer, Edward (of Tiptree), 182
Sayer, George (vicar), 33–34, **34**, 158; colour page **6**
Sayer, Martha, nee Potter (vicar's wife), 33; colour page **6**
Sayers, Dorothy L (author), 126, 137, 139, 168, 172; colour page **14**. See also 'Dorothy Sayers Cottages'
schoolmasters and schoolmistresses. See schools; teachers
schools, 34, 35, **36**, 36–37, 50–51, 60–61, 90, 100, 118, 127, 130, 132, 135, 137, 154, 156, 166, 176, 180. See also Bramston Secondary School (opened 1937); Chipping Hill (Board) School (Church Street) (opened 1902); Maldon Road School (also known as the British, Board or Council School) (1837-1966); National (Church) School (Church Street) (1866-1900); National (Church) School (Collingwood Road) (1813-1842); National (Church) Schools (Guithavon Street) (1842-1967); Rickstones Secondary School (opened 1977)
Scollan, Maureen, 73
Scoon, Robert (East India Company), 32
Scotland and the Scots, 32, 33, 43, 103, 104, 109, 111, 142, **153**, 171; colour page **20**
Scots Regiments, 103, 104, 109

Scott, Sir George Gilbert (architect), **59**, 74, 159, 181
seed drills and drillmaking, 67–68, 70, 79, 180; colour page **10**
seed industry, 88, 97, 141, **143**, 144
Segenhoe (New South Wales, Australia), 56; colour page **9**
serophine (musical instrument), **73**
servants, 28, 30, 60, 98, **99**, 154, **162**, 171, 172
sewage farm, 128
sewerage. See drains and sewers
Shaen, Samuel (gentleman and Congregationalist), 72
Sharp, 'old' (pauper), 48
sheep, **18**, 32, 50, 81, 127, 132, 136, 173
Sheerness (Kent), 81
Shelley family (various), **117**, 137, 171
shells (military), 135
shepherds, 19
Sherrin, George (architect), **147**, 154
ships, 32, 81, 83, 88, 94, 115, **134**, 135, **169**
figurehead, 141
shoemakers, 18, 19, 23, 53, 77, 104, 152, **161**, 174, 182
shooting, **92**, 163. See also guns
shop awnings and blinds, 162; colour page **16**
shops and shopkeepers, 7, **15**, 28, 37, 42–43, 65, 76, 98, 100, 112, 113, 114, 121, 132, 143, 180. See also Witham Co-operative Society
Shoreditch (London), 62
Shrewsbury, Earl of, 30
Sidney family (Catholics), 30
signalmen, 64, 94, 173; colour page **11**
sign, town, front **cover** and **reverse** thereof, **178**
silk and silkmaking, 57, 66, 167
Silver End, **112**, 114, 118, 123, 127, 131, 173, 185; colour page **14**
silverware, 19, 80, 113
Singapore, 138
skinners, 19
Skinner, William, 156
skittles, 180
slaughterhouses, 28, 144, 155
slaves and slavery, 37, 78, 97, **169**
slums and slum clearance, 83–85, 101–2, **124**, 124–25, 145, **153**, 165
Slythe family (monumental masons), 148
smallholdings, 183
small-pox, 50, 51

INDEX

Smith, Ebenezer (railwayman and councillor), 121–22, **124**
Smith, E C (grocer and draper), 173
Smith, Elizabeth (dressmaker), 99, 146
Smith, Harry (chauffeur), 96
Smith, John (Sir, of Cressing Temple), 21
Smith, Joseph (builder, and family), 86–88, **87**, **98**, 141, 154, 163, **179**; colour page **17**
Smith, R (researcher), colour page **11**
smiths, 19. *See also* blacksmiths; coppersmiths; tinsmith; whitesmith
Smith, Ted (councillor), 150
Smyth family (seed-drill manufacturers), 67–68, 70, 79, **180**; colour page **10**
Sneezum family (soldiers and park keeper), **108**
Snell, Frederick (artist), **49**
Socialism, 90. *See also* Communist Party; Labour Party
societies and clubs, 33, 50, 70, 76–77, **77**, 80, 81, 96, 100, **111**, 112, 129, **178**, **181**, 182. *See also* Constitutional Club; Witham Co-operative Society; Witham Literary Institution
soldiers, 10, 23, 25, 32, 35, 40, 52–53, **53**, **82**, **83**, 102–9, **107**, **108**, **109**, 112, 131–9, 146, 152, **153**, **155**, 162, **164**, 171, 184
solicitors. *See* lawyers
Somerset, 42
Somme, the (France), 108
soup kitchens, 76, 100, 114
South, Daniel (labourer and dissenter), 70–71
South Africa, 67. *See also* Boer War
Southcott family (judge and gentry), 21, 25, 27, 30, 34, 37, 158; colour pages **5, 6**
Southcott, Philip, landscape gardener, 33–34; colour page **6**
Southend, 81
South Midland Field Ambulance, **103**
Southwold (Suffolk), 67
Spa, the (Powershall End), 37–38, **38**, 151, 154, **187**
Spain, 22, 23
speed limits, 96, 118
spies, 42, 104, 177
spigot mortar emplacements and guns (also known as Blacker Bombards), 137, 170; colour page **15**
Spink, William (vet and horse dealer), 181
Spinks Lane, 181. *See also* Bramston School

spinning and spinners, 22, 48, 50
Spitalfields market (London), **147**, 154
Spooner, Samuel (brushworks salesman and manager), 66–67
sport. *See* games
Spread Eagle inn and yard (47-51 Newland Street), front **cover** and **reverse** thereof, 35, 39, 66, **77**, 167
Spring Cottage (nos.6-8 Powershall End), 152
Springett family (farmworkers), 152
Springfield, **41**, 156
Spring Lodge (house and Community Centre, 3 Powershall End), **21**, 58, 150–2, **151**
springs, 8, 84, 127. *See also* the Spa
Spurge (drapers), 174, 177
stables, 41, 85, 142, 144, 166, 167, 170
Station Maltings, 88
stationmaster, **145**
statues, 163, 168; colour page **14**
steam engines and machinery, 63, 69–70, 81, 86, 118, 141, 148, 176. *See also* railways
Steeple Bumpstead, 20
Stefre (White Horse Lane), 144
Stephen (king), 13, 14
Stephenson, Robert (railway engineer), **184**
Stevens, C, **80**
stockbrokers, 66, 98
stocks, 18
Stone, Richard (portrait painter), **86**
Stone Age, 8, 9
Stoneham family, **123**
stonemasons, 14, 148
Stourton (26 Powershall End), 75, 152
Stourton, Lord, 30, 152
street name plates, 168, 174; colour page **20**
street number plates, 156, 164; colour page **20**
strikes, 46, 88, 89, 109, 110, 113, 114, 116, 118
Strutt family. See Rayleigh, Lord
Stuart Witham, 22–28
Sudbury (Suffolk), 110
Suddards, Revd John (rector), **178**
Suffolk, 22, 24, 33, 40, 64, 67–68, 70, 99, 110, 116, 162, 180, **184**, 185; colour pages **5, 10**
suffragists and suffragettes, 100–101, **101**
suicide, 81
Sundays, 10, 23, 50, 59, 132, 143
Sunday Times newspaper, **45**
sun-dial, 35
surgery (129 Newland Street), **44**, 54, 96, **162**; colour page **16**

surplices, 24
surveys and surveyors, 13, 27, 73, 83–84, 102, 117, 124, 125, 162, 164. *See also* benchmarks; Domesday survey
Sussex, 37, 46
Swain, William (soldier), 53
Swan, Abraham (architect), **169**
Swan inn (153 Newland Street), 77, 94, **128**, 162
Sweden and the Swedish, 32
swimming, **128**, 162, 181

Taber family (seedsmen), 88, 141
Tabor, Margaret (author, suffragist and councillor, of Bocking), 100
tailors, 16, 19, 20, 55
Talbot family (gentry), 30
Talfourd, Thomas Noon (writer), 73
tanning and leather-making, 18, 19, 28, 43, **47**, **58**, 65, 99, 145, 175, 180, 184
Tarecroft Wood, Rivenhall, 13
tarmac, 117
Tavarez, Joseph da Silva (priest), 75
Taverner, James (doctor and proprietor of the Spa), 37, 39, 40, **187**
Taverner, Richard the (innkeeper), 15
taverns and taverners. *See* inns and innkeepers
taxes, 27, 30, 46, **86, 149**, 168, 173. *See also* rates and ratepayers
taxidermist, 136
Taylor, Edmund (nonconformist minister), 153
tea, 40, 64, 68, 90, 100, **171**
teachers, **31**, 35, 36–37, 51, 99, 108, 113, 115, 131, 132, **134**, 135, 180. *See also* schools
Technology Centre (White Horse Lane), 143
telegraph, the, 63, 65, 94, 96, 178
telephone box, 115
telephones and telephone poles, 96, 114–15, 130, 152, 154, 162, 173, **175**, 176, 178; colour page **20**
Temperance Hotel (9 Albert Road), **142**
Templar, Knights, **14**, 14–16, 17, 141, **161**, 166; colour page **3**
Templars estate (Cressing Road), **7**, 183
Templemead flats, 149; colour page **12**
Temples farm and estate, 86, **140**, 142, 148
tennis, **19**, 127
tenterfields, 22, 163

Terling, 24–25, 29, 38, 59, 79, 84, 101, **105, 133**, 185
Terling Place, 29, 106
Terling Road. *See* Powershall farm and manor
Territorial Army, **155**, 176
tetanus, 102
thatching and thatchers, 14, 19
theatre and plays, 38, 115, 129, 139
Thomasin family (brushmakers), 7, 47, 55, 66–67, **67**, 90, 164–65, 179, **182**
Thomasin Foster, Mark (High Sheriff of Essex, 2003-2004), **67**
Thompson, Albert and Kate (schoolteachers), 108
Thompson, Arthur R (tax officer and naturalist), 168
Thompson, George (coal merchant), 141
threshing, 19
Thurgood, John (member of British Resistance), **133**
Tilbury, 88, 153
tiling and tilers, **9**, 19, 141
timber, 17, 42, 58, 144, 156, 177. *See also* firewood
timber-framed buildings, 16, 17, **22**, 27, 35, 163, 165, 168, 169, 171, 174, 179, 182; colour page **2**
Times, the (newspaper), 80, 121
tinsmith, 178
Tiptree, 40, 68, 172
Titanic (ship), 94
Tite, William (architect), 74
tithes, 26, 152, 159
toilets and privies, 102, 120, 127, 138, 155, 167, 168, 176, **179**, 180
Tolleshunt D'Arcy, **115**, **148**
Tomkin, Thomas (doctor), 57, 84, 167
Tomlinson, Nicholas (Captain), 54
Tomtit (newspaper), **85, 177**
Tonbridge (Kent), 81
Totham, Great and Little, **72**, 104, **147**
Totscott (11 Church Street), 156; colour page **18**
Totteridge, Elizabeth, 24
town clock. *See* clock, town
town criers, 35, 92
Town Hall. *See* George inn (1st)
trade unions, 77, 88–89, **89**, 110, 113, 155
Trafalgar, Battle of, 52, 93, 172
Trafalgar Square (London), 163
Trafalgar Square (Maldon Road), 60, 85, 125

traffic lights, 120; colour page **14**
tramping and tramps, 66, 77
transportation (as punishment), 56, 58
trees, 30, 35, 94, 104, 112, 115, 125, 139, **145**, 146, **151**, 153, 154, 156, 158, 163, 167, 170, 171, 176; colour page **7**
Trew, wife of Thomas (pauper), 57
Trippe, Ellen (assault victim), 19
Trollope, Anthony (novelist), 164
True, Richard (clothier), 163
Tudor Witham, 20–22
tunnels, 153
turkey, 156
turnips, 48, 68
turnpikes, 39
Twain, Mark (American writer), 79
Tyndale, William (translater of the Bible), 20
typhoid, 84, 102
Tyrell family (shoemakers), 104

unemployment, 55, 57, 113–14
unions. *See* trade unions
Unions (Poor Law). *See* workhouses
United Reformed Church. *See* Congregational church

VAD. *See* Voluntary Aid Detachment
vagrants, 51
Vaux, Susannah (nurse and Poor Law Guardian), 101
VE day (1945), **138**, 138–39
Vestry, Select, 57–58
veterinary medicine, **28**, 181
viaducts, **8**, 62, 63, 145, 184; colour page **1**
Vicarage, Old (Chipping Hill), 26, 33–35, **34**, 158; colour page **6**
vicars of Witham (one of them known as the rector since 1994), 16, 23–26, 27, 33–35, **34**, 36, 56, 73–75, 101, 102, 110, 132, 157–58, **158**, **178**, 181
Victoria (queen), 66, **83**, 90, 94, 146
Victoria Cottages (Maltings Lane), 50, 68, 184
Victoria Cross, **82**, **83**; colour page **9**
Victorian Witham, 58–92, **140**
Virtue, George (publisher of engravings), colour pages **1**, **7**
VJ day (1945), 139
Voluntary Aid Detachment (VAD), 106, **109**
Volunteer Corps, 52
voting. *See* elections and the franchise

Wade, John (taverner), 40
Wadley family (shopkeepers), 156; colour page **19**
waggons. *See* carriers and carts
Wakelin family (farmers and librarian), 116, 128
Waldbrohl (Germany), 170
Wales, 66, 83, 111
Walford, Cornelius junior (writer and insurance expert), 79, 80
Walford, Cornelius senior (hairdresser and naturalist), 79
Walk Field, 151
Wall, Samuel (draper), 28
wallpaper, **54**
Walpole, Horace (writer), 34
war and wars, 23, 32, 81, 83. *See also* Boer War; Civil War; *Napoleonic Wars; Peninsular War;* World War, the First; World War, the Second
Ward, William (carrier and horseman), 167
Warley, Jonas (vicar), 27, 33, 34
War memorial, 108, 109, 171. *See also* Nurses' Bungalow
Warwick House (48 Collingwood Road), 146; colour page **19**
Warwickshire Regiments, 103, 104, 152
washerwomen and washing, 60, **61**, 98
watchmakers. *See* clockmakers
water engineer, 104
Waterhouse, Thomas (clothier), 48
Watering, the (Guithavon Valley), 21, 145
Waterloo (Belgium), battle of, **53**, 58
water supply, 28, **58**, 83–85, **85**, 94, 102, 103, 123, 127, 128, 138, **145**, 162, 172, 179
water towers, **85**, 94, 127, 172–73
Waterworks cottages, **128**
Watson, Robert (wig maker), 42
Watts, Thomas (cabinet and chairmaker), 42
weaving and weavers, 18, 22, 25, 27, 46, 172
Weil, Leo (German lawyer), 104
Weld, Thomas (vicar of Terling), 24–25
Welde, John (leather worker), 18
Wellington coach, 62–63
wells and pumps, 84, 94, 102, 153. *See also* the Spa

Wesley, John (Methodist leader), 70
West, Cissie (shopkeeper), 132, **149**
West Ham, 84
West Indies, **169**
Westminster (London), 163
Westminster, Catholic archbishop of, 75
wheelwrights, 19, 68, 180, **181**
whipping post, 23
whisky, **174**
whistles, 137
White, Thomas and Ann (soldier and his wife), 25
Whitehall (18 Newland Street, house, cinema and library), 32, 127, 129, 138, 172; colour page **14**
White Hart inn (Newland Street), 75, **77**, 78, 79, 167, 168
White Horse (2 Church Street), 144, 155
White Horse, 'New' (20-22 Chipping Hill). *See* Kings Head inn
White Horse Lane (formerly Hill Lane), 88, 143–44. *See also* Stefre; Technology Centre
whitesmith, 178
Whybrew family (farmworkers and shopkeepers), 88, 90
Wickham Bishops, 63, **133**, 183, 184
wigs and wigmaking, 30, 42
Wilkinson, Ellen (politician), 111
William I (king), 13
William IV (king), 81
Wilson, Carrington (ironmonger), 178
windmill, 182
windows and glaziers, 27, 28, 35, 85, 180. *See also* Crittall family
wine, 24, 26, 34, **36**, 38, 42, **43**, 80, **174**
wireless. *See* radio
Wiseman, Cardinal, 75
Witham, Little, manor. *See* Powershall farm and manor
Witham, place-name, 10
Witham Agricultural Society, 70
Witham Amateur Operatic Society, 129
Witham Building Society, 80
Witham Cartage and Coal Company, 117
Witham Co-operative Society, 7, 70, 85, 90, **91**, 99, 110, 130, 136, 163, 164
Witham Gas Company. *See* gas and gasworks
Witham half-hundred, 10
Witham House (57 Newland Street), 46, 70, 74, 79, **80**, 94, **166**, 167, 177

Witham Labourers Friend Society, 70
Witham Literary Institution, 78–79, 81, 94, 179
Witham Local Board of Health, 84, 94
Witham Lodge (Hatfield Road), 81, **93**, 98
Witham Place (Powershall End), **21**, 24, 27, 29–30, 34, **36**, 37, **150**, 150–52, **151**, 154; colour pages **5, 6**
Witham Town Council, **56**, 166
Witham Urban District Council, 56, 90, **91**, 94–96, 97, 102, 103, 106, 112–14, 116–18, 120-25, **122**, **123**, 127–30, 132, 137–39, 143–45, 150, **153**, 156, 164, 168, 173, 183; colour pages **15, 20**
Wombwald's Menagerie, 61
women, 78–79, 88, 97, 98–101, 104, 105–6, 110, 122, 128, 129, 135, 142
Women's Institute, 122, 128
Wood, George (town crier), 92
Woodbine Villa. *See* Woodhams
Woodgate, Thomas, 155
Woodhams (16 Guithavon Street), 176
woods and woodland, 13, 58, 103, 183. *See also* firewood; timber
Woodyards, James, and family, 73
wool. *See* cloth industry
wool carding, 22
woolcombing and woolcombers, 22
Woolf, Virginia (novelist), 106
wool merchants and woolmongers, 18, 22, 23
woolmongers. *See* wool merchants
Woolpack inn (7 Church Street), 156, **157**
Worcester, 25
Workers' Club, 129
Workers' Movement, **91**, 114
workhouse (Braintree Union), 61, 100, 114
workhouse (Witham parish, 24-40 Church Street)[, 48–50, 49, 52, 57, 59–60, 155–56; colour page 20
workhouse (Witham Union, Hatfield Road), 58–60, 59, 61, 71, 74, 83, 181
World War, First, 102–9, **103**, **105**, **107**, **108**, **109**, **115**, 116, 117, 121, 122, 128, 130, 146, 152, **153**, 154, **155**, 161–62, **164**, 171
World War, Second, 130–38, **132**, **136**, **138**, 142, 144, 154, 156, 162, 164, 170, 176, 184; colour page **15**
Wright, Francis (vicar), 23–26, **24**; colour page **5**
Wright, James (property owner), 179